Media, Market, and D

D1291285

The History of Communication

Robert W. McChesney and John C. Nerone, editors

A list of books in the series appears at the back of this book.

Media, Market, and Democracy in China

Between the Party Line and the Bottom Line

Yuezhi Zhao

University of Illinois Press

Urbana and Chicago

This book is printed on acid-free paper.

Library of Congress Cataloging-in-Publication Data
Zhao, Yuezhi, 1965–
Media, market, and democracy in China : between the party
line and the bottom line / Yuezhi Zhao.
p.   cm. — (The history of communication)
Includes bibliographical references and index.
ISBN 0-252-02375-7 (alk. paper). —
ISBN 0-252-06678-2 (pbk. : alk. paper)
1. Press—China—History. 2. Government and the press—
China. 3. Mass media policy—China. I. Title. II. Series.
PN5364.Z48 1998
079'.51'09—dc21 97-21144
CIP

In memory of my father

Contents

Acknowledgments

Numerous individuals, both in Canada and in China, have contributed to the completion of this book. A profound debt of gratitude is owed to the two co-senior supervisors of my Ph.D. dissertation at the School of Communication at Simon Fraser University, Bob Hackett and Pat Howard. Bob provided invaluable suggestions on the overall structure and arguments of the book. Pat offered many insights and made painstaking efforts to clarify my thoughts, tighten up my sentences, and correct my grammar. I am also very grateful to Rick Gruneau for his advice and encouragement. Mark Selden read an early version of the manuscript and provided a number of insightful suggestions for revisions. The University of Illinois Press's anonymous reviewers also offered many constructive criticisms. The final version was considerably improved thanks to their criticisms and suggestions. Jim Uhl volunteered many hours to scrutinize an earlier draft of the manuscript. I am profoundly grateful for his meticulous editing. I also wish to thank Richard Martin of the University of Illinois Press for the attention and care he has given to the manuscript. I take full responsibility, however, for remaining weaknesses and errors.

This study would not have been possible without the help of many individuals in China. I am grateful to them for their friendship, their enthusiasm for my research, their willingness to be interviewed, and their generosity in providing invaluable material and sharing insights. For reasons of confidentiality I cannot name them here, but I hope that my work is at least a partial repayment for my indebtedness.

My friends helped me in ways and moments that only friends can. Daniel Say kept me updated with books throughout the years and found me numerous electronic documents. Marie Cambon and Wu Xue provided me with material about the news media in China. Sun Wanning offered her comments and suggestions on an early draft of the book. Roger Howard, Ika Hackett, Lori Walker, and Carolyn Liu, among others, offered their friendship and support throughout the years. I thank them all.

I am also deeply indebted to my family in China and Canada. I am grateful to my parents, Zhao Ruqi and Qin Yujiao, and other members of my family in China for taking care of my daughter Linda during my research and writing. Sadly, my father passed away shortly before the publication of the book. I would also like to thank my sister Weichun for helping me make transcripts of television programs. Finally, I want to say thank you to my husband, Qian Jianxing, for his support and patience. I owe him much for the sacrifice he and our daughter Linda made over the past few years.

Media, Market, and Democracy in China

Introduction

When I was a journalism student in China in the early 1980s, our discussions about press reform were largely confined to technical issues. News must be brief—this was the central argument of an essay I wrote to fulfill requirements for my bachelor's degree. That argument made sense to me because the newspapers at the time were filled with tedious theoretical articles and lengthy news reports excerpted from government documents. A classmate advocated allowing international news to appear on the front page of Chinese Communist party organs. When another classmate wrote an essay about press freedom, rumors had it that he was criticized by the instructor for expressing "incorrect" views and received a low grade.

By the mid-1980s, press freedom and press legislation had become hot topics of debate within the Chinese journalism community. Articles that questioned the Party's monopoly of journalism began to appear in research journals. In 1989, Chinese journalists marched in the streets and demanded press freedom and a watchdog role to expose and discourage official corruption. Their sympathetic coverage of the student movement and their slogans, such as "We want to tell the truth" and "Don't force us to lie," won them heroic status. Their dreams and aspirations, together with those of students and many Chinese citizens, however, were crushed by tanks in Tiananmen Square and the streets of Beijing on June 4, 1989.

Democratization was the key issue in the struggle for media reform in 1989. By 1992, however, commercialization had become the order of the day. Market forces began to rapidly penetrate every aspect of news media operations in China. Indeed, Joseph M. Chan predicts that "1992 will be remembered as the year of commercialization." Chan argues that the importance of media commercialization "paralleled that of the organized demand for freedom of expression as witnessed during the pro-democracy movement in 1989."[1] Advertising, commercial sponsorships, stock market reports, TV-shopping channels, pay-TV, and, most important of all, corruption in journalism and red packets of cash in exchange for a promotional piece of reporting were the hot topics as I was doing research in China in late 1994 and early 1995. When I was chatting with a group of Chinese television university administrators visiting Vancouver in October 1996, one figure they were eager to share with me was that China Central Television, the state-controlled monopoly, paid 80 million yuan in tax revenue to the government in 1995. At a time when many other state enterprises bordered on collapse, China Central Television emerged as an economic power.

Despite the breathtaking speed of commercialization, journalism in China remains static in many respects. The Chinese Communist party still insists that the media are its mouthpiece and it continues to exercise blunt forms of media censorship. When copies of the U.S. newsmagazine *Newsweek* were sold in China in mid-1996, their pages containing stories about China were reportedly ripped out. Foreign news still seldom appears on the front pages of Party organs. "Protocol news"—Party General Secretary Jiang Zemin received foreign guests, Premier Li Peng and Standing Committee of the Politburo member Qiao Shi greeted Jiang Zemin on his return from a foreign visit, and the like—continued to appear on the front page of the *People's Daily* (Renmin ribao) before the death of Deng Xiaoping in early 1997. These seemingly routine news items served as an important means of communication in a tightly controlled political context and at a time of intense struggle within the leadership, signaling that no coup had overturned the government and the leadership was still unified. And of course, there was a total news blackout on the health of Deng until his death. In Beijing, more sophisticated news watchers based their speculations about Deng's health on various seemingly relevant signals, such as news reports about one of his daughter's overseas travels; in my home village in southern China, some peasants believed that Deng was already dead but that the media had not reported it. Both assumed that, despite the economic reforms, there had been no change in the way Chinese journalism operated.

News media in post-Mao China, in short, are in the paradoxical situation of at once being changed and remaining the same. Economic reforms and an open-door policy introduced market logic into the Party-controlled news media system and led to a fledgling journalism reform movement and the emergence of discourse on media democratization in the mid-1980s, which threatened to challenge the Party's monopolistic control. While the crackdown on the democracy movement in 1989 suppressed democratic discourses and reimposed tight political control, market forces gained momentum after the Party's unreserved embrace of a market economy in 1992. These developments produced the current mix of Party logic and market logic—the defining feature of the news media system. It is a scene full of contradictions, tensions, and ambiguities.

In this book I critically examine this intertwining of Party logic and market logic. I aim to contribute to current debates regarding prospects for democratization of the news media. I describe the twisted path that led to the current fusion of Party control and market forces and analyze new structures and practices, contradictions, tensions, and challenges as well as opportunities created by this fusion. I address the following questions: In what ways do market forces influence the media? How does the Party both introduce and attempt to contain the influence of the market? How does the commercial imperative both accommodate and challenge Party control? What are the political implications of the current fusion of Party control and market forces in the Chinese news media? To what extent does the market present a democratizing alternative to Party control?

The interlocking of Party control and market forces is part and parcel of China's unique approach to development in the post-Mao era: economic liberalization without political democratization. Reform and openness—that is, transformation of a command economy to a market economy and integration with the world markets of trade and investment—are the two key components of the post-Mao economic reforms. China has gone a long way toward them by expanding foreign trade and investment and instituting a series of market-oriented domestic reform measures: the semiprivatization of agriculture, the development of "special economic zones," the development of private enterprises and contracting out of small to medium-sized state enterprises, the decentralization of planning, the deregulation of prices, the marketization of state-allocated producer goods, the commodification of labor forces, and the introduction of stock markets, real estate markets, and capital markets.

On the political side, however, little progress has been made toward democratization. To be sure, attempts have been made to separate Party and government functions, to implement a legal system, to institutionalize and decentralize decision-making, and to reform cadre and personnel management systems. Efforts have also been made to increase social consultation and to implement local self-governance. There is, however, little change in the political structure. The Party still monopolizes power, informal and personal politics still prevail, the independence of the judicial system is still on shaky ground, and the bankruptcy of administrative and personnel reforms is evident in massive systemic official corruption. And although the culture of consumerism reigns there is still little change in the overall political culture. Power is still viewed as monistic and indivisible, and the politics of compromise that is vital to democratic governance is still not accepted.[2] Indeed, the Party still does not allow any form of dissent. The small number of democracy activists have been either jailed, forced into exile, or intimidated into silence. The Fifteenth National Party Congress in September 1997 further intensified the Party's policy of economic liberalization without political democratization. It embraced the sale of state-owned enterprises, the last bastion of a planned economy, amidst the old rhetoric of socialism and Party leadership. The Congress also underscored the old-style maneuver that codified Deng Xiaoping Theory and consolidated the personal power of Party General Secretary Jiang Zemin.

There are different interpretations of the implications of China's approach to development and the future directions of political, economic, and social reforms. Some deplore the fusion of totalitarianism and consumer capitalism. Some celebrate the triumph of a capitalist revolution and believe that this will eventually bring democracy. Some believe that China will institute a constitutional authoritarian government. Others fear the return of Maoism and powerful military control. Still others predict the total disintegration of China. The Chinese official line, on the other hand, has remained rather consistent over the past decade: China is firmly on the path of building "socialism with Chinese characteristics" or developing a "socialist market economy," whatever definitions these terms may have.

Instead of beginning with any of these lines of interpretation, I will pursue a "contextualized and concretized"[3] mode of understanding the news media scene in China. Nevertheless, some of the theoretical assumptions and normative commitments underpinning this study should be made explicit.

Beyond the Mass Propaganda and Persuasion Model

Before the economic reforms in the late 1970s, the dominant framework for analyzing the Chinese media was a mass propaganda and persuasion model.[4] According to this, the Chinese news media were tightly controlled instruments of political indoctrination and mass mobilization. Most notable in this tradition are studies of how the Party used the radio and press to propagate its goals and promote changes in the attitudes and behavior of the people in the early 1950s and early 1960s.[5] The Party's own conception of the media—as its mouthpiece—provided further evidence to support this interpretation. Within this model, the notion of ideology is narrowly defined as a set of comprehensive, totalizing dogmas, i.e., the doctrines of Marxism, Leninism, and Mao Zedong Thought, while the ideological process is seen as a process of intentional political propaganda and indoctrination.

Despite the Party's continuing grip on the news media and the persistence of old patterns of ideological control during the reform era, the mass propaganda and persuasion model is becoming increasingly inadequate. A growing body of literature has persuasively documented that the news media are moving away from the Party's prescription of political and ideological indoctrination.[6] Chin-Chuan Lee captures this change very well. First, according to Lee, while Mao ensured that state influence and radical revolutionary ideology pervaded every domain of social life, the state is now less intrusive. Second, the post-Mao regime's relative deemphasis of ideology has made it possible for various cultural genres, livelier media entertainment, and other less ideologically loaded materials to flourish. Third, while Mao repeatedly launched mass mobilization campaigns to pursue his ideological vision as well as to bolster his own power, his successors have encouraged the media "to focus on promoting economic modernization instead of class struggle," leaving China "far less totalistic in the ideological arena."[7] Lee also notes that "growing diversity in overall media structure and content coverage is gradually stripping away the ideological straitjacket imposed by the CCP [Chinese Communist party]."[8] Others have similarly noted the "de-ideologization" in post-Mao China.[9]

These changes are certainly significant, but they do not signify an "end of ideology."[10] Indeed, the dichotomy of the Party's control versus freedom from ideological constraints is rather one-dimensional. Although much of the recent scholarship has either explicitly or implicitly rejected the mass propaganda and persuasion model, its narrow notion of ideology as a set of rigid dogmas is still operative. There is, however, a broader concept of ideology in Western literature on the news media.[11] Although there is no single definition, current critical concepts of ideology share some characteristics. First, such a concept extends the analysis of ideology from the intentional to the unintentional, making ideology a function of social processes. Viewed from this perspective, the ideological function of the news media goes beyond the explicit promotion of ideological doctrines to the seemingly independent and autonomous codes and conventions of news production, including news values and the conventions of journalistic objectivity.[12] Moreover, instead of seeing ideology as merely an explicit and static set of doctrines, the critical literature perceives ideology as "an active practice"[13] operative on the level of common sense and everyday consciousness and discourses. It extends the analysis of ideology from the explicitly political to social and psychological dimensions. Finally, the critical literature typically relates ideology to relations of domination.[14] To point to something as being ideological implies a critique of relations of domination. John B. Thompson, for example, proposes to conceptualize ideology "in terms of the ways in which the meaning mobilized by symbolic forms serves *to establish and sustain* relations of domination."[15]

Although critical concepts of ideology have been developed largely within the context of media studies in the West, they are relevant for China for a number of reasons. First, although the Party has not relinquished Marxism, Leninism, and Mao Zedong Thought, it is counting on "delivering the goods" rather than on ideological doctrines alone for its legitimacy. Within this context, symbolic forms that serve to sustain Party domination, even though they do not explicitly promote political doctrines, are also serving an ideological function. For example, news reports about war and violence in the former Yugoslavia have persuaded many Chinese citizens that the price of ending Communist party rule would be political and economic chaos. The reports have thus served to "compel compliance to the current regime."[16]

Second, it is certainly true that the rise of mass communication, especially television, has brought profound changes to the ideological landscape. The increasing variety and liveliness of cultural and entertainment forms together with a reduced explicitly propagandist content has resulted in a proliferation of new symbolic forms. This does not mean, however, that the media are no longer doing ideological work or politically dominating. Indeed, the media's promotion of consumerism is no less ideological than their promotion of class struggle during the Mao era. Moreover, an argument can be made that while Marxism, Leninism, and Mao Zedong Thought have lost their grip on the population, the ideology of national and personal development through the market has replaced them. While this powerful ideology is more implicit, its grip on the people is no less totalistic.[17]

Third, a less reductionist understanding of ideology makes possible a broader critique of the ideological role of the media that perceives effects beyond the intentional control of the Party. Think again about the reporting of conflicts in the former Yugoslavia. It may be the result of deliberate political propaganda, but given commercialization and news values imported from the West, it may simply be considered as having audience appeal. A broadened concept of ideology makes it possible to see beyond the dichotomy between ideological control by the Party and the journalists' struggle for freedom and to analyze the political implications of recent media changes, including commercialization.

Finally, a structural critique of political domination based on a broad concept of ideology also helps to avoid common inconsistencies in analyzing the Chinese media. Although many analyses attempt a detached understanding, a political stance is always implicit. During the reform era, this political stance has exhibited two prominent perspectives: an overall rejection of the Party's ideological control as part of the "totalitarian" versus "freedom" characterization of the liberal perspective and a sympathy with the liberal reformers and their policy orientations in the "reformers" versus "hardliners" account of the Chinese domestic political struggle. Two different levels of analysis—a structural critique of the Party's overall model of political communication and an analysis of the struggle for control over the news media between different factions within the Party—are often fused, creating ambiguities and inconsistencies.

One case in point is Alison L. Jernow's interpretation of the Huang Fuping editorials in *Liberation Daily* (Jiefang ribao). In late 1991 and early 1992, while the rest of the Chinese press "was still belaboring the dangers of peaceful evolution"[18] following the 1989 crackdown, Shanghai's *Liberation Daily,* the organ of the Shanghai Municipal Party Committee, published a series of editorials under the pseudonym Huang Fuping calling for accelerated opening up and commercialization. These editorials were interpreted by Jernow as cracks appearing in "the wall of propaganda."[19] But if Huang Fuping "had the backing of Deng Xiaoping himself," as Jernow notes, then these articles do not represent a break from the nature of propaganda but are simply propagating a different line within the Party.[20] They signify a change in the *content* of news media rather than in the *nature* of the news media, which still operate as instruments of the Party's policy initiatives.

Such analytical confusion is also evident in Hsiao Ching-Chang and Yang Mei-Rong's analysis of the struggle for press freedom by the Shanghai *World Economic Herald* (Shijie jingji daobao) (1980–89), a semi-independent newspaper at the center of the political struggle in 1989.[21] To be sure, the *Herald* published some articles that other newspapers would not have dared to print, but Hsiao and Yang fail to explicitly define what they mean by press freedom. It is clear from available evidence that the degree of freedom the *Herald* enjoyed was a direct result of its acting as an informal mouthpiece for the Zhao Ziyang faction within the Party and had Zhao's protection for some time. Freedom, therefore, must be contextualized and qualified. While the paper was able to survive several political storms with the help of Zhao in 1987, by the end of 1988 nobody in the Party could protect it anymore and it was forced to close down.[22] The freedom it had enjoyed was taken back by the Party.[23]

While Hsiao and Yang view editorial intervention by Jiang Zemin and the Shanghai Municipal Party Committee as problematic, they fail to examine a set of "complex relationships that often put the *Herald* closer to Zhao Ziyang's administration than were other newspapers."[24] If the *Herald*'s freedom is defined as its ability to pursue a particular editorial orientation vis-à-vis conservative elements within the Party, then such freedom ended in April 1989, when Jiang Zemin's Shanghai Municipal Party Committee attempted to censor the newspaper and eventually forced its closure. If press freedom is defined as freedom from political intervention and patronage, then such freedom had ceased to exist long before 1989, when Zhao Ziyang rescued the paper from conservatives who had wanted to close it. Zhao at different points acted as an irresponsible patron of the newspaper and used it as an instrument to advance his own causes.

The point is not to discredit the *Herald* and the heroic struggles of its staff against certain forces within the Party. But it is important to make a clear distinction between evidence derived from structural analysis and content analysis in the study of press freedom. What China needs is a news media structure that works fairly for not just one newspaper with a specific editorial orientation but for a wide range of news media outlets that speak with a plurality of voices.

The Liberal Press Model as a Normative Standard?

The analysis of media systems inevitably invokes explicit or implicit normative models of the press. Consistent with the mass propaganda and persuasion model and its narrow conception of ideology, much of the analysis of the news media in

China has been informed by Fred Siebert, Theodore Peterson, and Wilbur Schramm's influential *Four Theories of the Press*.[25] Within this narrative, the historical development of "a free and responsible" press in the West went through three stages: the authoritarian stage in which the press was subject to overt state control and functioned to support the state; the libertarian stage in which the press became politically and financially independent from the state and accountable to the public through the market mechanism; and a third stage in which the press became less partisan and more socially responsible with commitment to professional values of objectivity and balance. With the collapse of the Soviet model, this grand narrative of evolution from an authoritarian to a libertarian and finally to a social responsibility model of the press seems to have claimed world historical relevance, together with the celebration of the triumph of liberalism and capitalism on a global scale and of the "end of history."[26]

Consequently, the transformation of the Chinese press is approached as a comparable process. This is most explicitly articulated by Mark R. Levy in his "Editor's Note" to the *Journal of Communication*'s summer 1994 symposium on mass media in China. Levy asks, "Is the practice of journalism in China changing? and if so, what are the chances that a western, liberal model of the press will take hold?"[27] Implicitly, this grand narrative has informed much of the research and interpretation of changes in the Chinese news media: the focus on the struggle for press freedom against state control, the concern over whether economic development will eventually lead to press freedom, the dichotomy between Party control and market freedom, and the relevance of Western-style professionalism.[28]

While this narrative holds much explanatory power, it tends to oversimplify the complicated process of transformation in the Chinese news media. For example, notwithstanding the presence of liberal reformers, whose voices have been heard in Western media and academic articles, some other protagonists in the Chinese journalism reform movement do not easily fill the roles assigned to them by the script of the liberal narrative. Within the Party establishment, for example, some ideologues have found that talk show hosts in the newly commercialized media outlets are more effective ideological workers than those in the Party's ideological departments. Within the reform camp, some have argued that China must develop its own form of "socialist press freedom," rather than simply follow the Western model.

The core concept in the Western liberal model is "freedom of the press," which is defined in negative terms as freedom from state interference. But a Western liberal model means more than this. C. B. Macpherson, in discussing liberal democracy, notes that what is often overlooked is that it "and capitalism go together," a fact that "some people find admirable and some people would prefer not to have mentioned."[29] The same applies to conventional invocations of the liberal press model.

In the West, freedom of the press from direct government control goes with the organization of the press as a privately owned, profit-oriented commercial enterprise. Thus, a "libertarian" or simply "free press" model is actually a "press market model of editorial freedom." The essence of this model requires that there be no restraint "in the form of advance censorship, screening or licensing, nor any retribution for what is published, aside from what any citizen might have to answer for before the law." Within this model, however, "the freedom offered is essentially an individual right to free speech that has been translated into an economic right to run a publishing business with as much freedom as any other business, and often with certain special privileges added."[30] The public's right to free speech is typically equated to the property right of media owners.

As China struggles for democratization in media communication, an important question needs to be asked about the adequacy of a Western liberal model as a normative ideal, regardless of its feasibility in China.

While definitions of democracy abound—and I shall return to this issue later—even a minimal definition requires the realization of basic rights, such as freedom of opinion, of expression, of speech, of assembly, and of association.[31] There is no question that liberal democracy and its companion model of press freedom through the market is in many ways superior to the political system and the media system of China today. State control remains the most important obstacle to democratization of communication. Indeed, if there is one single important idea that is offered by a Western liberal model it is the relative autonomy of the press. The struggle for this autonomy must be the first step toward democratizing the news media in China. But equally important are these questions: How can relative autonomy be achieved? On what basis? Who should have control over and access to the means of communication? While the news media should definitely not be left exclusively in the hands of the Party, can and should they be left to private entrepreneurs and the market alone?

Having studied journalism in China and North America, I have seen firsthand both the dangers of a Party-dominated authoritarian media system and the limitations of a heavily commercialized media system. I have also learned firsthand the risks of binary thinking in the dominant political culture both in the East and in the West—the reduction of freedom of the press to either unaccountable Party or corporate control of the media, the conflation of democracy with either the rule of a vanguard Party or the market, and the conceptualization of the news media either as instruments of Party propaganda or as generating an objective, value-free reflection of reality and public opinion. In this book I attempt to transcend such either/or thinking in analyzing the interlocking of Party control and market forces in the Chinese news media. While I am critical of the fundamentally undemocratic nature of Party journalism and sensitive to the liberalizing impact of commercialization, I do not equate democracy with the market. Instead of treating commercialization as a precondition that will sooner or later lead to democratization of media communication in China, I will describe the commercialization of the Chinese news media as a complicated process of challenge, accommodation, and containment. Instead of constructing a one-dimensional narrative of liberation from the Party's ideological domination through the market, my analysis draws attention to developments that may have contributed to a shift in the Party's ideological work from crude political indoctrination to more subtle forms of ideological domination. Instead of taking the Western liberal press model as the normative standard in analyzing changes in the Chinese news media and speculating about the possibility for the emergence of a liberal model of the press, I insist on the relevance of Western critiques of the limitations of the liberal press to the struggle for the democratization of political communication in China and on the need for other alternatives.

Scope and Organization of the Book

Without doubt, the news media system in China is in a state of great flux. It is far from a monolithic and unified propaganda machine. In a way, it can be characterized as a multifaceted creature undergoing a process of rapid transformation, with different parts of the body straining in different, even opposite, directions. Indeed, because of the specific ways the news media intersect with the political and economic structures of a society, they are at the heart of the contradictions and tensions that characterize China's current reform program. It is virtually impossible to provide a comprehensive portrayal of "the system"—if such a term can be used at all. There are practices of Party journalism as usual. There are striking examples of unrelieved systemic corruption. But there are also instances of cutting-edge journalistic innovation and evidence of increased autonomy, although these developments co-exist with extreme forms of commercialism. These are all aspects of Chinese journalism in the mid-1990s. I have been selective, focusing on what I consider the most relevant and representative of dominant and emerging forms and practices. My choice of topics and case studies were largely based upon the findings of my fieldwork. For example, I did not plan to write a whole chapter on corruption in journalism until I realized the scope of the problem. And while I had some knowledge of Guangzhou's Pearl River Economic Radio and Shanghai's East Radio before going to China, I had not even heard about the innovative programs at China Central Television or, for that matter, the story of *Beijing Youth News* (Beijing qingnian bao). They became the subject of my case studies on the basis of my exposure to the Chinese academic and trade literature, my discussions with various people inside and outside the media industry, and, in particular, recommendations of Chinese media scholars I interviewed. Although I discuss the mass media in general and analyze both print and broadcast media, I focus mainly on the journalistic aspects of the news media operations. I provide overviews of media development in the country and discuss two cases of media reform in Beijing, but I also analyze cases of journalistic innovation in news organizations in Guangzhou and Shanghai—two regional centers of reform in China—and discuss how these innovations have been or are likely to be diffused throughout the country. Even here, I have to make choices. For example, I focus on developments in radio broadcasting in these two cities, rather than on television. This is not because I regard television as being less important but because initial reform and commercialization were carried out in radio broadcasting and have an impact not only on the patterns of reform and commercialization of radio broadcasting throughout the country but also on reform and commercialization in television. Finally, while I focus on actual developments in media policy and practices, I also try to convey a sense of the ongoing theoretical debates regarding the news media inside China and address various media reform arguments raised by those inside China.

I begin my analysis of the current interlocking of Party control and market forces in the Chinese news media with an overview and critique of the Party's model of political communication and of the Party's journalism theories and practices. In chapter 1 I describe the general structure and characteristics of the media under Party domination. If the whole study is conceived as an analysis of the accommodations and tensions between Party logic and market logic, then this chapter is about Party logic. Instead of simply invoking abstract labels such as "authoritarian" or "Leninist totalitarian," however, I try to provide as much historical and contextual detail as possible about the Party's media theory and practices.

In chapter 2 I analyze the twisted path of media reform since the early 1980s and the political and economic developments that led to rapid commercialization of the media in 1992. I critically examine the media reform literature during the political ferment of the mid-1980s. In particular, I examine the extent to which this literature challenged the Party's model of political communication. I then discuss the suppression of this discourse on media democratization in 1989 and the subsequent turn to the market both in media theory and practice.

In chapters 3 and 4 I analyze the different ways in which market forces influence existing media institutions and practices, particularly the traditional Party organs and broadcast stations. Chapter 3 has a more general discussion of media commercialization in terms of financial and organizational structures. In it I focus on such aspects as increasing reliance on advertising and sponsors for financing and the growth of media organizations into business conglomerates. I also discuss the implications of commercialization for the overall structure of the news media system. In chapter 4 I explore the impact of the coexistence of the Party principle and the market principle on the level of news reporting; in particular, I center on corrupt forms of journalism that go beyond China's own legal and ethical boundaries. The issues raised are no less structural.

In chapters 5 and 6 I examine newly established commercialized media institutions, formats, and content in broadcast and newspaper sectors. Through detailed case studies of media reform and commercialization in Guangzhou, Shanghai, and Beijing, I explore the accommodations and tensions between Party control and market forces in the emerging commercialized media sector. Although these newly commercialized popular media outlets are not outside the Party-controlled media system proper, unlike traditional Party organs they are completely dependent on the market for financial support. They have gained more autonomy either as a result of deliberate reform efforts initiated by these media organizations themselves or by default—that they are on the margins of the existing Party-controlled system.

In chapter 7 I discuss the implications of the intertwining of Party control and market forces in the Chinese news media. In particular, I provide a critical assessment of the emerging popularized commercial media sector and explore the possibility for emergence of a propagandist/commercial model of journalism. In chapter 8 I outline internal and external challenges to the current media structure and analyze the Party's most recent responses to these challenges. The concluding chapter is more speculative and hypothetical. In it I look beyond the current interlocking of Party logic and market logic and take issue with those who advocate for further commercialization of news media in China. I outline a theoretical framework for the democratization of news media and discuss alternative possibilities.

The primary data for this study was gathered during fieldwork in China between 1994 and 1995. The research involved three aspects: the monitoring of print and broadcast media content, documentary research, and interviews.

Monitoring of Media Content

In addition to television viewing, radio listening, and newspaper reading, my monitoring of media content involved several specific projects for analysis in different chapters. These projects included a survey of national and provincial Party organs available in a university newspaper and periodical reading room in Beijing, the monitoring of two China Central Television news and current affairs programs, as well as a survey of newspapers from newsstand operators in Beijing, Shanghai, and Hangzhou.

Documentary Research in China

Documentary research involved an extensive examination of Chinese books, Party and government documents, press reports, and academic and trade journals published between the late 1980s and 1994. Journalism and broadcasting yearbooks, academic journals published by journalism schools and research institutions, and trade journals published by major news organizations served as primary sources for tracing trends. They also provided the basic material for analyzing the debates in journalism theory and for describing the specific reforms carried out by different media organizations.[32] Journalism trade journals and internal policy publications of government media administrations provided a particularly rich source for policy instructions by Party and government authorities and for views and comments about media theory and practice by media critics, media officials, and rank-and-file reporters and editors.

Without doubt, the debates and discussions in these publications were published under various constraints and thus have to be read "between the lines" just as a perceptive reader would probably do with Chinese newspapers. Nevertheless, they not only contain rich and detailed factual descriptions but also reveal a considerable level of critical discussion of issues concerning the news media and journalists' reflections on work practices. By publishing under pen names, many writers are able to convey their perspectives on various issues confronting the news media.

Interviews

Media monitoring and literature research were supplemented by extended in-depth interviews with a wide range of people from Beijing, Hangzhou, and Shanghai. Among them were top journalism and broadcasting scholars, journalism educators, media administrators, radio and television producers, and ordinary journalists. Interview data provided valuable material by which I could critically evaluate and contextualize print sources. Due to the politically sensitive nature of the subject, however, the interview data has been used either as background material or cited anonymously to respect the desire for confidentiality of most informants. Whenever possible, I use comparable material from trade journals.[33]

1

Party Journalism in China: Theory and Practice

James Curran observes that the Soviet media before Gorbachev "was at times more restricted in theory than in actual practice (thus reversing the pattern of the West where the media has long been more restricted in practice than in theory)."[1] What was true in the former Soviet Union is true in China, particularly during periods of relative political stability. Neither Chinese journalists nor readers and audiences are passive dupes. They have ways of communicating that contravene Party tutelage and surveillance.[2] In this chapter I will provide an overview of the evolution of Party journalism, the structure and control of news media under the domination of the Party, and the Party's media theory and practice. Although it begins with a brief narrative about the evolution of the Party press, this chapter is organized around key aspects of the Party's journalism theory and practices.

The Legacies of Party Journalism

The Party press can be traced back to radical journals of the late 1910s and early 1920s in which students and intellectuals voiced their opposition to imperialism and to Chinese warlords. Many future Party leaders, such as Chen Duxiu, Li Dazhao, and Mao Zedong, were involved in publishing radical journals before the founding of the Communist party in 1921.[3] The first Party organ, the *Guide* (Xiangdao) was published in 1922. During its first united front with the Nationalist Party between 1924 and 1927, the Party created a number of labor, peasant, women, and youth journals in an organizing effort. From the beginning, therefore, the Party established organs and non-Party publications that were nevertheless under its leadership. This is still the dominant feature of Chinese journalism today.

On November 7, 1931, the Party, engaged in rural-based guerrilla warfare with the Nationalist government, established the central government of the Chinese Soviet Republics in the town of Ruijin, Jiangxi Province (known as the Jiangxi Soviet). On the same day, the central government established the Red China News Agency, the predecessor of today's Xinhua News Agency. The agency not only sent reports to the outside world but also used the army radio to collect outside news, mainly dispatches of the Nationalist government's Central News Agency. These

were edited and printed in *Reference News* (Cankao xiaoxi), which was distributed to Party leaders. This practice of news organizations providing intelligence for
high-level Party leaders continues today.

Central-level Party, government, army, youth, and labor organizations established their own organs. By the fall of 1933, there were thirty-four newspapers and
journals in the Jiangxi Soviet. The most influential was *Red China* (Hongse zhonghua), which was established as the organ of the central soviet government on
December 11, 1931. It later became the joint organ of the Party, the government,
the All-China Labor Union, and the Communist Youth League. Until its demise
at the start of the Long March in October 1934, it was important for the Party's
war effort as well as for political and economic construction of the revolutionary
bases.[4]

The Long March ended most of the Party press. But army units continued to
publish journals and pamphlets reporting war news and celebrating the bravery
of soldiers. Party journalism revived as soon as the Red Army reached northern
Shaanxi and established a revolutionary base. *Red China* resumed publication in
January 1936. In deference to the newly formed united front with the Nationalist
Party against the Japanese, the name was changed to *New China Journal* (Xinzhon-
ghua bao). At the same time, the Red China News Agency became the New China
(or Xinhua) News Agency.

Yan'an, capital of the Party-controlled zone in the border areas of Shaanxi,
Gansu, and Ningxia, became the Party's press center. There, newspapers and journals for cultural affairs, youth, women, and peasants were published in addition
to the main Party organs. In 1941, the Party combined *New China Journal* and a
Xinhua publication to establish its first daily newspaper, *Liberation Daily*, which
soon became the organ of the Party Central Committee. The theories and practices developed by the Party in Yan'an as reflected in this paper are still relevant.[5]
In 1942, *Liberation Daily* reformatted its pages. Originally, the four-page paper
carried international news (mainly about the Soviet Union and international communist movements) on its first two pages. Domestic national news and local news
were on pages three and four, respectively. In an effort to make it more relevant
to its readers, and as part of the Party's attempt to assert independence from the
tutelage of Stalin and the Comintern, news about the revolutionary base areas was
moved to the front page, local news to the second page, and international news to
the third page. News about revolutionary activities gained primary importance.
For example, the creation of a new form of peasant self-organization, which would
be of interest to other peasants, was front-page news.[6] This innovation was revolutionary at the time.

On December 30, 1940, Yan'an Xinhua Radio began trial broadcasting. The Party's first, the station was affiliated with the Xinhua News Agency, which provided

all broadcast material. It aired important Party documents, editorials and articles from the Party's main newspapers and magazines, news, speeches by well-known personalities, revolutionary stories, and music.

The Party press continued to grow during the anti-Japanese war (1937–45) and the civil war (1945–49) in the areas controlled by the Party. The Party also continued underground publications in areas not under its control. It gained concessions during the anti-Japanese war allowing it to establish publications openly in Nationalist-controlled areas. Most notable among these was *Xinhua Daily* (Xinhua ribao) issued in the Nationalists' war capital, Chongqing, under the leadership of Zhou Enlai.

The News Media in the People's Republic

News media after 1949 were established mainly on the basis of the Party's journalism cadres and the material and technological infrastructures left over from the old regime. Some of the Party organs created in the revolutionary base areas were moved to big cities and became central and provincial Party organs. The Party's journalism during the revolutionary war years became the journalism of the party state without much change either in conceptualization or in structure.

The Party press, however, did not initially monopolize journalism. The Party realized the necessity of keeping a few independent commercial newspapers in major urban centers because the Party press, so long rural-oriented, might not satisfy urban tastes. A small number of commercial newspapers and radio stations were thus allowed to continue into the early 1950s.

Eventually coexistence proved impossible. The commercial newspapers became part of a planned Party-dominated system but with special roles. A private national newspaper, for example, was required to devote 60 percent of its coverage to local affairs of Wuhan, the city where it was published.[7] These newspapers were forced to design their coverage to support the Party's guidance in political and social life. Moreover, the interviewing style of reporters from commercial newspapers was considered too intrusive by Party and government officials and thus journalists were often refused access to news sources. Private newspapers were also unable to get much advertising. As a result, although the Party encouraged them in theory, privately owned commercial newspapers could not survive. More importantly, as the journalism scholar Sun Xupei notes, the Party did not have a long-term plan for the continued existence of commercial newspapers. Party committees were established in them and socialist transformation was soon carried out in them. Their numbers dropped from fifty-eight in March 1950 to twenty-five in August 1951 to zero in 1952.[8]

Private commercial radio stations suffered a similar fate. In early 1950, there were thirty-three but by the end of 1953, they had all disappeared. A network of "people's radio" stations run hierarchically by central, provincial, and municipal governments, monopolized radio broadcasting. At the county level, wired broadcast stations were set up. When television was introduced in 1958, the same hierarchical and monopolistic pattern was followed.

In 1949 and in the early 1950s, some political and social organizations, as well as government departments, started special interest newspapers. China's democratic parties, which have weak power bases, had some voice in the press in the early years of the People's Republic. The Chinese Democratic League began its official organ, *Guangming Daily* (Guangming ribao), on June 16, 1949, in Beijing.[9] *Wenhui Bao,* begun by non-Communist progressive intellectuals in Shanghai's foreign concessions in 1938 and closed by the Nationalists during the civil war, resumed publication on June 21, 1949. These two nonaffiliated newspapers were both supported by the Party and considered integral parts of the socialist press system.

Publications of the Party's mass organizations also become an important arm of the system. The All-China Workers Federation began *Workers' Daily* (Gongren ribao) on July 15, 1949. The Chinese Communist Youth League created two newspapers in 1951, *China Youth News* (Zhongguo qingnian bao) and *China Juvenile News* (Zhongguo shaonian bao). Government departments put out their own newspapers as well. The Ministry of Health, for example, initiated *Health News* (Jiankang bao) in 1950. By 1954, in addition to 151 Party organs, there were 17 newspapers aimed at workers, 23 at farmers, 17 at youths and juveniles, 14 at specialized trades, and another 15 published by social organizations and other political parties.[10]

During the Cultural Revolution (1966–76), almost all of these ceased publication, as did many Party organs. Although Red Guard tabloids flourished, there were only forty-three regular newspapers in the whole country in 1967.[11]

Since the launching of economic reform in the late 1970s, China has experienced an unprecedented media boom. Radio and television stations, which were mostly limited to central and provincial levels in the 1970s, were established on the municipal/prefecture and county levels. By the end of 1992, there were 812 radio stations and 586 television stations.[12] The network of Party organs was also extended. Non-Party special interest newspapers, published by government departments, business enterprises, and other political and social organizations, came back with unprecedented vigor. Some catered to specific readers—workers, farmers, women, youth, seniors, police, students, minority language or English readers. Some specialized in particular subject areas—sports, economics, science and technology, health, culture, education, law and order, the environment. Still others were general interest evening papers and digests. By the mid-1980s, their total numbers had already far exceeded the number of official Party organs. Of the 1,008 new newspapers published between 1980 and 1985, for example, there were only 103

Party organs.[13] By 1992, there were 1,230 non-Party newspapers.[14] However, Party organs still dominated the press by their size, frequency of publication, and number of employees.

By the end of the 1980s, China had developed a rather elaborate media network. Xinhua was the largest news organization with three major departments: domestic with bureaus in all provinces; international with more than ninety foreign bureaus; and translation, providing reports from foreign countries for restricted distribution among Party and government bureaucracies. *People's Daily* is the organ of the Party Central Committee. Central People's Radio (CPR) and China Central Television (CCTV) are monopolies. CPR's 6:30 to 7:00 morning news and CCTV's 7:00 to 7:30 evening news are transmitted nationwide every day, making them the most important news programs in the country. These four outlets are at the very top of the Chinese news hierarchy.

In addition, there are a number of important special interest national newspapers. *Guangming Daily,* originally published by the democratic parties, is now the Party organ for the country's educated elite. *Reference News,* published by Xinhua, carries mostly material from foreign news agencies. *Economic Daily* (Jingji ribao) is the organ of the State Council; it specializes in economic policy and economic issues. *People's Liberation Army Daily* (Jiefangjun bao) is the organ of the Party's Central Military Committee and the General Political Department of the Chinese People's Liberation Army. In addition to *Workers' Daily, China Youth News,* and *China Juvenile News,* the special interest category has been expanded to include such titles as *Farmers' Daily* (Nongmin ribao), affiliated with the agriculture department, and *China Women's News* (Zhongguo funu bao), published by the All-China Women's Federation. Many government bureaus, such as culture, sports, education, health, industry and trade, and science and technology, have their own organs.

This media structure is more or less reproduced at the provincial and municipal levels, although without as much complexity. The structure is both hierarchical and monopolistic. Typically, a province and a city (or prefecture district) has a Party organ, a radio station, and a television station. As the most important local news outlets, they are under the direct control of a local Party committee.

The four major national organizations are the agenda-setters. Xinhua's reports of major national and international events are carried all over the country. Important editorials in *People's Daily* are frequently transmitted by Xinhua News Agency, summarized on the national radio and television broadcasts, and sometimes reprinted by provincial Party organs. On October 14, 1994, for example, *Hainan Daily* (Hainan ribao), the Party organ of Hainan Province, China's newest and arguably most liberal province, reprinted the entire *People's Daily* editorial of the same day under the headline: "Strengthen and Improve the Construction of the Party's Grass-Roots Units."

The Party Principle

The central concept that underlies the Party's domination over the media is the "Party principle" (*dangxing yuanze*). A typical journalism textbook describes it as comprising three basic components: that the news media must accept the Party's guiding ideology as its own; that they must propagate the Party's programs, policies, and directives; and that they must accept the Party's leadership and stick to the Party's organizational principles and press policies.[15]

The Party exercised strict control over its publications from the very beginning. The first resolution of the Party's founding congress in 1921 stated that "journals, daily publications, books and booklets must be managed by the Party's central executive committee" and that "no central or local publications should carry any article that opposes the Party's principles, policies and decisions."[16]

Lenin's notion that the Party newspaper should be the Party's collective propagandist, agitator, and organizer was also instrumental in shaping the Chinese Party's journalism policy. In an April 1, 1942, note to its readers, *Liberation Daily* explained that to be the Party's propagandist, a newspaper must not only make *all its contents*—each commentary, each feature, each news item—embody the Party's views but also make the newspaper an advocate for every single policy and campaign. At the same time, it must educate the people, raise their consciousness, and guide and support them in their struggles. The Party proclaims itself to be the vanguard of the proletariat representing the interests of the people. Within this ideological construct, the media serve as the mouthpiece of the Party and, by definition, serve as the mouthpiece of the people, too.

The Party principle and the mouthpiece theory are constantly being emphasized and reinforced as the Party struggles to maintain control of the media. Because the Party's many local authorities were scattered during the war years, the central authority had to partially rely on newspapers to spread its policy directives and maintain unity. Mao Zedong himself issued many directives to high Party leaders on the importance of maintaining complete control of the press and overcoming tendencies toward independence among propaganda workers. In 1942, he criticized high-level Party organizations for paying little attention to directing the Party's news organizations. Again in 1948, in criticizing Party leaders for allowing "erroneous" ideas to spread, he insisted that the press must unconditionally propagate the Party's policies and he suggested strict measures of press control. Mao proposed that a leader with a correct understanding of Party's policies read galley proofs before a newspaper is published.[17]

The post-Mao leadership continues to stress this theory. Even Hu Yaobang, considered the most enlightened post-Mao leader, in a widely publicized speech in 1985 stated that "the Party's journalism is the Party's mouthpiece,"[18] including both

Party and non-Party news outlets. While writers of literature are free to choose subjects and develop themes with "completely comradely suggestions and advice" from the Party, journalists must speak strictly on its behalf.[19] In November 1989 Jiang Zemin gave a speech on the Party's leadership in journalism that could have been taken from a Party document of the pre-1949 era: "Party Committees at various levels should frequently discuss and study news work. Issues such as propaganda policy, guiding ideas, focus of news reporting, effects of propaganda in each period must be discussed in Party Committee meetings. The chief responsible comrade of the Party Committee must take personal charge of news work. He must provide timely information to the media, issue orders, [and,]. . . moreover, he must personally preview important editorials, commentaries, and news reports."[20]

The Party has developed a number of mechanisms for directing the media.[21] General rules and parameters for news operations can be found in Party resolutions, directives, announcements, internal bulletins such as *Propaganda Trend* (Xuanchuan dongtai) (issued by the Party's Propaganda Department on a weekly basis), and speeches and informal verbal messages of leading Party figures. Some rules, such as a 1953 resolution prohibiting a Party organ from criticizing the Party committee with which it is affiliated, have been strictly enforced.[22] In 1980, the Party reiterated that the media should unconditionally propagate Party policies and may not put forward any views opposing the Party's major decisions or discuss important theoretical and policy issues about which the Party has already made a decision.[23]

In addition, the Party sometimes sets specific guidelines on news reporting. A 1987 document issued by the Party's Central Secretariat provided detailed instructions for reporting important domestic political and social issues. For example, the deaths of leaders and important personalities should be reported to both domestic and international audiences on the same day; traffic accidents involving foreigners and overseas Chinese citizens should be reported to overseas audiences on the day they happen. If the situation is not clear, the event should be reported in a "brief and objective" manner right away, with detailed reporting to follow after more thorough investigation.[24]

Similarly, Party leaders' speeches have been important for transmitting the Party's ideas about news reporting because they define the nature of journalism and set out general and specific guidelines. They have been carefully studied by media workers and constantly interpreted and reinterpreted by media theoreticians.

In addition to setting general rules, the Party often defines topics to be given attention for a specific period that become the focus of campaigns. Although their subjects can be very broad, like economic construction, or more specific, like eliminating pornography, they always reflect the Party's priorities. Since major media organizations are an integral part of the Party apparatus, their leaders occasionally participate in meetings at which they learn the Party's agenda firsthand. But more often, topics for attention are passed down from the Party's Propaganda Department. Although officials of major media organizations are all appointed by the Party, news directors and chief editors do not always have the final say. Important items are often previewed by Party officials in charge of propaganda.

Party propaganda departments, however, are not necessarily the highest media authority. On crucial issues or at crucial moments, the Party secretary at each level will directly supervise media work. Thus, when Qin Benli, editor-in-chief of the *World Economic Herald,* refused to accept the censorship of material ordered by the Shanghai Party official responsible for propaganda, it was Jiang Zemin, then Party secretary of Shanghai, who talked to Qin and forced him to accept censorship.[25]

On important occasions, Party leaders become directly involved in news and editorials. During the war years, Mao wrote many news dispatches for Xinhua and published many unsigned editorials in *Liberation Daily.* During the political struggles in the 1950s Mao, apparently unhappy with the moderate tone of *People's Daily* editorials on certain issues, also penned a number of editorials.[26] More recently, the notorious April 26, 1989, *People's Daily* editorial that defined the student demonstrations as "counter-revolutionary turmoil" was widely believed to have been written by Party officials.

The Party closely surveys media content. Media monitoring (*shendu, shenting*) is usually performed by special teams of veteran Party ideological workers. For editors and journalists, the danger of postpublication retribution is omnipresent. Punishment ranges from being forced to write self-criticisms to demotion to unemployment. Under constant pressure to avoid political "mistakes," many professionals learn to play it safe.

Even non-Party newspapers are still published under the ideological leadership of the Party. In 1956, Mao called for constructive criticism, saying, "Let a hundred flowers blossom, let a hundred schools of thoughts contend." *Guangming Daily,* then jointly run by China's eight democratic parties and other nonpartisan coalitions of industrial, commercial, and political forces, published some of the boldest criticism of the Party in a truly democratic fashion. Its editor-in-chief, Chu Anping, and other non-Communist intellectuals openly challenged the Party's monopoly of political power. *Wenhui Bao,* an influential non-Party newspaper oriented toward Shanghai's intellectual and cultural elites, also voiced harsh criticism. As a result, both were severely attacked by the Party and forced to make self-criticisms. During the subsequent anti-rightist campaign, the critical writers from these two papers, together with many other intellectuals, were labeled "rightists." Their careers were ruined and their personal lives were affected for more than twenty years.[27] *Guangming Daily* is now under direct control of the Party's central Propaganda Department, while *Wenhui Bao* is controlled by the Shanghai

Municipal Party Committee. The prominent role of these two non-Party news-papers in the early 1950s, their containment, and their eventual takeover by the Party serve as an important footnote to the Party's ascendancy to ideological monopoly. The 1993 *China Journalism Yearbook* (Zhongguo xinwen nianjian) listed only two obscure newspapers under democratic parties, with average circulations below fifty thousand per issue. Indeed, one of these two, *Unity News* (Tuanjie bao), published by the Revolutionary Committee of the Kuomintang, is perhaps one of the most boring newspapers in the country.

Organizations such as trade unions and women's federations are not autonomous civil organizations but considered "mass organizations" that serve as "bridges" and "transmission belts" between the Party and special social groups. Although special interest newspapers under the control of these organizations sometimes struggle to speak for their audiences,[28] they are obligated to accept Party policies uncondi-tionally and propagate them in their specific areas.

Similarly, although Party committees are not directly involved in the operations of special interest newspapers, these papers do not constitute an independent public sphere. They are all ultimately subject to Party control. The *World Economic Herald,* the best known non-Party special interest newspaper in the 1980s, for ex-ample, was eventually forced to close down. Its fate is illustrative of the Party's monopolistic control of the news media.

Government Administration of the News Media

The intricate relationship between the Party and the state in China makes media administration especially complicated. Before 1949, the Party controlled all me-dia operations in areas under Communist control. When the Party came to pow-er in October 1949, the administrative and technical operations were shifted to the government, while the Party controlled ideology. The government set up the Gen-eral Press Office on October 19, 1949, making it responsible for administration of print and broadcast media. Xinhua News Agency changed its official affiliation from the Party to the state, under the direction of the General Press Office. The Party's Central Broadcasting Bureau became the Broadcasting Bureau under the General Press Office. In 1952, however, perhaps as recognition that private com-mercial media outlets had disappeared and that the Party had never stopped ex-ercising control, the General Press Office was dismantled. Xinhua became a de-partment under the State Council, China's cabinet, but its daily operations rely heavily on instructions from various levels of the Party bureaucracy, from the Politburo to the central Propaganda Department. It is thus under the dual lead-ership of both the Party and the government.

The Broadcasting Bureau has evolved into the Ministry of Radio, Film, and Television.[29] Unlike any other government department, however, it has a dual identity as both a news organization and a broadcasting administrative bureaucracy. Like Xinhua, it also is under the leadership of the Party and the government. The ministry directly controls the three national broadcast networks: CPR, CCTV, and China International Radio (Radio Beijing). Its editorial board, under the leadership of the ministry's Party committee, is directly in charge of the news, features, and arts programming of the three stations. Under the minister's leadership, the editorial board includes responsible deputy ministers, heads of the three radio and television networks, and leaders of other departments, such as the Film Bureau, the Broadcast Publishing House, and the Television Arts Committee. The board's duties include delivering Party and government directives to the news outlets; drafting strategies for carrying out these directives; organizing and coordinating large-scale media campaigns; approving major media activities, propaganda plans, and program changes initiated by the broadcast networks; and exercising editorial control of important news items and programs. For example, if CCTV wants to make a major change in its programming, its proposals will typically go through the following power hierarchy: the ministry's General Editorial Office, which is responsible for the day-to-day work of the editorial board, the editorial board itself, the ministry's Party committee, the Propaganda Department of the Party Central Committee, and possibly the member of the Standing Committee of the Politburo in charge of media and ideology.

The ministry is also a huge government bureaucracy in charge of every aspect of the country's broadcast operations—issuing regulations, setting technical standards, training personnel, and coordinating research. Its policy directives can be as specific as the number and qualifications of staff in the smallest unit of the broadcast network because staff members are considered government employees.

For the print media, the government in 1987 established a bureaucracy that is similar to the dismantled General Press Office, the State Press and Publications Administration (SPPA).[30] Among other things, it drafts and enforces press regulations and policies, licenses publications, and monitors texts. However, this semiministerial-level government agency is under the supervision of the Party's Propaganda Department and thus has no authority over central Party newspapers, such as *People's Daily* and *Guangming Daily*. But if a Party organ at the provincial or county level wants to expand or change its publication schedule, it must get approval of this agency.

Just as the media structure on the national level is more or less copied on local levels, the administrative structure is also replicated. Each province and municipality has its own broadcast bureau, which is under the dual leadership of the government and the Party. Only the SPPA does not have offices below the provincial level.

Party Journalism as a Form of Political Communication

The Chinese Communist party's notion of the role of the media in the political process is based on its theory of political communication; that is, the "mass line." As Pat Howard points out, the mass line defines three distinct power relations: between cadres (Party workers in the field) and the "masses" (the people as a whole), between Party cadres and ordinary Party members, and between the Party as the revolutionary vanguard and the masses.[31] Although elements of the basic concept can be found in Lenin, Mao provided the most definitive statement of its essence:

> In all the practical work of our Party, all correct leadership is necessarily "from the masses, to the masses." This means: take the ideas of the masses (scattered and unsystematic ideas) and concentrate them (through study turn them into concentrated and systematic ideas), then go to the masses and propagate and explain these ideas until the masses embrace them as their own, hold fast to them and translate them into action, and test the correctness of these ideas in such action. Then once again concentrate ideas from the masses and once again go to the masses so that the ideas are persevered in and carried through. And so on, over and over again in an endless spiral, with the ideas becoming more correct, more vital and richer each time. Such is the Marxist theory of knowledge.[32]

Thus, the people provide the raw material for policy-making by the Party on their behalf. Although their concerns, their aspirations, their well-being are supposed to be the sole concern of the Party, they do not participate in decision-making. Nor do they exercise control over policy formation. The Party, composed of the most farseeing and revolutionary elements of the people, is supposed to be able to define the general interests of the people by remaining close to them. The people themselves, on the other hand, are often muddle-headed and short-sighted. The Party leaders study their situation, collect their opinions, and turn these into systematic policies. The Party's task is to educate the people, to win mass support for and active participation in carrying out the policies. During the process, of course, the peoples' creativity, initiatives, and concerns will again be noted by the Party and incorporated into policies.

Journalism, which is an integral part of Party work, is one means of communication whereby the Party implements the mass line. As Timothy Cheek puts its, journalism has both transformational/agitational and administrative roles under the Party.[33] *Resistance News* (Kangzhan ribao), a newspaper published in the Jinchaji base area (in northern Shanxi Province), clearly articulated the basic concept of Party journalism, or "mass line journalism," as early as 1938 during the anti-Japanese war:

Of course, the production of *Resistance News* has its mission. It must become the pro-
pagandizer and organizer of the border region's mass resistance [and] salvation movement, it must represent the needs of the broad masses, reflect and pass on the real conditions and experience of the broad masses' struggle, promote various aspects of work,
[and] educate the masses themselves. At the same time, from the promotion and assistance of the broad masses, [the paper] itself progresses. . . . It teaches others, and at the
same time is taught by others.[34]

This symbiosis between the newspaper and the people is mediated by the Party.
Although the newspaper facilitates communication among the people, the Party
decides what experiences are to be exchanged and which are to be promoted or
condemned.

The dominant mode of communication is supposed to be a two-way process.
The media are supposed to report the people's opinions, concerns, and aspirations
and to inform the leadership of the performance of cadres who are working directly with the people. They are supposed to describe concrete realities. In mass
line theory, the greatest threat to the leadership of the Party is its detachment from
the people.[35] Liu Shaoqi, when he was the Party's general secretary in 1948, provided a good explanation of this in a speech to the northern China press corps. In
his view, the Party had nothing to fear but its detachment from the people. Among
the Party's links with the people, journalism is key. "You travel to all locations. The
people depend on you to voice their demands, difficulties, experiences and even
to describe mistakes in our work. You turn them into news, features, and reports
to Party Committees at various levels, and to the Central Committee. In this way,
you make a connection between the Party and the masses."[36]

To fulfill their role as a bridge between the Party and the people, journalists, according to Liu, must serve the people with their whole heart, must convey the truth
without exaggeration, sensationalism, or prejudice. He even provided detailed advice on how to write a comprehensive rather than a one-sided report, an in-depth
rather than a superficial one. And he suggested how to conduct interviews so that
people would tell the truth. Clearly, his purpose was not to inform the people but
to provide information for decision-making. Thus, Andrew Nathan has interpreted this function of the press as an intelligence mission for the leaders.[37]

While Liu provided journalists with a good description of the media's role in
facilitating bottom-up flow of communication, Mao Zedong in the same year
provided the clearest expression of the top-down flow required by the mass line.
In a talk to the editorial staff of *Jinshui Daily* (Jinshui ribao), a Party organ in a
revolutionary base area in northwest China, Mao defined the function of newspapers in this way: "The role and power of newspapers consists in their ability to
bring the Party program, the Party line, the Party's general and specific policies,
its tasks and methods of work before the people in the quickest and most exten-

sive way."[38] Mao insisted, "Your job is to educate the people, to *let them know their own interests,* their own tasks and the Party's general and specific policies."[39]

This propagandist and instrumentalist concept of the media was given full play in practice. However, as Timothy Cheek has argued, the concept of propaganda in the Chinese context should not be understood in the pejorative sense but in the literal sense of the word: "Propaganda is nothing more than the attempt to transmit social and political values in the hope of affecting people's thinking, emotions, and thereby behavior."[40] The media are instruments to propagate the Party's policies and directives, to persuade people about the correctness of a policy, and to tell them the good results of a particular policy. The news functions to mobilize people and sustain morale as in the case of war propaganda, which definitely left a legacy for the Party's approach to journalism.

Indeed, notions such as "stimulating" and "encouraging" often appear in discussions about the functions of the media. For example, in a note to Guangxi provincial Party leaders in 1958, Mao wrote: "When it comes to the work of the whole province, a newspaper has the greatest effectiveness in organizing, stimulating, criticizing, and motivating."[41] The Party Central Secretariat in 1981 defined the "basic nature and role" of broadcasting in a similar fashion: "Radio and television are the most powerful modern instruments to educate and stimulate the whole Party, the whole military and people of all nationalities in the construction of socialist material and spiritual civilizations."[42]

This notion of "education" is also significant for an understanding of the paternalistic role of the media. China has a long tradition of scholar-officials "propagating" the moral teachings of the dynasty and fostering a good and moral society.[43] Journalism emerged at the beginning of the twentieth century in a context that ensured the "polemical and educational nature of the venture." Indeed, "Chinese journalism was already educational journalism" before Marxism had any impact.[44] The Party infused this Confucian belief with the Leninist concept of a vanguard whose task is to enlighten the people and help them to see their own interests. Providing role models is one responsibility of journalism as defined by the Party. Journalism must have a "guiding character" (*zhidao xing*). Journalism professor Gan Xifen summarizes this notion quite well: "Being a powerful tool of opinion, news media should guide the people to elevate their consciousness and spirit, to become more united, and to make improvements. News media must not do the opposite by publishing wrong materials to create political division or ideological backwardness among the people. This is the lofty sense of responsibility of our socialist journalistic enterprise."[45]

Such a definition leads to a particular notion of news. As early as August 1942, a *Liberation Daily* editorial had made it clear: "We already know that newspapers do not only report the news, they are also sharp weapons in constructing our nation and Party and in reforming our work and our lives."[46] News in typical Party journalism is about Party and government policies, creative experiences and local adaptation of policies, and the achievements of individual and institutional role models.

The lead story in the January 17, 1995, issue of *People's Daily* (overseas edition) is typical of the administrative role of journalism. It reports how Party and government authorities in Shandong Province try to increase farmers' incomes. According to the paper, the province "correctly deals with the relationship between increased productivity and increased income," "makes the production of grain and cotton its central task," and takes as a goal the development of high-output, high-quality, and high-efficiency agriculture. It concludes with a summary of five concrete measures for increasing income. The story, of course, is designed not merely to praise Shandong Province and boost its image but, more importantly, to provide an example for others.

News, therefore, is often selected on the basis of its relevance to the central task of the Party and the government and reported from the Party's perspective. As a result, subject matter is narrow and sometimes technical. News is usually not about breaking events but about trends, tendencies, and achievements over time. Often stories summarize quarterly and annual reports of production units and government departments. By providing an overview of an industry, a unit, or an aspect of the Party and the government's work, news is conclusive and comprehensive. The prototype of a typical news item is the government report, rather than an engaging story about an event, as is often the case in the West.

While Western media scholars, through painstaking critical analysis, have concluded that news is not completely objective and value-free as advertised but actually carries ideological orientations and embodies a set of enduring values, the Chinese Communist party openly declares that news is value-laden. Indeed, the Party demands that news carry its ideology and value orientations. The Party contends that values can be and should be expressed through the selection, juxtaposition, and presentation of news; indeed, a "good" news item has a clear political orientation, advocates or criticizes, makes an explicit or implicit value judgment.[47]

Even a seemingly innocent weather report can carry a political message. A textbook example is a 1957 Xinhua dispatch about extremely cold weather in Shanghai.[48] It describes a pre-Liberation snowstorm in 1947 that caused the deaths of hundreds of children on the streets overnight and compares it with the much colder conditions in 1957, when nobody froze to death. The story reports how the city's welfare department helped the poor and elderly. The message: the current system is better than the previous one.

The typical news story is thus highly positive, didactic, and openly value-oriented. An article in *China Journalism Yearbook 1993* provides a good example of Party journalism in action, from the initial identification of a story to its intended effects.[49] A team of three reporters, one from *People's Daily,* one from CPR, and one from a local military newspaper, covered a contemporary role model, Su Ning, a young army officer in the northeastern city of Harbin. The reporters initially learned that Su had died while rescuing a comrade and that he had led a simple life and had served the people as did Lei Feng, a soldier role model before him. But these elements alone, the journalists decided, were not enough to make Su the most desirable model in the current context of reform and openness. Then they learned that Su had written a number of research articles on military affairs, including three on the Gulf War. Thus, the journalists reasoned, Su was not only loyal and selfless but also served his country with knowledge and intelligence and with a spirit of exploration and a sense of dedication. These elements in his character made him a contemporary hero who met the demands of modernization. Moreover, although Su's father and father-in-law were both senior military officials, he did not take advantage of these facts. In the context of current widespread corruption and excessive pursuit of material pleasure, Su could be considered a role model in opposing corruption and "peaceful evolution."

The reporters decided that Su was worthy of emulation. Moreover, he would provide a useful reference for the Party and the military in setting the political and moral qualifications of the next generation of Party and military cadres. According to the *Yearbook* article, the journalists had a number of other reasons for pursuing the story. First, they had been looking for contemporary role models for many years.[50] Second, the editor-in-chief of *People's Daily* had called on journalists in early 1991 to focus on discovering new models. Third, to improve the credibility of the Party and to raise morale, reforms as well as new role models were needed.

The first reason is a reflection of the professional values of Party journalists. To promote a role model is to do a good job as a journalist. Just as the journalist watchdog who exposes wrongdoing is a hero in the West, the journalist who discovers a role model is a hero in China. The second reason suggests the journalists' assimilation of specific priorities transmitted from news organizations. The third is consistent with the party's tradition of reporting positively.

What is significant is the journalists' effort to contextualize, to relate an event to the broader political situation, and to take into consideration the Party's propaganda needs as well as its current concerns (modernization, corruption, legitimacy). The construction of a news story is a process of abstraction, of elevation, of injection of political meaning into a news personality—or, more bluntly, of developing an example to fit the propaganda needs of the Party. Because it tests the sensitivity of a journalist's "nose for the news," this process is crucial for "good" journalism. Of course exaggerations, twists, and distortions are common in this process. Many of the role models set up during the Cultural Revolution were twisted to meet particular political needs.

In any event, the three reporters spent two weeks gathering material and writing the Su Ning story. This is characteristic of the cooperative, noncompetitive relationship among news organizations. The journalists believed that they must have a "high sense of responsibility" in treating the story and that their report must be "in depth," "truthful," and "vivid." They took their fourth draft to Beijing, where the top editors of *People's Daily* told them the story should emphasize Su's dedication to modernizing China. Their fifth draft was published in *People's Daily* and broadcast by CPR.

People's Daily made an organized effort to promote Su as a hero. Considerable space was devoted to the story, three commentaries on it were published, and a special editorial team including department heads led by the editor-in-chief and his two deputies took charge. In addition to the original three, two more *People's Daily* reporters were sent to Harbin to gather more material. Following the first feature story, the newspaper published at least six more features on Su with commentaries and photographs.

The *Yearbook* article suggests that these reports had a major impact on people. General Party Secretary Jiang Zemin was "deeply moved" by them. University students said that they had "found a true model." Elementary school pupils determined to be like Su when they grew up. "Workers speeded up their production; military officers became more devoted to national defense, the study of science and modernization; private entrepreneurs improved their service and put trust before money." The article concludes: "Many facts demonstrate that to put forward a model such as Su Ning is indeed a big boost to the construction of two civilizations!"

In the spring of 1993, the Party's Central Military Committee and the military's General Political Department launched a movement to learn from Su Ning. Jiang Zemin, who was also chairman of the Party's Central Military Committee, named Su as a model cadre in the modernization of China's defense. At the same time, *People's Daily* published an editorial and a long feature on the social effects of Su Ning on people of all walks of life.

The credibility of the *Yearbook* article is unimportant for this discussion. Here we are presented with a casebook example of Party journalism "at its best," a social engineering effort described as having changed people's beliefs and behavior.

Limitations, Attempted Reforms, and Disasters

As Pat Howard points out, the Party's mass line process is paternalistic and far from democratic in either a representative or a participatory form. "It does not mean democracy in the sense of autonomous self-government. Rather, it is government on the people's behalf by leaders who, in the final analysis, are not responsible to the people, but to the Party."[51] The mass line "does not extend to allowing 'the masses' to organize autonomous interest groups or political forces that could challenge, check, or even supervise the Party's exercise of state power."[52] Neither do the news media play such a role because they do not act independently to mediate between the civil society and the State. Rather, they are totally assimilated into the Party state apparatus and act "in the service of the state."[53] Of course, there is room for criticism and self-criticism in the media, but this is different from acting as independent watchdogs. Once a decision is made, dissenting views cannot be reported. Consequently, media criticism is insubstantial and operates in a top-down fashion. Criticisms tend to be aimed at lower-level Party officials and bureaucracies for failing to carry out Party directives adequately, for poor working style, and for failing to live up to Party standards.[54]

In practice, the two-way mass line model has been severely lopsided in favor of top-down communication. That Liu Shaoqi, who provided the most definitive statement on the journalists' role in bottom-up communication, was purged by Mao, who emphasized top-down communication, is in itself significant. But even if it were implemented in a more balanced way, the model itself is fundamentally flawed. Like the mass line, journalism under the leadership of the Party is undemocratic and paternalistic.

First, since policy formation remains the Party's prerogative and policy-making is highly centralized, the mass media, as channels of communication between the top Party leadership and lower-level Party cadres and the ordinary people, do not play a significant role in reporting the policy-making process, especially debates within the Party on important issues. Because they report only the final policies, their implementation, and their impact, there is no concept of a people's right to know or of an informed citizenry in a representative or participatory democracy. Although journalists provide important information relevant to policy-making, the practice of restricting this to internal reference reports or "intelligence" means that citizens are systematically excluded from vital information that would enable them to participate in policy-making.

Second, just as there is no right of recall and no mechanism by which the people can make the Party accountable, there is no institutional mechanism that ensures the media's accountability to the people. Mass line journalism, therefore, is highly paternalistic in theory. In reality, its performance is shaped by irresponsible and unaccountable Party leaders and their power struggles. At the height of the Cultural Revolution, even columns such as "letters from readers" were canceled. Reporters who had written "internal reference" material to report problems to the Party were investigated and sometimes prosecuted.[55]

Third, notions of "the masses" and of "the people" homogenize needs and interests and conceal fundamental conflicts. They "sabotage prospects for building a socialist society on a foundation of pluralist solidarity and diverse democratic forums for the articulation of differing needs and negotiation of agreements (plans and policies) for the utilization of productive resources."[56] Notwithstanding the Party's claim that there are no fundamental conflicts of interest among the people, the process of "taking from the people" is unavoidably selective. The interests of urban dwellers, for example, have always been primary and are often promoted at the expense of the rural population.[57]

Indeed, constant struggles within the Party over the control of the media suggest that it is difficult enough for the news media to be the voice of *the Party*. It is thus impossible for the media to speak for *the people*. The existence of different newspapers for different political and social groups is potentially conducive for democratic communication, but these newspapers are unable to articulate independent perspectives within the current power structure.

To be sure, there is a certain form of participatory journalism in China that, in theory at least, provided some grass-roots access to the media. The amateur correspondents system derived from Mao's notion that the press must be run by "all the people, the whole Party," rather than by a few professionals behind closed doors (*quandang banbao, qunzhong banbao*).[58] Although elements of this practice were already in place in the 1930s, *Liberation Daily* in Yan'an first systematically articulated and instituted this model. It declared in an editorial that the Party's newspapers are also the newspapers of the people. Therefore, "our newspapers should not only have capable editors and reporters, but more importantly, should have correspondents who live among the people and participate in various kinds of practical activities."[59] In 1944, there were approximately two thousand amateur correspondents in the Yan'an area, more than half of them workers and peasants.[60]

Because grass-roots correspondents extend the news net and broaden the horizons of news reporting, they could, theoretically, play an important role in democratizing journalism. But they work within a context of Party control. Grass-roots correspondents are not the same as freelance writers in the West since most are affiliated with low-level Party committees. Conventionally, they must first get their reports approved by propaganda departments in their own units.[61] Just as journalists at a Party newspaper may not criticize the Party committee to which it is affiliated, a correspondent in a factory cannot criticize the factory's Party committee. Often, amateur correspondents are mere publicists for their Party organizations.

Like the history of the Party itself, the history of journalism under the control of the Party has been twisted. At times, the Party engineered media reforms in an attempt to make the news closer to the people.[62] However, when the Party becomes totally detached from the people and acts against the interests of whole sectors of the population, the media, without any relative autonomy, can only rise and fall with the Party. Two historical episodes are noteworthy: the media reform movement in 1956 and the media's role in the Cultural Revolution.

As noted previously, Leninist press theory was important in the formative years of the Party. After the Party came to power in 1949, the media copied the Soviets in every aspect. However, the Party gradually realized that there was a negative side to this. In 1956, after the Soviets criticized Stalin's mistakes, the Party sought more indigenous ways of developing socialism. A media reform movement was initiated.[63]

People's Daily, under close leadership of the Party, solicited opinions from a wide range of citizens and studied other newspapers, including Chinese commercial newspapers before 1949 and a number of Western newspapers.[64] A *People's Daily* editorial called for expanded news coverage, free discussion and debate of different opinions, and better writing. The editorial expressed a desire to reflect people's lives and concerns and provide more diverse content.

Significantly, this editorial revised *Liberation Daily*'s rigid concept of a Party organ. *People's Daily* suggested that instead of making every article reflect the Party's perspective, only editorials and those articles written by members of the Central Committee should. It even proposed that opinions opposing the Party could be published. At the same time, following its tradition of participatory journalism, it urged the people to participate in newspaper work: "Newspapers are opinion institutions of the whole society." Furthermore, "Our name, *People's Daily*, means that it is the common weapon and property of the people. The people are its masters. We will run a good newspaper only if we depend on the masses."[65]

Xinhua and broadcast stations also acted to broaden their coverage to reflect a wide range of opinion and topics, including providing more informative, service-oriented, and entertaining programs. Although these reforms did not alter the basic news media structure, there was a significant shift toward a more pluralistic press and an attempt to redress the emphasis on top-down communication. This reform movement, however, ended in 1957 with the anti-rightist campaign. By 1958, the media had abandoned commitments to reform.[66] Like the Party, the media became even more divorced from the people during the Great Leap Forward as demonstrated in news reports of absurdly high outputs and of impossible achievements. They became unquestioning tools of Mao's movement.

The Cultural Revolution was the dark age of Chinese journalism.[67] The undemocratic tendencies in the Party's concept of the media were fully exposed and amplified. Control of the media was chaotic. The Party's instrumentalist concept of the media, when taken to its extreme, excused deliberate manipulation, falsification, and exaggeration, so long as they met political objectives. The emphasis on the media's function of organizing and mobilizing people led to a situation in which a single editorial in *People's Daily* could shape a whole mass movement. The polemic tradition of Chinese journalism was also taken to its extreme.

The media were full of single-minded expressions of opinion and sweeping generalizations. A narrow notion of policy relevance led to a particular form of didactic media presentation. Political slogans, "great criticisms" (*dapipan*), and "falsehood, big talk, and empty talk" (*jia, da, kong*) became the daily media fare. "Quotation journalism" (*yulu xinwen*) emerged in which remarks, usually printed in bold typeface, by Marx, Lenin, and Mao were used in news reports. The required political uniformity and the lack of any editorial independence led to local newspaper night editors checking central Party papers to determine the placement of political news, the wording of headlines, the choice of type fonts, and the size of photos.[68]

Party orthodoxy now insists that the Cultural Revolution was a deviation, a mistake, and, indeed, the Party itself was made a victim of "ultra-leftist" political groups headed by Lin Biao, once Mao's designated heir, and Jiang Qing, Mao's wife. The Cultural Revolution is interpreted as a period when the "glorious traditions" of "the Party and people's journalism" were violated, when the press was not under the leadership of the Party but in the hands of a few individuals in pursuit of power.[69] However, that ten years of Cultural Revolution happened at all and that the media system only amplified ultra-leftism suggests that something was fundamentally wrong with both the political system and the media system. Such fundamental flaws eventually fueled movement toward media reform in the post–Cultural Revolution era.

2

The Trajectory of Media Reform

Chinese media reform in the late 1970s and early 1980s began as an attempt to correct specific theories and practices of the Cultural Revolution and return to the earlier ideals of the Party press, such as "seeking truth from facts" and having relevance to the everyday lives of the audience. The media were still viewed as instruments of the Party, but the objective was different in the new era of economic reform and openness. The definition of the media as instruments of class struggle was officially dropped. Instead, the media were promoted as instruments of economic and cultural construction, with a new stress placed on business information and entertainment.

Reporters began to emphasize "truthfulness," "brevity," "timeliness," "liveliness," and "readability." The scope of reporting was broadened; human interest stories, disaster news, and crime news, for example, became acceptable. News that criticized the daily work of authorities and the wrongdoing of officials increased. In 1980, major national media exposed a 1979 oil rig accident, leading to the State Council decision to punish a vice premier and remove the petroleum minister. Instead of relying on government handouts for news, journalists were encouraged to investigate situations and produce on-the-spot reports.

In discussions, such ultra-left media theories as "facts should serve politics" were criticized. Journalism professor Gan Xifen's assertion that "facts are thus primary and ideology secondary" in news reporting may sound naive to critical media scholars in the West, but in China, it was subversive and emancipatory.[1] Early mainstream American communication theory, with its seemingly scientific character, its abstraction of the communication process, and the absence of "class" and "ideology" found a receptive audience among Chinese journalism students in the early 1980s. Concepts such as "information transmission," "sender," and "receiver" gained considerable circulation in media reform literature, as did the role of the audience. The media, it was said, should be more "reader-oriented than leader-oriented."[2] The Western concept of "news value" as a set of professionally determined standards for news selection, such as importance, proximity, and timeliness, received considerable attention.

Despite changes in media content and practices, however, the Party's fundamental concept of political communication and the role of the media remained the same. The Third Plenary Session of the Eleventh National Party Congress in 1978, a historic meeting that ushered in Deng Xiaoping's economic reform and open door policy, explicitly reasserted the mouthpiece theory. For the most part, media reform in the early 1980s was a case not only of "loud thunder, small raindrops" but also of "old bottles, new wines."[3] Much of the effort was concentrated on operational and technical levels.

The Struggle for Media Democratization in the Mid-1980s

The media reform movement reached a new stage after the mid-1980s. As Judy Polumbaum observed, by 1985 attention had shifted to the media's role and structure.[4] Although technical and operational reforms had brought some change, it was difficult to advance any further. Even such seemingly easy goals as timeliness were formidable. Despite efforts to make reporting more professional, the media were still required to meet the Party's propaganda objectives. Professional values like timeliness were considered secondary. In the West, timeliness is closely connected to competitiveness. Without such an environment, there was little incentive to pursue it. Propaganda for economic prosperity simply replaced or, more accurately, supplemented the previous narrowly defined task of political propaganda, while the patterns of news reporting remained the same.

After economic reform, political reform was pushed onto the Party's agenda. Steps were taken to separate government administration from Party ideological leadership. The Party's dominant role in nearly every aspect of life was declining. Also discussed were such issues as the need for more openness in the government process, democratic decision-making, and public participation.

The years 1986, 1987, and 1988 were a period of theoretical ferment. Although Hu Yaobang, then Party general secretary, reaffirmed the role of the media as the mouthpiece of the Party and warned against excessive controversy and critical reporting in 1985,[5] just a year later the Party leadership was tolerating discussion of ideas that he had explicitly discouraged.[6] Chief editors of national newspapers openly expressed their desire for greater editorial independence and relative autonomy.

Under the leadership of Zhao Ziyang, the Thirteenth National Party Congress in October 1987 put political reform and, as part of it, journalism reform on the national agenda. Significantly, in Zhao's report to the Party Congress, mention of the press's role as the mouthpiece of the Party, which reportedly had been in early drafts, was dropped after extensive debate.[7] "Political transparency," a glasnost-like phrase, was used to advocate greater openness in government and more reporting of the political process.

Zhao affirmed three significant concepts: that the Party should have "supervision by public opinion" (*yulun jiandu*), that the Party and the government should inform the people about important events (*zhongda shiqing rang renmin zhidao*), and that the people should participate in the discussion of important issues (*zhongda wenti jing renmin taolun*). While these notions did not challenge the Party's fundamental assumptions, they did suggest significant moves toward less paternalistic and more democratic communication and decision-making. News organizations were given more editorial autonomy. As one journalist in a major national news organization recalled to me in late 1994, Party control over the media was relatively relaxed during 1987 and 1988. Well-known investigative journalist Liu Binyan even suggests that "by the mid-1980s the expanded freedom to publish made it possible for several Party organs to have taken on the character of private newspapers."[8] Zhao not only provided "rhetorical ammunition that sanctioned more aggressive reporting" and ushered in significant openness and attention to sensitive issues but also invigorated theoretical discussions. Some reformers began to raise fundamental questions about the process of political communication itself. The Party principle was challenged by an emerging discourse on the democratization of media communication.

Freedom of the Press

By the mid-1980s, freedom of the press had become an overt issue for advocates of media reform.[9] While journalists pursued press freedom by asserting more editorial autonomy, theorists tried to define press freedom and to elaborate its grounds. They stressed that press freedom means freedom within the constitution and the law, which in fact suggested that the press should be free from the arbitrary power of the Party. Such freedom, some of them further pointed out, was for all the people as part of their democratic rights. Hu Jiwei, former editor-in-chief of *People's Daily,* argued: "The kind of press freedom we want to advocate is press freedom for all the people and not just press freedom for news workers. Freedom of the press for citizens is the right to be kept informed as masters of the country, their right of political consultation, their right of involvement in government and their right of supervision over the Party and government."[10]

Underlying such an argument is an assumption contrary to the Party's long-held notion of the press as a tool for educating and mobilizing the people for the causes it has chosen. By introducing the concept of "rights," Hu went further than Zhao's enlightened paternalism of "letting" (*rang*) the people have more information and more participation.

Addressing the Party's concern that greater freedom would cause instability, some reformers based their arguments on utilitarian grounds. They reasoned that press freedom is not only a right but also conducive to political stability. Wang

Ruoshui, known for his theory of Marxist humanism and alienation under social-ism, claimed that instability is caused by bureaucratism, corruption, and degen-eration, which can be checked by a free press.[11]

This point was carried further by Hu Jiwei. In an article widely circulated dur-ing the student movement in May 1989, Hu contended that "there will be no gen-uine stability without press freedom."[12] He asserted that a free press can not only prevent and correct Party and government wrongdoing, and therefore eradicate destabilizing factors, but also promote mutual understanding between the peo-ple and the government and among different segments of society. It provides a safety valve for people to vent their dissatisfactions. His points were summarized in an introduction to his essay by the *World Economic Herald*.

> Without freedom of the press, the people are helpless in the face of policy mistakes and the phenomenon of increasing corruption. If what they say is moderate, it serves no purpose. If what they say is tough, it is not published in the press. As time goes on, many people will cherish an attitude of saying and thinking nothing, and even taking things as they come, bending to fate. Such a phenomenon gives a false impression of stability and unity. But it actually has people's numbness, indifference and their repression as a price. Hidden therein is an even greater risk. Can a leader with a head for modern pol-itics really be reconciled to this kind of superficial stability and unity?[13]

In a direct appeal to the Party and the government, Hu argued that press free-dom would help to establish the democratic authority of the Chinese political leadership. He believed that only a leadership authority established under the condition of a free press is a democratic authority truly supported by the people. Otherwise, he warned, there can be only an unstable autocratic authority.[14] The reformers, therefore, attempted to persuade the leadership that not only had they nothing to lose by allowing a freer press but they also could actually increase their credibility and, consequently, their legitimacy.

The People Principle

While calls for a freer press appealed to the people's democratic rights, the argu-ments were often couched in the context of the Party's own agenda to preserve political stability and its authority. But another debate, this one between the "Party principle" (*dang xing*) and the "people principle" (*renmin xing*) contained a more radical challenge to the Party's control.

The people principle was put forward by some scholars in the early 1980s and criticized by the Party in the middle of the decade during the campaign against "bourgeois liberalization." It resurfaced after the Party's Thirteenth National Congress in 1987, when it was widely discussed in academic and trade journals. Instead of unconditionally following the Party even when it makes mistakes, this principle contends, the media should speak for the people and represent their interests. As Gan Xifen maintains:

> the lesson of the holocaust of the ten-year Cultural Revolution has taught us that the Party's leadership, even the Party Central Committee, may commit mistakes. When mistakes are made and when the Party's press blindly executes the leadership's intentions, newspapers themselves are committing serious mistakes. Therefore, upon discovering mistakes, editorial departments should not blindly implement their instructions. Newspapers should put the interests of the people above everything else and be run accordingly. . . . When a communist society is attained, even the Party will be eliminated. Yet the people are permanent, they live forever![15]

While Hu Jiwei had appeared to advance this concept as the antithesis of the Party principle, many others viewed it less radically as a supplement to the Party principle. For example, Qian Xinbo, deputy director of the Journalism Research Institute under the Chinese Academy of Social Sciences, argued that the media in a socialist country should represent both the Party and the people, which are not identical as the Party maintains. When the Party was in a political struggle and needed to publicize its ideas, it was justified in insisting that the media speak only for it, but this was no longer appropriate since the Party was in power. According to Qian in a socialist country the media should instead be the people's watchdog by overseeing the Party and the government. He criticized those who "take too lightly the Western concept of the press as the Fourth Estate" and dismiss this idea as bourgeois.[16] Gan Xifen similarly asserted that newspapers should belong to both the Party and the people and that "socialist newspapers are also the papers of the people."[17]

Underlying this seemingly innocent call for representing the people is a fundamental challenge to the Party's vanguard role. As the theoretical ferment reached a climax just before the 1989 student movement, some authors were already calling the mouthpiece theory into question. Journalism researcher Wu Tingjun, for example, cited a number of limitations in practice.[18] First, because the theory was the product of political struggle, it subjects the media to narrow political calculation; news and propaganda become one and the same. News content becomes overly politicized; even sports, science, and human interest stories are no exceptions. Second, the theory leads to an emphasis on top-down, one-way communication. Third, the media become completely dependent on the Party, just as the tongue is subject to the control of the brain. Consequently, the media have not only failed to point out Party mistakes but have also amplified those mistakes. Thus, he concluded that "the tragedy of Chinese journalism is perhaps rooted in this theory."[19]

Journalism Laws and Western Media Concepts

While some theorists confronted the Party directly, others took an intellectual detour by promoting journalism as a science and by advancing the notion of "laws" in the positivist tradition, one consistent with the Chinese interpretation of Marxism. Instead of subjecting journalism to the arbitrary control of the Party, they argued, journalism should follow "laws" of its own.

An article in the Xinhua Agency–sponsored trade journal *Chinese Journalists* (Zhongguo jizhe), for example, contended that such laws include some of these principles: "News is a report on an event that has occurred recently and that people are generally concerned about. News is intended for the broad masses of readers. If enterprises regard their customers as 'God,' then news media should view readers and audiences as their 'God,' serving them, satisfying their needs, and winning their confidence. A news medium is an important means by which public opinion in society is expressed, or we may say that it in itself is a major component of public opinion in society."[20]

Gan Xifen acknowledges that it is "the very fundamental law of journalism" that it is "subordinate to politics" and is always "an opinion tool of a given class"; nevertheless, he argues, there is more to it than this because of the "most frequently observed universal laws of journalism":

1. Reporting must be objective and true, reflecting reality.
2. Reporting must be speedy and timely.
3. Journalism must reduce its distance from the audience, making itself easy for the audience to accept.
4. Audience evaluation and feedback should determine who survives in journalism.[21]

Clearly, these laws, except for Gan's first "very fundamental law," are implicitly drawn from liberal press theory in the West and are abstractions based on Western mainstream news media practices.[22] There is even a touch of the consumer sovereignty concept. Whether there are indeed such laws of journalism is highly debatable, of course. What is significant is that all are missing from current dominant theory and practice in China. Underlying the various arguments for journalism to follow its own laws is a call for recognition of the internal logic of news discourse and for the relative autonomy of journalism practices.

Independent Newspaper Ownership

Theoretical challenges to the Party's theory and practice were accompanied by a more concrete demand for an independent media sector free of Party and state control. However, this was such a sensitive issue that even the outspoken Hu Jiwei did not treat this issue as a top priority in his speeches and writings, although it was clearly on his agenda: "At first we thought the Party had to lead everything, including the press. We used to think the press was equivalent to the Party press. But this is wrong, because the Party's news operations—such as *People's Daily*— is only a part of the press work."[23] Implied is the understanding that Party journalism is only one form of journalism and that there can be and should be other forms.

Technically speaking, there were already a large number of non-Party newspapers by the mid-1980s, but they were still under Party control with "unified propaganda lines."[24] The reformers were instead asking for independent newspapers that would not have to follow the Party line.

In fact, arguments for people-run or independent papers (*min ban*) had been advanced during the "hundred flowers" movement in 1957, but they were criticized as the most extreme example of rightist views during the anti-rightist campaign in the same year.[25] The topic remained taboo until the mid-1980s, when the Party's reform policy encouraged the growth of private industrial and trade enterprises. The Party's call for supervision of the Party and the government by public opinion made some outspoken intellectuals feel that it was again time to raise the issue, and some managed to get it on the public agenda.

Wu Zuguang, a dramatist and a member of the Chinese People's Political Consultative Conference (CPPCC, which could be described as the upper house of China's parliament), proposed at a CPPCC meeting in 1987 for the government to allow publication of independent newspapers and journals.[26] An opinion poll in 1988 by the Journalism Research Institute of the Chinese Academy of Social Sciences and the Capital Journalism Society among all members of the National People's Congress and the CPPCC was bold enough to venture a new interpretation of the constitutional guarantee of freedom of the press. It asked whether respondents agreed that freedom of the press means that citizens may publish newspapers.[27] The idea was also written into one of the drafts of the proposed press law.

Theoretical proposals for independent newspapers also involved a rejection of the Party's fundamental concept of the media as tools for class struggle. Chen Lidan, a senior journalism researcher with the Chinese Academy of Social Sciences, for example, argued that the class struggle notion is wrong and the Party should define the media as an "information dissemination industry."[28] With such a redefinition, of course, ideological barriers to independent newspapers are removed. If the media are an industry, then the Party should certainly allow different forms of ownership to exist, as it has in many other economic sectors.

As is a common strategy in political discourse in China, advocates for independent newspaper ownership found theoretical ground in the Party line of the day—that is, the Party's argument that China is still in an "initial stage of socialism."[29] During this initial stage, the central task is supposed to be industrialization, which requires coexistence and competition between various forms of ownership, wherein the market should be the main mechanism for mobilization and allocation of resources. This became the ideological underpinning of economic reform and in a de facto way has been interpreted as the basis for social diversity and ideological pluralism.[30] Proponents of independent newspaper ownership, therefore, based their arguments on this theory. As Chen Lidan wrote: "Since the initial stage of socialism will extend for more than 100 years, during which various types of economic reforms and interests will coexist with one another, we should also allow divergent views to coexist with one another. This is because a particular ideological form should always be compatible to a particular social structure and a particular economic structure."[31] He argued that the existing government-controlled structure would inevitably clash with the idea of ideological pluralism and thus independent newspaper ownership would be unavoidable.

Contextualizing the Democratization Discourse

The crusade for press freedom, the articulation of the people principle, the construction of journalism laws, and the call for independent newspapers constituted some of the main thrusts of an emerging discourse on the democratization of media communication. Underlying these was a common desire to break away from the Party's monopolistic, arbitrary control. In their call for a freer press, democratic forces within the news reform movement desired a more independent public sphere, where different interests could be better communicated and through which the public could exercise some control over the Party and the government. The media thus would become an important force in recasting the relation between political and civil society and in reshaping Chinese society in a more democratic form. It would significantly change political communication.

On the other hand, since most of these ideas were in their formative stages and their expression was limited for political reasons, they remained elementary, fragmentary, and unsystematic. The intellectual project of redefining communicative relations in Chinese society and the media's role was only begun. For example, press freedom is primarily conceived as freedom from overt editorial intervention by the Party but within the constitution and the law. Virtually nobody asked whether the press could advocate changing the fundamental structure of the state. Because many ideas were slogan-like, it was not clear how they could be institutionalized and implemented. For example, how is the people principle to be made operational? Should the Party simply loosen its control and allow journalists to represent the interests of the people, or should there be new institutional arrangements that make the principle secure? Can the people rely on professional journalists to reflect their interests? If the Party's claim to represent the people is elitist, and if its use of the term "the people" conceals differences among the people, the same can be said of others who might claim to speak on behalf of the people. There are a number of unexplored questions regarding independent newspaper ownership as well. What about financing? How should such newspapers be organized? Does people-run (*minban*) simply mean private ownership by an entrepreneur, or does it include other forms of nonstate ownership, like cooperatives of journalists or citizens? Can it also mean a new form of public ownership?

Indeed, this emerging democratic discourse was burdened with potential contradictions and inconsistencies. Residues of and overreactions to the Party's media theory and practice were apparent. In proposing his laws of journalism, for example, Gan was not bothered by the potential contradiction between his first "very fundamental law" conceding the class nature of journalism—and, hence, the inevitable subordination of journalism to politics—and his more operational laws, especially the notion that news reporting must be "objective and true."[32] In fact, while proposals for laws of journalism underscore a critique of the Party's political reductionism that acknowledges journalism only as a political instrument, they do not pose a critique of the Party's model of political communication as such. Moreover, democratic sensibilities often intermingle with elitist sensibilities. For example, while Hu Jiwei's theoretical arguments for "press freedom for all the people" appear democratic, his ideal newspaper of the future—established and run by entrepreneurs who are at the same time politicians or have the power to influence politicians[33]—is elitist.

Such inconsistencies reflect not only the preliminary nature of the discourse but also the broad political and intellectual divisions in China. During the mid-1980s in addition to the conventional "reformers versus hardliners" division within the Party, there were different strands in the reform camp, most notably neo-authoritarians, technocrats, and democrats. Although the Western media often use the single label "liberal reformers" to describe all reformers, different groups held various perspectives on politics and modernization, especially from mid-1988 to the government crackdown in the spring of 1989.

Neo-authoritarians insisted that China was not ready for democracy, claiming the people have inadequate political skills and a weak sense of citizenship after centuries of paternalist rule. They maintained that democracy can be achieved only after a transition period of authoritarian rule and that economic growth cannot be achieved simultaneously with democratization.[34] According to their thinking, the development of a market economy under neo-authoritarian rule will necessarily lead to a democracy because "a democratic regime and a market economy are like twins."[35] They promoted the idea of the need for a middle class of independent entrepreneurs, bureaucrats, and technological and cultural elites capable of securing and maintaining the foundations for democratic governance to become the dominant forces of society.

Technocrats have three traits—scientific training, professional occupations, and actual or putative positions of power. As Li Cheng and Lynn T. White have argued, political development in China in the 1980s was primarily technocratic because dramatic shifts in cadre policy since 1978 had promoted technocrats to practically all top posts, thus fostering a technocratic movement.[36] Their elitism, technological rationality, and antidemocratic ideals frequently resonate with the views of neo-authoritarians.

Democratic reformers, on the other hand, asserted that democracy is the essential prerequisite to Chinese modernization. They declared that China needs to move to forms of participatory democracy immediately and that "enough of a foundation for a viable pluralistic system is in place to make democratization possible."[37] Instead of seeing democracy as an end product of a market economy developed under neo-authoritarian rule, democratic reformers insisted that democracy is both a means to shape and motivate political development and an end to political governance. As a result, this school argued that "economic growth, political stability, and democratization are different aspects of modernization that are both interdependent and interactive."[38] To the claim that the Chinese were not ready for democracy, democrats countered that only by participating in policy-making will the Chinese people come to understand democracy and make a commitment to it. Instead of relying on a middle class for democratization, democrats saw mass-based political pressure from below—students, workers, and others who participated the 1989 democracy movement, for example—as the agents. According to democrats, "mass-based political pressure must be deployed to stimulate, coordinate, and facilitate political and economic reforms."[39]

Many reformers who took part in the pro-democracy movement were neo-authoritarians and technocrats.[40] There is a fundamental gap between these reformers, many of whom are within the Party, and grass-roots elements:

> While the students, workers, and intellectuals demanded participatory democracy and freedom of assembly, of expression, and of the press, the neo-authoritarian Party members advocated iron-fisted rule with only a modicum of democracy. Reformists in the Party openly opposed mass democracy; they considered the powerful, the entrepreneurs, and the intellectual elite to be the backbone of China. Seeing the mass of people as backward, these Party reformists decided that "only a majority of the best may represent the interests of the majority, only this elite may be leaders and control the direction of the nation's development for the near future."[41] Lacking a theoretical foundation for discussion, the reformists and the democracy movement participants had no basis for communication and could not ally against conservatives.[42]

While reformers within the Party initially provided an opening for democratic reformers, in the fall of 1988 Zhao Ziyang and his followers attempted to avoid a crisis in economic reform by sacrificing political democratization and embracing neo-authoritarianism. During the political struggles in the spring of 1989, Party reformers failed to make alliances with democratic forces, failed to promote conscientious dialogue with the democracy movement, failed to legalize their reform activities, and failed to make full use of the news media to gain popular support.[43] As a result, the movement was defeated. Even reformers within the Party were crushed by more conservative elements, as symbolized by the downfall of Zhao.

The media reform movement, and especially the debate about press legislation, was illustrative of the different perspectives within the broader reform movement. Despite the 1982 Chinese constitution's formal endorsement of free speech and free expression for all citizens, the Party continues to exercise press freedom on "the people's behalf." As the media reform movement progressed, journalists felt the need for a press law to protect them from the Party's arbitrary power. They wanted details as to what they could and could not do.[44] Democratic reformers wanted press reform to be legalized as part of the transition from the rule of individuals to the rule of law. Discussions had been underway since 1980, but actual drafting of legislation did not begin until 1984, when Hu Jiwei, in his capacity as a member of the Standing Committee of the National People's Congress and vice-chairman of its Education, Science, Culture, and Public Health Committee, was entrusted with the task. But there were major differences of opinion, particularly over the role of the media and the purpose of the proposed legislation.

Liberal and democratic reformers wanted to change the structure of the media system, defining and protecting the rights of journalists and the public to present their views and offer criticisms. They wanted at least part of the media to become independent of the Party/state apparatus and a law that would allow nonofficial publications. For example, Yu Haocheng, a legal expert, argued that "the tools of information must be independent of the rulers, otherwise the people will not be able to enjoy freedom of expression and publication, the two freedoms that guarantee their rights to know what is happening, engage in political discussion and supervise the government."[45]

Similarly, Sun Xupei, a prominent journalism scholar with the Journalism Research Institute of the Chinese Academy of Social Sciences, believed that the primary objective of press legislation was to define a notion of socialist press freedom that would maintain the leading role of the Party press but would include independent publications.[46]

This democratic perspective fundamentally challenged the Party's monopolistic control over political communication. Hu Jiwei consulted scholars with the Journalism Research Institute of the Chinese Academy of Social Sciences and soon gained the backing of Sun Xupei and "a majority of newspaper editors, journalists and the public."[47]

Neo-authoritarian reformers, however, insisted that the Chinese people, including journalists, were not ready for press freedom. The deep division between them and the democrats was clearly reflected in the issue of independent newspaper ownership. A 1988 survey found that 60.1 percent of National People's Congress (NPC) delegates and 30.7 percent of CPPCC delegates disagreed that press freedom means that citizens could publish independent newspapers.[48] Conservative Party ideologues, of course, were even more adamant in rejecting this idea.

In January 1987, with the creation of the State Press and Publications Administration, the responsibility for drafting press legislation shifted. Under the leadership of Du Daozheng, who was believed to be a conservative, this agency saw the press law mainly as a means of control. Du stressed the duties of journalists and obligations to the government and society, focusing on order and control. He wanted a law defining the limits of journalists and protecting the government from them and reportedly opposed the idea of independent publications.

In addition to fundamental disagreement over the role of the media and the reason for a press law, Hu and Du also disagreed over the procedures by which press legislation should be drafted. Hu wanted wide discussion and public participation in the process and the law passed by the NPC as a whole; Du wanted it passed by the more restricted NPC Standing Committee after consultation only with specialized groups.[49]

With the political openness created by the Thirteenth National Party Congress in October 1987 and the regrouping of the top leadership, Hu resumed drafting the law, sharing the responsibility with Du.[50] As a result of deep divisions, different drafts of the press law were circulated in 1987 and 1988. After many delays and intensive debates, in early 1989 a draft law—reportedly Du's conservative version—was put on the agenda of an NPC Standing Committee meeting for discussion scheduled for late June. But suppression of the pro-democracy movement led to its removal from the agenda.

Media Reform after June 1989

With the crushing of the pro-democracy movement in June 1989, the media reform movement suffered a major setback that was apparent both in journalistic practice and in theoretical discussion. The Party attributed the movement to the influence of "bourgeois liberalization," a Western strategy of "peaceful evolution," and the partial takeover of the media and the ideological front by liberal and democratic reformers. With this view reinforced by the collapse of the Soviet Union and socialist regimes in eastern Europe, the Party tightened up. Combatting "bourgeois liberalization" and "peaceful evolution" remained priorities until 1992.[51]

Two speeches, one by Jiang Zemin, the other by Li Ruihuan, a member of the Standing Committee of the Politburo in charge of propaganda and ideology who was appointed in June 1989, effectively reimposed the Party's principle and closed any theoretical debate on reform. Both speeches were made at a seminar for high-level media officials, including editors-in-chief of provincial Party organs. The seminar was designed to reflect on media performance before and during the pro-democracy movement and to unify thinking among media officials.

Jiang basically reiterated the mouthpiece theory. He claimed that serving the Party and serving the people were invariably one and the same and criticized those who advocated the people principle and press freedom, charging them with maliciously trying to overthrow Party leadership. Party committees were asked to actively supervise the media.[52] Even Zhao Ziyang's popular notion of political transparency was criticized.

Li not only stressed the Party principle but also emphasized the Party tradition of positive propaganda. The media were again instructed to fulfill didactic and exhortatory responsibilities by providing "correct" direction to the public and arousing people's confidence in and enthusiasm for the socialist system. Li's outline for media reform did not touch on any of the substantial issues that had been pushed onto the political agenda before and during the democracy movement. A press law was not even mentioned; nor was the issue of separation of Party and government in media administration. There was not going to be any structural reform redefining the relationship between the media and society, just a focus on operational and technical levels with minor improvements in content and style of presentation.[53] Media reform, after a decade of intense debate and struggle, seemed to have returned to its starting point of a decade earlier.

The Party also made new senior appointments in the media and ideological fields.[54] Hu Jiwei was stripped of his position in the National People's Congress and expelled from the Party. Work on drafting a press law was suspended. As many news organizations were criticized for the "liberal" tendencies in their reports and for their sympathetic reporting of the student movement, some publications were closed and some reorganized at the top. Journalists and theorists who were active in the pro-democracy movement were subjected to investigation, work suspension, job reassignment, and even imprisonment.[55]

Restrictions on editors and journalists increased. Although it had been relaxed considerably during the mid-1980s, the preview system was enforced more strictly so that adherence to the Party line could be ensured. *People's Daily,* for example, was required to report its main news content to the Party's Propaganda Department before its daily four o'clock editorial committee meeting. The two most important news programs on the national radio and television networks faced similar supervision. The relaxed control of the mid-1980s, it was now decided, had been a mistake. Zhao Ziyang was blamed for not exerting equal force with both hands; while his grip on economic development was firm, his grasp on the ideological front was considered "soft." A special Leadership Team on Ideological and Propaganda Work was set up, consisting of top leaders of the major media under the leadership of Politburo member Ding Guan'gen. For two years there was little substantive discussion of media reform as a political project in Chinese journalism studies. The people principle became taboo again and press freedom and supervision by public opinion virtually disappeared from discourse on reform. Despite the resistance from rank-and-file journalists, the media were dominated by positive propaganda.

The Turn to Rapid Commercialization in 1992

Although introduction of a market mechanism had been part of media reform from the beginning, the issue of media commercialization was not a focus of the movement. Demands for more press freedom centered on loosening Party control. Nor did those who advocated Western press concepts, like a watchdog role for the media, explicitly advocate commercialization. Even those who favored independent newspapers did not pay much attention to financial issues. This changed dramatically when, after two years of economic consolidation and readjustment, the Party decided to speed up economic reform once again. In 1992, a resolution was issued on faster development of tertiary industry, which officially included the media.

The most important turning point was the publication of Deng Xiaoping's talks during his inspection tour of south China in early 1992. Subsequently, the Fourteenth National Party Congress, in October 1992, officially adopted Deng's proposal for more economic openness and formally embraced the concept of a "socialist market economy." Joseph M. Chan provides an excellent account of the main thrusts of Deng's talks:

> Brushing aside the conservatives' urge for taking anti-peaceful evolution as the central task, Deng reiterated the primacy of the policy of "one centrality, two basic points": Of central importance was economic construction, whereas reform and an open-door policy, and maintenance of the Four Cardinal Principles were the two basic points. Deng called for faster economic growth and boldness in experimenting with reforms. At the same time, he directed that practice should take precedence over theoretical debates and that controversies over the nature of Chinese reforms and other historical-political issues should be shelved. While he continued to maintain that rightism was an undesirable tendency, he unprecedentedly emphasized that leftism was posing a more imminent danger.[56]

In typical pragmatic fashion, Deng overcame ideological barriers to commercialization by arguing that the market is only a mechanism for economic development that does not determine whether a system is capitalist or socialist. With this new claim, China completed its fifteen-year journey from a planned economy to a market economy. In the early 1980s, the economy was planned but supplemented by the market mechanism. During the mid-1980s, this shifted to a planned commodity economy. Now the market had finally triumphed. It was to have a dominant role not only in the allocation of consumer goods and services but also in the allocation of production goods and resources. Deng's talks defined the new mood of the country. Suddenly, commercialization assumed an astonishing pace in every aspect. The speed of economic growth reached unprecedented levels.[57]

While Deng himself brushed aside ideology and single-handedly closed the debate on whether the reform was capitalist or socialist, Minxin Pei, a Harvard-trained political scientist, has put a definitive label on the nature of the change. According to Pei, Deng's 1992 speech had the effect of "re-energizing China's capitalist revolution after Tiananmen" and marked the "semiformal takeover" of capitalism.[58] Pei provided a number of reasons for his claim that "the economic developments in China in 1992–1993 marked the near total victory of its society-led capitalist revolution." (1) China's political leadership openly endorsed the market economy despite the rhetoric of a "socialist market economy." (2) The government permitted the takeover of small and medium-sized state-owned enterprises by private entrepreneurs and foreign investors. (3) There was a huge exodus of technical and political elites from the state sector into the private sector. (4) The private sector dramatically expanded into previously closed areas such as real estate, commercial aviation, and the financial market. (5) Many provincial and local governments passed liberal laws expanding the formal private sector. (6) There was a massive infusion of new foreign investment.[59]

The changes in the economic sphere were indeed profound. The media, however, were still in the paradoxical situation of both remaining the same and being changed. Although the Party had gone a long way toward yielding control of the economy to the market, it had not yielded political control or changed the pattern of political communication. To be sure, there has been change in the content of propaganda in the media since Deng's talks. In responding to Deng's call for accelerated economic growth and for taking economic construction as the central task, Li Ruihuan instructed that the key point of propaganda work in 1992 was to emphasize economic construction without dry and empty sermonizing. He pointed out that the media should be more informative and should meet the needs of various audiences.[60]

But the Party has not changed its pattern of control over the media. Thus Anne Thurston is partially right when she observes that since Deng's talks, everything and everyone has changed except the press.[61] Indeed, one media researcher in Beijing suggested to me in late 1994 that Party control was tighter than during the Cultural Revolution. Although this is perhaps an overstatement, it contains some truth. The media's handling of a 1994 shooting incident in Beijing is revealing. In the early morning of September 20, a frustrated, heavily armed military officer managed to hijack vehicles all the way from his camp in Tong County to the eastern suburbs of Beijing. Unable to reach Tiananmen Square on his suicidal mission, he went on a shooting rampage, killing more than ten persons, including foreigners, until police shot him to death. This happened during the morning rush hour in a busy traffic area; moreover, it involved foreigners and attracted foreign media reports.

This story would definitely not have been reported during the Cultural Revolution, but now is the age of reform and openness. In fact, in 1987 the Party prepared clear instructions for breaking such stories. These events "should be reported openly in a timely and a continuous manner; moreover, effort should be made to report it before foreign media do."[62] However, neither the national nor the local Beijing broadcast media were allowed to report the event. Brief reports did appear in *Beijing Daily* (Beijing ribao) and *Beijing Evening News* (Beijing wanbao), but they were identical, apparently prepared by some outside authority. The news desk at Beijing People's Radio received at least three orders from above, the first from the station's news director, the second from the station's president's office, the third from the city's propaganda department, all prohibiting reporting the event.[63] The argument here is not that such an event should be the focus of the national news nor that a media system that gives maximum coverage to such an event is necessarily desirable. The important point is whether a news outlet has the autonomy to decide whether to report (and if so, how) or not to report it. The way the story was handled in the two Beijing newspapers that did carry it illustrates the extent of "openness" available.

News reports in the major media in late 1994 and early 1995 remained typical of Party journalism—monolithic, positive, and highly predictable. A scanning of front-page stories in thirty-six different national and provincial newspapers reveals little variation.[64] The leading stories included policy directives from provincial and national leaders; visits of Party and government leaders to various provinces; study of government policies and the works of Deng Xiaoping; achievements of individual factories, counties, or persons; good agricultural harvests despite drought; the openings of a construction project and a highway; how banks serve the economy; education in patriotism; model Party members; and an expert in economics who wished to join the Party in the last minutes of his life.

Similarly, domestic news on CCTV's main evening news program consists of the daily activities of Party and government leaders; meetings, plans, or announcements of various government departments and agencies; and achievements and prosperity in various areas. During the five days between January 16 and January 20, 1995, for example, four of the five lead stories were about the daily activities of Jiang Zemin, the Party general secretary, whether they were important or not.[65] Reports of the activities of the premier and other leaders followed. There was not a single example of negative news or analytical reporting in the five newscasts. Although a January 16 item about court decisions on two corrupt officials came the closest, it was initiated neither by the crime nor by the trial; the case had already been decided.

And yet, something has changed. Rapid commercialization is evident. Although the Party and the government still reject such terms as "commercialization" (*shangyehua*) and "commercial radio stations" (*shangye diantai*) and prefer to use terms such as "industrialization" (*chanyehua*) or "go to the market" (*zuoxiang shichang*), the market has taken a more prominent role on the level of media policy. During the National Working Conference on Press Management on October 21, 1992, three days after the closing of the Party's Fourteenth National Congress, Liang Heng, an official responsible for newspaper management at the State Press and Publications Administration, openly talked about the "commodity nature" of the press and the imperative of "eventually pushing newspapers to the market."[66] Liang proposed a process of gradual transformation. Party organs, general interest national newspapers, special interest newspapers run by social organizations, enterprise newspapers, and army newspapers would be subsidized initially; evening papers, news digests, papers specializing in culture and lifestyles, as well as trade newspapers would be "pushed to the market" first, when their subsidies were cut.[67] In November 1992, Liang declared that "conditions are ripe for newspapers to be marketized."[68]

Liang's discussion lagged far behind actual practices. Many newspapers, including some provincial Party organs, had lost their subsidies long before 1992. As Liang himself reported to the meeting, of the 1,750 newspapers in 1992, one-third had already achieved financial independence.[69] Nevertheless, Liang's statements were significant.

In the area of theory, media scholars quickly began to push for commercialization. Much of the energy for media reform is now being channeled into commercialization. The reform discourse has changed dramatically with a new vocabulary informing discussion about news media reform in academic writing and trade journals. While lip service is still paid to the Party principle, the focus is on commercialization. "The market economy and news media reform" has become the hottest topic in Chinese journalism circles. Nationwide seminars that include the country's top media scholars, essay competitions in academic and trade journals, as well as numerous individual articles all focus on the same theme.[70]

Media theorists advance their arguments for commercialization in a typical orthodox Marxist fashion. The base is being transformed from a planned economy to a market economy. As a result, the current media system, whose basic principles and operating mechanisms are largely the product of a planned economy, must also be changed to make it compatible with the economic base: so the argument goes. Moreover, since the news media have been officially designated as part of the tertiary sector, they are also part of the economic base and should be treated as such, that is, commercialized and developed in accord with market principles. It has become fashionable to assert the commodity nature of the news. Some even cite Marx to support this view. In favoring organizing news production in accord with the demands of the market, they call for a cognitive shift from media as "propaganda instruments" to media as an industry, from being "tools" to being "service providers," from "leading the masses" to "serving the consumers."[71] Some have even gone so far as to say that the Party and the government should pay a fee for media services.[72]

While this embrace by theorists of commodification is quite striking and several steps ahead of the official Party line, it is in the actual practice of journalism that the extent and significance of the cognitive shift is most apparent. Media organizations and journalists have gone even further in subjecting themselves to the forces of the market than any theorist has actually recommended. Media practitioners took the road to commercialization long before 1992, but Deng's talks provided a catalytic rationale.

3

Media Commercialization
with Chinese Characteristics

Until the beginning of economic reform in 1978, the media in China were completely subsidized by the state—except, that is, for a brief period in the early 1950s when, by accepting advertising, some Party organs, including *People's Daily,* became financially independent.[1] Although the Party has continued to attach great political and ideological importance to the media, as the economic reforms were implemented, it became increasingly clear that the state could no longer bear the entire burden even if it wanted to.

Reform and openness since the 1980s had created a growing demand by foreign and domestic enterprises for effective advertising channels. Media commercialization, therefore, is also part and parcel of the development of a market economy. In addition, two important developments have made commercialization an economic necessity for media organizations. First, although reform has brought prosperity in the overall economy, governments at all levels have been relatively deprived. As part of the early measures to encourage local initiatives, the government pursued a policy of economic decentralization, which led to redistribution of wealth from the central government to local governments, enterprises, and individuals.

The effect of economic decentralization on national government budgets is amplified by the unauthorized flow of wealth away from the state (most of this never made it into government accounts) and into private pockets as a result of fraud, massive tax evasion, and theft. As Robert Weil observes, these losses have been staggering.[2]

> As a consequence of these developments, while in 1981 the share of revenues going to the central government was 57 percent, by 1993 this had dropped to under 39 percent. Thus the national state bodies of socialist China are greatly underfunded compared with the United States and Japan, the leading capitalist countries, where the percentage of taxes going to the centre is 55 and 70 percent, respectively. It is this massive loss of revenue that has fueled the almost desperate drive to cut government responsibility for social security, health and education, and to force all state institutions to make their own way economically.[3]

With limited revenue, the government's investment priorities have been in such areas as science and education rather than in the media.

The government's increasing inability to invest in the media has been compounded by a second development: the public's growing demand for more media services. With increasing prosperity, people have more money to spend on culture and entertainment. Indeed, one of the first things many Chinese families, urban and rural alike, buy with their savings is a television set. There were only 3.4 million television sets in China in 1978; by 1992, the number had reached 230 million.[4] "Television villages"—where every household has a television set—were still treated as news in the early 1980s; by the middle of the decade they were commonplace.

The rapid growth in the number of viewers stimulated investment in new stations, in more channels, and in the extension of daily broadcasting hours. The state, with a shrinking purse, was increasingly unable to provide funds for the usual media operations, not to mention new technologies and expansion of services. Throughout the 1980s, government funds could provide only 50 to 70 percent of what was needed to maintain the regular operation of existing broadcast channels. It could provide only 9 percent of what was needed by the newspaper sector for technological improvements.[5] Media organizations, especially broadcasting, suffered severe financial difficulties. To end complete dependence on state subsidies and to find other sources of financing was thus more an economic necessity than an espoused political principle.

In fact, economic reform of the media began almost as early as the overall economic reform. Although the first appearance of advertising on Shanghai Television in February 1979 is often considered the beginning of media commercialization in China, market mechanisms in the media actually began a year earlier. In 1978, the Ministry of Finance approved the introduction of a business management system at *People's Daily* and at a number of other newspapers published in Beijing. Although these newspapers were still regarded as political and cultural institutions and still received subsidies, they began to be managed as business enterprises. In addition to adhering to the Party line, they had to pay attention to the bottom line as well. They were forced to save money by streamlining operations and were subjected to cost analysis, profit targets, and government taxation.

The government adopted a policy of gradually cutting subsidies and encouraging commercialized financing. Some newspapers lost all subsidies in the early 1980s.[6] Production materials such as newsprint and ink, which had previously been allocated by the government, were gradually left to the invisible hand of the market. At the other end of the news process, the return of newspaper vendors to city streets in the early 1980s served as a reminder that newspapers had indeed become commodities. The monopoly that the post office had held in the distribution of newspapers was challenged when *Luoyang Daily* (Luoyang ribao), the Party organ of Luoyang City, started its own delivery system in an attempt to increase subscriptions in 1985. By 1987, more than five hundred medium-sized to small newspapers had set up their own distribution networks.

In the broadcast sector, although governments at all levels continued to invest, the central government encouraged broadcast organizations to earn money and fill the gap between what the government could provide and what was needed. In a 1983 document, the Party suggested that broadcast organizations at all levels should explore other sources of income. In 1988, the Party and the government for the first time clearly stated that broadcasting should depend on multiple channels of financing.[7]

Although the majority of broadcasters have not adopted an enterprise management system, they have in one way or another established responsibility contracts with their respective government financial departments. Under these contracts, the government provides certain funds, while the broadcast station—or bureau with its affiliated stations—projects a set amount of self-generated income. These become the operating budget of the organization. If a station or bureau earns more than anticipated, there are rules for how it can use the surplus. But if it falls short of the projected revenue, it has to cover its own losses.

To meet financial objectives, many news organizations set up internal financial responsibility systems and sign financial responsibility contracts with subordinate units. Thus, different departments are required to generate a given amount of income. Here again, if a department earns more than projected, it can spend the surplus itself. In some organizations, not only advertising departments, but also editorial departments and even individual journalists, are assigned revenue quotas.[8] Indeed, since the mid-1980s, "creating income" (*chuangshou*) has become one of the most frequently used terms in the Chinese media industry. Gaining wide circulation are slogans like "running on two wheels [publishing and making money] at the same time" (*liangge lunzi yiqi zhuan*), "one hand on editorial quality, one hand on creating income" (*yishou zhua zhiliang, yishou zhua chuangshou*), and even "an editor-in-chief who does not know how to make money is not a good one." Indeed, the media have explored all means of "creating income," and this movement toward financial independence has brought profound changes.[9]

Advertising: The New Lifeblood

Advertising has become the single most important nongovernmental source of media revenue since it was reintroduced in early 1979. Once condemned as the tool of capitalism, advertising has not only been rehabilitated but also promoted by the Party and the government as "a potential tool for economic reform, the four modernizations, and social change."[10] In 1982, the government formally stated that advertising has the capability and responsibility to "promote production, increase commodity circulation, guide consumption, invigorate the economy, increase consumer convenience, develop international economic activities, serve the needs of socialist construction and promote socialist moral standards."[11]

The Party's and the government's great enthusiasm for advertising culminated in China's hosting the Third World Advertising Congress from June 16 to June 20, 1987, in the most prestigious political meeting place in China, the Great Hall of the People in Beijing. "Admen in China Get Red Carpet," an article in *Advertising Age* exulted. During the congress, China's then head of state, President Li Xiannian, paid a surprise visit to the nearly fifteen thousand delegates from all over the world, and Acting Premier Wan Li celebrated advertising as "an indispensable element in the promotion of economic prosperity."[12]

With favorable government policies and a rapidly expanding market economy, advertising has become China's fastest growing industry since the early 1980s. Between 1981 and 1992, the national advertising sales volume grew from 0.118 billion yuan to 6.786 billion, with an annual growth rate of 41 percent. During the same period, the number of businesses involved in advertising grew from 2,200 to 16,683, with an average annual growth rate of 20 percent, while the number of people employed by the industry grew from 16,000 to 185,000, with an average annual growth rate of 26 percent.[13]

The mass media, with their special status as the producers, solicitors, and exhibitors of advertising, have been able to grab a lion's share of advertising revenue. In 1992, the four major media—television, newspapers, radio, and magazines—received 4.00 billion yuan of advertising income, or 64 percent of the total advertising revenue of 6.78 billion yuan. Television alone accounts for 2.05 billion, or 30.2 percent.[14] This was close to the 2.38 billion yuan of broadcast operating funds provided by governments at all levels in the same year.[15]

The rate of growth in the advertising industry has accelerated since 1992 along with the wave of economic growth inspired by the Party's and government's unreserved embrace of a market economy. In 1993, advertising revenue in the whole country reached 13.4 billion yuan, a 98 percent increase over 1992.[16] As a result, news media's advertising income increased dramatically. In 1992, the ten biggest advertising revenues for newspaper organizations ranged from 27 million to 81 million yuan.[17] In 1993, the top figure was 170 million, more than double 1992's highest.[18]

It is worthwhile to note in this context that although the first commercial advertiser in post–Cultural Revolution China was a domestic firm, transnational advertising and marketing play a significant role in media commercialization. Just a few weeks after its airing of the first commercial advertisement, Shanghai Television aired the first foreign commercial, for Swiss Rado watches. Foreign companies, eager to access the huge and newly opened Chinese market, soon learned that they could place advertisements virtually anywhere. Japanese consumer goods producers were particularly aggressive. The centralized and monopolistic nature of major Chinese news media institutions make them ideal and effective advertising vehicles for brand name products. Companies such as Seiko, Citizen, Casio, Hitachi, and Toyota began to pour money into the Chinese news media in the early 1980s even though there was no apparent sign of a market for their products. By 1982, foreign advertising had already accounted for about 10 percent of the nation's total advertising revenue (approximately U.S. $7.7 million).[19] American advertisers were not far behind. By 1987, mainly U.S.-based multinationals such as Coca-Cola, Pepsi-Cola, Gillette, Maxwell House, IBM, and Procter and Gamble were spending about $16 million on television advertising in China each year.[20] Due to their financial strength and marketing expertise, multinational companies and joint ventures between foreign and Chinese companies continue to be the most aggressive and effective advertisers.

Transnational commercial media organizations and entertainment program providers played an instrumental role in bringing foreign advertising to Chinese television, especially through the well-known barter formula whereby Chinese television stations provide advertising time to foreign media companies in exchange for free television programming. Between 1982 and 1984, CCTV signed barter agreements with six American media companies. In one of these agreements, CBS provided sixty-four hours of "off-the-shelf" information and entertainment programming to CCTV in exchange for 320 minutes of advertising time, which was sold by CBS to nine foreign advertisers, including several Fortune 500 firms.[21] The scope of the barter business has since grown dramatically. A 1995 agreement between CCTV and the American entertainment giant Encore Entertainment, for example, involves ten hours of a week of feature films, drama, music, and variety programming.[22]

Transnational business and media firms are keen on accessing the huge Chinese market. That China's advertising rates are among the lowest in the world, especially on television, further enhances the attractiveness. In the words of an American media consultant, "Where you may have a US $5 CPM [costs per thousands] for a national evening prime broadcast in the United States, it's only about nine cents in China. . . . You get a lot of bang for your buck here."[23] Chinese media organizations, on the other hand, are hungry for hard foreign currency and, in the case of television, content, and have become interdependent in this relationship. Indeed, to be able to attract foreign advertising is the symbol of commercial success. The following description, provided by a Chinese media researcher, is illustrative:

> He [publisher Cui Enqing] opened the day's paper and turned directly to page 8, the "Special Advertising Page." A sense of joy burst into his heart as he was gazing at the glossy

Jeep Cherokee photo. . . . This was January 15, 1994, a noteworthy day in the history of *Beijing Youth News.* . . . Together with two more (foreign) advertisements on page 3, the revenue derived from foreigners this day alone surpassed *Beijing Youth News'* entire advertising revenue in 1991.[24]

The rapid increase in advertising revenues has significantly altered the nature of news media operations. Newspaper publishing, for example, has become so potentially profitable that many institutions are jumping in to make money, not to play politics.[25] On December 5, 1925, Mao Zedong, in an inaugural editorial for a new political journal, asked, "Why publish the *Political Weekly* [Zhengzhi zhoubao]?" His answer? "To make revolution."[26] In the 1990s, the same question gets a completely different response: "It is a money-making business. A newspaper with 20,000 or 30,000 subscribers can well support its employees with advertising income alone."[27]

The growth in advertising has feuled a boom in all media sectors since the latter half of 1992.[28] The number of radio and television stations increased from 724 and 543 in 1991 to 1202 and 837 in 1995, respectively.[29] At the end of 1991, the number of registered newspapers in China was 1,543 but had grown to 2,039 by the end of 1993.[30] During the 1980s, the average rate of newspaper growth was one new title every three days. Between 1992 and 1994, the rate increased to one every one and a half days. By the end of 1995, the number of newspapers had reached 2,200. A total of 72 million copies were sold daily.[31]

In addition, existing newspapers expanded their pages to meet advertisers' demands for more space. In 1992, the four-page broadsheet format, which had been typical of Party organs since *Liberation Daily* in the early 1940s, shifted to eight pages. Dailies published special weekend supplements, while weeklies increased their frequency of publication. In 1992 alone, more than 200 newspapers added pages or increased the number of issues.[32] This trend continued in 1993 with 130 newspapers increasing pages or issues. Another 150 did so simultaneously on New Year's Day, 1994.[33] Some jumped from four pages to eight pages and then to twelve pages in just two years.

Advertising has left no media space untouched. "Too much advertising" has become the most common complaint of television audiences. Because television stations are reluctant to insert commercials into programs, advertisements are packed between them. Commercial breaks average seventeen minutes on some local stations. A four-hour session of prime-time television viewing includes one hour of advertising.[34]

CCTV is the hottest advertising medium in the country, thanks to its protected status as the only national television network. In 1992, its advertising revenue was 500 million yuan, accounting for 25 percent of the total national television advertising revenue.[35] Because of its monopolistic access to a national audience, CCTV was able to increase its advertising prices rapidly in 1993 and again in 1994.[36] The station introduced a bidding system in prime-time advertising pricing for 1995, with a beginning price of 7 million yuan for a five-second spot over a period of one year. By 1996, this beginning price had increased to 12 million yuan. Still, competition was fierce. A Shangdong-based liquor advertiser ended up paying 38 million yuan a year for a five-second prime-time advertising contract.[37]

Although the time devoted to advertising on CCTV was only eighty-two minutes daily in 1993 (out of more than fifty hours on four different channels at the time), 50 percent was during prime time on the most watched general interest channel, CCTV-1, which has an estimated audience of more than 600 million.[38] Nightly between late 1994 and early 1995, in the seventy minutes running from 7:00 P.M., the beginning of its main news program, and 8:10 P.M., the start of the popular drama series "The Story of the Three Kingdoms" (Shanguo yanyi), CCTV managed to sandwich eighteen minutes of advertising spread through eight breaks. This accounted for nearly half of the total advertising time of the whole evening. With the length of each advertisement between five and thirty seconds, the viewer was bombarded with more than *seventy* messages touting all kinds of products. Sometimes there were ten to twenty commercials in one slot. CCTV offers perhaps the most intensive advertising viewing hour in the world.[39]

But this is not the whole story. In addition to the eight commercial breaks, the weather forecast at the end of the 7:00 P.M. national news was also completely commercialized. The television screen was divided into two parts. While the larger part carried the national weather map and satellite weather pictures, a smaller portion, usually at the bottom or right part of the screen, flashed advertising messages.[40] Moreover, the picture that accompanied weather reports for most provincial capitals was also a hidden commercial. Rather than taking a bird's eye view of the whole city or a picture of a scene that symbolizes a city—Beijing's Tiananmen Square, Shanghai's waterfront, or Hangzhou's West Lake, for example—each picture focused on a specific hotel, shopping center, company tower, industrial zone, or other spot with obvious advertising value.[41]

In newspapers, advertising has conquered the political and ideological aloofness of the traditional Party organ. Although advertising accounts for only between 25 and 30 percent of total newspaper space, still far less than in North American commercial papers, the enthusiasm for advertising and the treatment of advertising by major Party organs would make even the most commercially aggressive North American newspapers appear timid.[42]

Unlike North American newspapers, the masthead of a typical Chinese newspaper does not run across the whole page but occupies only the left half of the top. The right half is an empty space, which is often called the "eye of the newspaper," a tribute to its eye-catching position as the first spot seen by most readers. During the Cultural Revolution, this space was reserved for Chairman Mao's quotations or political slogans. Today, advertising has taken over. My survey of twenty-four provincial Party organs in October 1994 found a third of them with advertising in this space. Moreover, as in the CCTV weather forecast, advertising has even entered the square containing the date of publication next to the newspaper title. In the October 17, 1994, issue of *Shaanxi Daily*, for example, this square carried a drug advertisement in the form of a classified ad, with company logo, telephone number, and the name of a salesperson.

Perhaps the most radical advertising practice is that of Party organs selling their entire front page to an advertiser for a day.[43] A Tianjin Party organ even created a series of ongoing news reports about its month-long auction of its advertising space for a particular day and thus turned all its readers into spectators of its advertising sale. The highest bidder paid 1 million yuan for one day's exclusive use of all the advertising space in the newspaper. Many other bidders got publicity through news reports. A commentator in a trade journal characterized this as an exercise in the "the emancipation of the mind" and an important step toward the introduction of market mechanisms in advertising pricing: "As a special commodity, newspaper advertising must be marketized and Party newspapers must take a leading role in this regard."[44] According to this writer, the Party newspaper should no longer fix a reasonable advertising price so that a small business might get a chance to publish an advertisement, but instead function strictly in accord with the rule of the market. In other words, "sell the advertising space to the client who can pay the most."[45]

Chinese Infomercials

The commercialization of the Chinese media, however, goes far beyond conventional advertising. Since the economic reforms, media organizations have gradually developed into an information industry serving government and business clients. One important aspect of this is paid information services that are integrated into regular media content. Just as with advertising, the media charge clients for displaying such information. But no advertising agency is involved and audiences usually do not know that what they are seeing or hearing was paid for. In broadcast media, such programs are called "type II advertising" (*erlei guanggao*), but this term circulates only inside the industry. These programs are in fact a form of infomercial.

In the broadcast media, paid information services usually appear in the same format as regular news or current affairs programs, with regular announcers. The names of these programs usually contain the word "economy" or "market," such as "Economic Kaleidoscope," "Economic Overpass," "Economic Life," "Golden Bridge over the Sea of Businesses," "Consumer Guide," "Information Service," and

"Television Market," all of which were current in 1992. They usually contain both paid and unpaid parts. Unpaid reports focus on macro-economic policies and overall trends in economic development. Paid sections have micro-business information with advertising value. The clients either send in their own material to be edited by the station staff or the station sends reporters for on-site interviews and videotaping. Each piece of information is assessed a price, which is usually less than that for regular advertising.

For many years, the flagship business information program was CCTV Business Department's "The Economy in Half an Hour" (Jingji banxiaoshi), which charged three thousand yuan for thirty seconds of time. It began in late 1989 and soon became very popular with certain audiences, especially the business community and individual entrepreneurs.[46] The program, as described by CCTV,

> closely ties itself to the country's central task of economic construction, propagates the Party's and the government's economic policies and directives, promotes model individuals in all walks of the country's economic life; introduces successful business management and the experiences of individuals who have recently become wealthy; transmits various kinds of domestic and foreign business information; makes connections between producers, distributors, and retailers, and serves the socialist market economy and consumers.[47]

The program is thus the most direct expression of the use of news media as instruments of economic development. Among the many features in the half-hour daily program, some achieved almost legendary status for providing useful business information for individual entrepreneurs and enterprises. "May You Become Wealthy," a short segment of practical wealth-generating information and advice to farmers, was praised as the "farmers' golden key to become wealthy through science and technology."[48]

Since 1992, the program has organized an annual four-day television trade fair. By turning the television screen into a huge trade mall, the program aims to serve as a "matchmaker" in the marketplace and provide a "golden bridge" between businesses.[49] Broadcast live nationwide from a huge exhibition hall in Beijing, the program showcases new inventions, patented technologies, equipment, and personnel files. Twenty telephone hot lines let viewers participate. In 1992, the anticipated trade volume during the fair was more than 1 billion yuan.[50]

CCTV's "Joint Business Information Broadcasting" (Jingji xinxi lianbo), a cooperative effort among CCTV and provincial television stations, was another well-known program.[51] Initiated in August 1992, it was inspired by Deng's talks.[52] This thirty-minute show carries more than seventy items of business information each day divided into five categories: macro-economy, new products, finance, services, and international. Each category is further divided into segments according to subject. Most of the information is provided by provincial television stations and CCTV shares the fees it collects with them.[53]

This program is also popular with government departments and the business community as demonstrated by the more than fifteen thousand letters in its first three months on the air. A county Party committee in Hunan Province even issued a circular requiring government officials and the business community to watch it regularly and to use it to publicize local products.[54] The program's fame can also be attributed, at least partially, to Deng Xiaoping, whose secretary phoned CCTV on October 21, 1992, to say that Deng watched it almost every day. Deng's widely circulated comments were reputed to have been: "The 'Joint Business Information Broadcasting' program discusses business exclusively, its creation is very timely. Although the program is not very long, only thirty minutes, the content is very rich, fast-paced, with a high volume of information. It will be conducive to the economic development of the country and to the cultivation of the market economic system."[55] CCTV President Yang Weiguang explained that CCTV's aim was to make the program "a propagandist of the Party's economic policy and a promoter of factory products."[56]

Local broadcast stations have gone even further in serving business. In Beijing TV's "Television Market," a reporter takes the audience directly into department stores and introduces commodities on display.[57] A survey of the *China Broadcasting Yearbook*'s (Zhongguo guangbo dianshi nianjian) listing of selected new programs reveals that almost all provincial stations added at least one such program in 1992. These programs are politically both safe (in that they do not explicitly deal with politics at all) and expedient (in that they fulfill the Party's and government's objective of making the media instruments of economic development). They are also easy to produce. Most importantly, they generate revenue. Thus, it is perhaps no surprise that some have suggested that broadcasters should condense regular news content, cut news broadcast time, and increase paid business information broadcasting. Zhuang Hongchang of Dalian Broadcasting Bureau, for example, suggested that regular news programs be divided into two parts, the first half for regular news, the second half for paid business information.[58]

Commercial Sponsorship of Media Content

Commercial sponsorship of specific media content is another form of media commercialization. In the newspapers, company name, logo, product, and sometimes address, name of salesperson, and phone number are packed in a small square and attached to a news story, a commentary, or a column and become an integrated part of the journalism. The work of journalists thus often carries a specific business "stamp." It is "specially printed" (*teyuan kandeng*) by a company or "print-ed with the assistance" (*xieban*) of a business firm or a government department. In this way, even tobacco manufacturers, who are barred from regular advertis-ing, are able to get their message across in major news outlets. If paid broadcast information is "type II advertising," then it is fair to say that commercial spon-sorship of news and opinion in newspapers is the ultimate form of advertising because it makes a direct link between the leading news story of the day and a specific business or product.

Commercial sponsorship of specific media content in China began in the mid-1980s but was originally limited to entertainment and educational programming in broadcasting.[59] After gradually spreading to news programming and across different media, it has become pervasive since 1992, apparently another "bold step" on the road to commercialization. Just as almost all newspapers in China carry advertising, almost all in one way or another carry some sort of sponsorship. Dif-ferences are only a matter of degree. For example, the Ministry of Health's organ, *Health News,* carried one sponsored item on October 13, 1994. On the same day, *Xinhua Daily,* the provincial Party organ of Jiangsu, carried sponsored news items and columns on seven out of its eight pages. The only exception was page five, which was devoted exclusively to regular advertising.

There are several ways of sponsoring news and information content. A spon-sor can put its stamp on news, photos, feature articles, and opinion pieces on ev-ery page by promoting some sort of competition, usually paying the paper for organizing the contest and providing the cash awards. The most popular is for "best leading news story," in which a sponsor puts its stamp on the day's leading item. A survey of twenty-four national newspapers and provincial Party organs between October 15 and October 18, 1994, turned up eight, or one-third, with "best leading news story competitions." Some were named for the sponsor. For example, *Shaanxi Daily* (Shaanxi ribao) on October 16 held the Hanzhong Cup Leading News Com-petition cosponsored by the Hanzhong Prefectural Party Committee and the Hanzhong prefectural government; *Qinghai Daily* (Qinghai ribao) on October 15 held the Welding Flower Cup Leading News Story Competition, sponsored by a welding materials factory. In a space not smaller than the news story, its stamp carried details about the factory's current stock, product specifications, address, and telephone number. On October 17 *Gansu Daily* (Gansu ribao) held the Con-struction Bank Cup Leading News Story Competition, which included the logo of the Construction Bank and a small line "celebrating the fortieth anniversary of the Ganshun Branch of the Construction Bank." *Zhejiang Daily*'s (Zhejiang ribao) competition stamp carried a company name, products, and a telephone number. *Ningxia Daily*'s (Ningxia ribao) included a factory name, the name of the factory director, and a phone number. *Guizhou Daily's* (Guizhou ribao) was sponsored by a tobacco manufacturer, also with the name of the factory director.

The news stories in competition are regular news items, usually written by staff reporters or amateur correspondents. Usually the news is not related to the sponsor. But in the case of *Gansu Daily,* the story appeared to be a public relations piece for the sponsor because it lauded the bank's Lanzhou Railway branch for providing funds for railway construction. There is an old Chinese saying that "big awards produce heroes" (*zhongshang zhixia you yongfu*). With all these prizes from businesses, it might be thought that journalists would strive for superior news reporting. But, in fact, the opposite appears true: "Some units, after providing money, attach specific conditions to the newspaper's propaganda, for example, in the form of a requirement that the newspaper carry specific content or a specific number of items provided by the unit itself. Even without these specific conditions, the two parties may reach some sort of agreement. . . . Thus, the newspaper must take special care of news reports about the sponsoring unit: down-playing critical reporting, making a big deal of any good news."[60]

In addition to competitions, sponsors can also support regular newspaper columns or create special columns on chosen subjects under their own names. Examples of the former include the October 13, 1994, issue of *Economic Daily,* the organ of the State Council, in which the page one "Reports on the Asian Games" column was sponsored by a tobacco manufacture; its page two feature column "I Am the Same Age as the Republic" was sponsored by a medical equipment supplier; and its page six "Stock Market Reports" was sponsored by a real estate company. On the other hand, the Personnel Bureau of the Ministry of Culture sponsored a specific column in *China Culture News* (Zhongguo wenhua bao) publicizing personalities in literature and the arts.

Thus, a sponsor can buy space virtually anywhere in a newspaper. Even the most sacred parts of the newspaper, the commentaries and news analyses written by reporters and editors, are sometimes supported by sponsors. In the October 21 issue of *Liberation Daily,* the page four "Special Commentary" on the diffusion of nuclear power in northeast Asia was "specially printed" by a Shanghai laundry equipment manufacturer. On the same day, *People's Daily* carried a page six "International Forum" commentary about Russia's presence in the Middle East that was "co-sponsored" by the China Golden Coins Corporation.

Since many news and editorial departments have a direct responsibility for "creating income," they have to look elsewhere than advertising, which is the province of the advertising department. Among the many popular sayings among media workers is "if you want to get rich, solicit sponsorships" (*yao xiang fu, la zanzhu*).[61] As will be discussed in the next chapter, since reporters and editors often receive bonuses from sponsorships, there is a strong incentive to attract them.

In the broadcast media, a common form of commercial sponsorship is joint production of feature and information programming. Broadcast officials have actively promoted this practice. Xu Chonghua, deputy minister of Radio, Film, and Television, for example, instructed local broadcasters in the following straightforward language in 1992: "Government departments want to expand propaganda; enterprises want to promote their products. They are willing to spend money on programs. . . . There is no problem with joint program production."[62]

In these joint programs, government departments or businesses typically provide money and material; stations produce and broadcast the program. CPR, for example, ran a feature program called "Shanming City in Progress" for a fairly long period in 1994. Insiders suggested that it was cooperatively produced, with money and at least some of the broadcast material provided by the city. The city, in turn, may have obtained most of the money from local enterprises.

Local stations usually take this practice one step farther. The president of a radio station in Hunan Province, for example, reported how his station invited "nearly eighty factory leaders, managers, and directors to the studio to be interviewed and to co-sponsor programs."[63] A local radio station in Sichuan Province contracted with a number of government departments to provide money and broadcast material on a regular basis, although the radio station accepted full responsibility for airing them. Another station in the same province has even established a special editorial committee consisting of representatives from forty-eight government departments and businesses. These organizations pay an annual fee and provide program material.[64]

All of these examples are presented as successful cases in academic and trade journals analyzing the broadcast industry. There is no discussion whatsoever of the political and social implications of these forms of commercialized financing. That the media have become the mouthpieces of whoever can pay has not been a subject of concern.

Business Involvement in the News Media

Some enterprises are not satisfied with merely sponsoring a particular newspaper column or broadcast program or publishing newspapers for circulation within their enterprises ("enterprise newspapers," or *qiye bao*). Although the government prohibits direct business investment in the media in general and allows businesses to operate only internal media outlets aimed at its own employees, businesses have entered the industry in one way or another. In Guangdong Province, thirty newspapers, or 29 percent, have some sort of open or behind-the-door "cooperative" relationship with business enterprises. These take various forms. For example, an enterprise may provide both financial and editorial input. Its investment may be returned either in the form of advertising space or having its name included in the masthead.[65]

On February 5, 1993, *Wenhui Bao* reported in a page one story that the first shareholding newspaper in the country, *Sichuan Sports News* (Sichuan tiyu bao) had been established in Sichuan Province with investment from a musical instrument manufacturer. According to the story, the business would provide money and management expertise and the two parties would "jointly run the newspaper and explore business opportunities in sporting goods and culture."[66]

There are also many unconfirmed, but authoritative, reports that some newspapers and radio stations have leased entire pages or time blocks to specific businesses, together with editorial rights.[67] For example, *Chinese Journalists* reported a remark by Zhang Changhai, chief editor of *Guangming Daily*, that a Beijing-based newspaper had sold the editorial rights to two of its pages for a year, one to a Guangdong company, one to a Beijing sporting goods company, at a cost of fifty thousand yuan per page.[68]

In such a situation, a business takes over content production, advertising sales, and salaries. Thus, the purchasing company can buy a segment of the Party's mouthpiece and turn it into its own mouthpiece while still making a profit.[69]

Government authorities have ignored these developments, except in a few extreme cases. In 1994, the State Press and Publications Administration suspended the publication licenses of six newspapers for illegally transferring and selling editorial rights to private businesses. Among these six papers, *Jiangsu Health News* (Jiangsu jiankang bao) had signed a twenty-year cooperation contract with a private company in which the newspaper sold the publication rights to some of its pages, including the final editorial rights. The private business twice published fabricated news reports regarding one of its products. The stories were even accompanied by photos of six persons falsely claiming to be Ph.D.'s returned from studying overseas who were supposedly responsible for research and development of the product.[70] In another case, a trade newspaper managed by the Anhui provincial light industry bureau sold its registration number and advertising permit to the Wuhan-based Changjiang Culture Promotion Center for ten thousand yuan. The deal was exposed when the purchasing company published an unregistered supplement with sensational crime stories that caught the attention of the authorities.[71]

Turning Party Organs into Business Consortia

While the media are now inextricably linked with business through advertising, sponsorships, and other market relationships, news organizations themselves have expanded into noninformation and nonentertainment businesses to broaden their bases of revenue in a way that is "analogous to the diversification of investment by media consortia in capitalist societies."[72] Business expansion has evolved through several different stages. Initially, news organizations increased broadcast channels or created subsidiary publications, usually smaller market-oriented ones focusing on business information and entertainment.

As a result, although the government does not allow cross-media operations between publishing and broadcasting, national media organizations have grown into huge operations with multiple outlets. As of 1996, Xinhua News Agency put out a total of thirty-nine dailies, weeklies, and monthlies.[73] Its important recent subsidiaries have been *China Securities* (Zhongguo zhengquan bao), a daily that specialized in business news and the stock market, and *Xinhua Daily Telegraph* (Xinhua meiri dianxun), a general interest daily that carried the agency's own news dispatches. CPR ran seven diverse channels. CCTV operated eight channels in 1996. CCTV-1 emphasized news and current affairs; CCTV-2 focused on business; CCTV-3 featured traditional Chinese operas; CCTV-4 catered to overseas audiences. Two pay-TV channels focused on sports and movies; a third offered children's, military affairs, and educational programming; another specialized in arts and culture.

People's Daily ran five subsidiary newspapers, including its overseas edition, which is the official organ for propagating the Party line among the Chinese-reading public overseas. The other four were much more market-oriented. *Market* (Shichang bao) is a tabloid with specialized market information and consumer news. A more elaborate version of the comic page in Western commercial newspapers, the tabloid *Satire and Humor* (Fengci yu youmo) appeared three times a month and was edited by the paper's Literature and Art Department. *Global Digest* (Huanqiu wencui) was a weekly tabloid run by the newspaper's International Department, specializing in feature reports on international hot spots and human interest stories. *China Economic News Bulletin* (Zhongguo jingji kuaixun), launched in 1992, was a joint venture between the *People's Daily* overseas edition and the American high-tech company Dela-Global Inc. Unlike the others, this paper, with Chinese and English editions and flexible delivery methods through fax, express delivery, and airmail, apparently targeted Chinese- and English-speaking business elites both inside and outside China. Its offering of "direct, timely, reliable and accurate, and practical" information was unlike the usual fare of *People's Daily*.[74] *People's Daily* also published four magazines: *Journalism Front* (Xinwen zhanxian), *Earth* (Dadi), *People's Forum* (Renmin luntan), and *Tide of the Times* (Shidai chao).[75]

Today, Party and government organs are no longer simple mouthpieces; they have become business conglomerates. The appearance of the *People's Daily* headquarters is perhaps symbolic of this increasing media involvement in other aspects of the economy. If one approaches the huge newspaper complex from its main entrance on the west, one still gets a feeling of impressive status and the political weight of the institution with its armed guards and the *"People's Daily"* inscription in the familiar calligraphy by Mao. But at its gate to the south, the scene is rather different. Although an armed guard stands watch under a sign of the paper's name, above the sign is a more impressive, eye-catching sign across the whole gate: Shanghai Volkswagen Designated Maintenance Department. The garage, just inside the gate, sprawls out into the complex, with rows of cars and busy workers. Run by the newspaper's transportation team, it is reportedly making a lot of money for the newspaper. To attract business, of course, it is necessary to have a sign, and what can be more impressive than a huge sign over the familiar name *People's Daily?*

Initially, a 1988 provisional regulation jointly issued by the State Press and Publications Administration and the State Administration for Industry and Commerce limited the media's business operations to information and publicity-related areas, such as advertising, information services, sponsorship of trade fairs, and cultural and educational activities, or to technically related businesses, such as radio and television repair shops, photo-finishing, printing, and broadcasting, photography or printing equipment supply and service centers. The regulation prohibited operations that are unrelated to the media.

Such barriers, however, have broken down since 1992, although there is nothing official revoking the 1988 regulation. The media have expanded into areas such as tourism, transportation, real estate, manufacturing, and trade. *Liberation Daily,* for example, has moved into real estate, computers, and taxis. Similarly, the Shanghai Broadcasting Bureau has its hand in real estate, tourism, telecommunications, and taxis.[76] In prosperous Jiangsu Province, local broadcasting administrations have established hundreds of small industrial enterprises. By August 1993, they had even initiated sixteen joint-venture enterprises with overseas business interests, attracting U.S. $7,830,000 in investments.[77]

Implications of Commercialization

Although the media are still owned by the state, their economic basis has been shifted from complete reliance on state subsidies to increasing dependence on commercial revenue from advertising, sponsorships, and business operations in other areas. At the same time, the media have evolved into business organizations with interests in many aspects of the economy. Many newspaper organizations have achieved complete financial independence and contribute profits and taxes to the state treasury. Most broadcast stations still receive government aid, but the percentage of government funds in overall expenditures is decreasing. Of the Ministry of Radio, Film, and Television's 1.1 billion yuan expenditures for the 1993 fiscal year, for example, government subsidies accounted for only 36 million.[78] In the economically developed areas of Shanghai, Guangdong, Jiangsu, and Zhejiang, the ratio of self-generated funding versus government funding is even greater. In 1992, at the Shanghai Broadcasting Bureau, for example, commercialized financing provided ten times the funds the government did.[79] By 1993, the ratio was estimated to have reached 20 to 1.[80] Some broadcasters actually contribute more to the state in taxes and profits than they receive in subsidies. Indeed, for them, the meaning of government funding is more symbolic and political than financial.

This increased dependence on advertising and sponsorship has obviously greatly altered the media landscape. To be sure, Party organs and broadcast stations are almost guaranteed stable advertising income by virtue of their monopoly and their long-established advantages in the market. Moreover, because Party organs rely heavily on institutional subscriptions purchased with public money, they can still more or less practice Party journalism as usual and at the same time receive handsome advertising and sponsorship income.

Nevertheless, advertising and sponsorship have had a significant impact. On older radio and television stations and in Party organs, less and less emphasis is put on political issues. New programs and added pages are mostly devoted to business information and infotainment. And as we will see in chapters 5 and 6, many newly established newspapers and broadcast channels are almost exclusively devoted to business and entertainment. Although political news has become more tightly controlled, it has also become less prominent and less pervasive. Newly established business publications have gained a steady readership, thus effectively challenging Party organs like the *People's Daily*.

Although China has not developed standardized systems of audience and readership surveys, with readership statistics and audience ratings available to potential advertisers, such statistics have become increasingly important to the news media industry.[81] Many news organizations conduct surveys on an ad hoc basis; some, however, have began to contract with outside organizations, such as the survey teams affiliated with various levels of the government statistic bureau on a regular basis. CCTV, for example, contracts out its audience survey to a national survey team under the State Statistics Bureau and publishes a weekly report on audience ratings. The television industry in Shanghai has even developed a relatively independent system of surveying. Administrated by the Shanghai Radio, Film, and Television Bureau, television audience surveys in Shanghai are contracted out to the Shanghai Population and Information Center, which produces regular television ratings in the Shanghai area on the basis of thirteen hundred sample households by using the diary method.[82]

Advertising has also caused a power shift within the Party media system, as reflected in the relative decline of national and provincial Party organs and the rise of metropolitan organs. National and provincial organs have more responsibility for propagating Party and government policies. They have to cover a wide range of political, economic, and social issues and must take into consideration a wide audience, both urban and rural. In contrast, municipal media outlets have fewer political responsibilities and their subject matter is closer to the daily life of the urban population. Although their circulation is smaller than national and provincial outlets, their readers are mostly urban dwellers, who are currently the main force in the growing consumer society in China. In addition, advertising rates of municipal newspapers and broadcast stations are generally lower than those of national and provincial outlets. Thus, they are ideal advertising vehicles for consumer goods and services. Since 1993, the newspaper with the nation's highest advertising revenue has not been *People's Daily,* nor the Guangdong provincial Party organ, *Nanfang Daily* (Nanfang ribao), but *Guangzhou Daily* (Guangzhou ribao), Guangzhou City's Party organ. It has the highest rate of private subscriptions (based on individual consumer choice, in contrast to institutional subscriptions, which are compulsory in many cases) among all Party newspapers in the country. Its daily street sales alone total two hundred thousand.[83]

The structural impact of commercialization can also be seen in the decline of papers for peasants. Although these newspapers were relatively underdeveloped to start with, reflecting the lack of political and cultural capital of peasants, nevertheless there was a small boom of peasant papers in the 1980s as a result of initial reforms in the news media. By 1989, there were twenty-six national and local peasant papers, published either by government agricultural departments or by main provincial Party organs in the form of a rural edition. But with the rapid commercialization of the newspaper industry since the early 1990s, peasant papers have suffered a drastic decline both in number and in circulation. In 1993, circulation dropped more than 20 percent. *Liaoning Peasant News* (Liaoning nongmin bao), which once set a national circulation record of 1,300,000 for newspapers of its type, for example, dropped to 100,000 in 1993. Peasant papers are usually not profitable because of difficulties in distribution, increased production costs, failure to attract advertising, and lack of other commercial revenues.[84] With increased emphasis on commercial success, some Party organs simply stopped publishing peasant papers or reoriented them toward the more profitable urban market.[85] Shanghai's *Liberation Daily,* for example, has stopped publishing its rural edition. *Jilin Peasant News* (Jilin nongmin bao) was changed to *Jilin Business News* (Jilin shangbao) in 1992. *Anhui Daily* (Anhui ribao) changed its rural edition to an entertainment-oriented evening paper catering to the urban population in the provincial capital. As a result, this huge agricultural province was left without even one special newspaper for peasants.

Commercialization in newspaper distribution has further contributed to this decline.[86] To be sure, the end of the post office's monopoly in newspaper distribution has increased the income of newspapers in densely populated cities. But the subsequent reduction of profits for the post office has also made cross-subsidies for rural distribution less viable.[87] Thus, "the end of the post office's monopoly in distribution may ultimately deprive remote rural areas of ready access to city publications, further widening the rural-urban disparity."[88] Similar developments can also be seen in the radio sector. Wired-radio networks have deteriorated in some rural areas due to lack of public investment since the introduction of market mechanisms.[89] This means that households without television have been further deprived of access to information, especially since wired-radio has traditionally provided the bulk of local news and agriculture information.

Because the state controls the number of media outlets, advertising remains largely a sellers' market in the mid-1990s. Advertisers have to push to get spots on major Party organs and broadcasting stations. For this reason, their power to directly interfere with editorial content is limited. But the pressure of advertisers has already been felt by editors. Yuan Hui, an editor with the Shanghai People's Radio network, for example, has revealed that the biggest pressure he faces is from advertisers. After the airing of a critical report, a well-known department store threatened to withdraw its 1 million yuan annual advertising account. Another company offered to buy one hundred thousand yuan of advertising in exchange for canceling a critical piece. When editing any negative item, Yuan had to notify his superiors as to whether the subject was an advertiser and, if so, the amount of advertising involved.[90] With growing media competition and increasing rates, which leave only a few large—and powerful—advertisers in the market, the influence of advertisers will be even more strongly felt by journalists.

In the competitive local and small media markets, news outlets have to put forth extra effort to get advertising, and during the process all kinds of exchanges can occur. For example, one may offer to publish a promotional piece in the form of a news story or feature in return for an advertisement. This kind of offer to advertisers has become common, as we will see in the next chapter.

At the same time, the explosion of opportunities for commercial involvement in the media means that financially resourceful businesses and government departments will have the best access to the channels of communication. While a small and rich city in the coastal region is able to get national media exposure and promote its businesses through sponsorship or coproduction of media content, poor cities in the interior or government departments and social organizations that have less financial resources, especially those devoted to noncommercial causes such as environmental protection, social welfare, and justice, will still have to rely on the goodwill of the Party and journalists to promote their investment opportunities and causes.

So far, the media are generally uncritically enthusiastic about almost all forms of commercialization. Commercial revenues have enabled them to improve working conditions, expand services, introduce new technologies, and, of course, improve the welfare of staff members. The news media have become major businesses. At the same time, they have turned themselves into the mouthpieces and instruments of domestic and international businesses. The media's use of their influence to promote business interests, including their own, is not only tolerated but celebrated. After all, they fulfill their role as instruments of economic construction as prescribed by the Party. The following is a passage from *China Journalism Yearbook*. It summarizes the experience of *Yichang News* (Yichang bao), the Party organ of Yichang City in Hubei Province, in setting up an enterprise fund as a way of realizing "businesses' participation in the running of newspapers and newspapers' provision of services to businesses." It reveals the media's new role and is significant because it was published and promoted by the country's most authoritative book of record on journalism.

> Upon the advice of entrepreneurs, we have introduced two columns [one on business strategies and one on successful entrepreneurs]. . . . In news reporting, we reflect the difficulties and demands of businesses, cheer for them and appeal on their behalf. We support and protect their reforms on the public opinion front. At the same time, we use our connections to build bridges between enterprises and the society at large. Whenever news organizations all over the country come to Yichang city to have activities [such as meetings of newspaper editors], we provide opportunities for members of the enterprise fund to connect with the news media. In June 1987, forty chief editors came to Yichang city. Some of the main enterprises in the fund received them. . . . Later, these newspapers carried reports of these enterprises. . . . In short, our principle is, newspaper sets the stage, businesses sing the opera.[91]

4

Corruption:
The Journalism of Decadence

Although commercialization has undoubtedly brought more financial freedom, the media are deeply confused over guiding principles and professional values. There is a growing uneasiness about widespread practices that exchange access to readers and audiences for money, whether the exchange is mediated by individual journalists, editorial units, or news organizations. While the Party principle is still constantly being reaffirmed, the commercial imperative has become important operationally. The Party's exercise of power is often crude; but the media's submission to the power of money is crass. As in many fields in China, corruption has become "not an aberration, but the very way the system works, deeply imbedded in the government itself."[1] In journalism it is not just a few individuals but an institutional and occupational phenomenon involving the majority of journalists[2] and the majority of media organizations from the smallest to the very pinnacle of the Party's propaganda apparatus, *People's Daily*.[3]

The following is a telling example. On August 1, 1994, Li Wenhuai, a reporter of the provincial radio station in Hebei, became the subject of a feature story in *Press and Publications News* (Xinwen chuban bao), the official organ of the State Press and Publications Administration, a national news outlet. Li was newsworthy because he does not accept money or gifts for reporting. According to the story, since the 1980s Li has refused to promote commodities and has declined gifts worth as much as two thousand yuan. As a result, although he has been a journalist for more than thirty years, he remains poor—and newsworthy.[4]

Forms of Corruption in Journalism

Corruption has been part and parcel of the process of media commercialization. It emerged in the mid-1980s and, like a virus, has spread to every part of the media, penetrating deeper and deeper. There are many forms of corruption, ranging from unethical practices to criminal activities. Journalists, media officials, editorial departments, and the subsidiary businesses of the media often take advantage of their connections with news organizations to pursue their own financial gains.

All-Expenses-Paid News Reporting

The most innocent form of corruption is perhaps "three-warranty reporting" (*san-bao caifang*), whereby journalists' travel, accommodations, and meals during out-of-town assignments are paid by the news source. This is also called "invitation journalism" (*qingjie xinwen*) because journalists are invited by government departments and, more often, business enterprises and other institutions. Their reports, of course, are always "good news"—opening of a construction project, an anniversary party, high efficiency in production. Reporters have a pleasant tour guided by their hosts. They travel by the best and most comfortable means, stay in fancy hotels, and are wined and dined. They see what their hosts want them to see, meet those their hosts want them to meet, and, of course, report what their hosts want them to report.

In many such cases, reporters travel in a pack under the sponsorship of one host. They even agree to publish on the same day. Such a group may be organized either by the host or by an intermediary. For many journalists, three-warranty reporting is a pleasant vacation. The sponsors get not only publicity but also an opportunity to say "thank you" to journalists who have been supportive in the past and, of course, to ensure their continued support. A few lucky journalists (lucky not by chance, but because of past performance) have been sent overseas. Their sponsors are China's newly emerging state-owned multinationals with subsidiaries in foreign countries.

Because the practice is so common, news organizations and journalists have largely taken it for granted. The business division chief of *Economic Daily* reported that it had become so pervasive that whenever a reporter is going out of town, colleagues will usually ask, "On whose invitation?"[5] In general there are three different perspectives within journalism circles regarding this. In the first it is viewed positively because during three-warranty reporting reporters do not have to worry about transportation and accommodations and are not subject to the budget constraints of their own news organizations; the writing is easy and it benefits both parties. According to the second perspective, this type of reporting puts journalists on their host's leash because they are obligated to report the good and not the bad. Moreover, working in a group, they cannot do in-depth reporting; the practice is thus bad for journalism. A third perspective seeks middle ground and is obviously an attempt by journalists to find psychological comfort: "You can participate, but the principled thing to do is not to hand your leash to your host. After completing the 'required program,' you can add some 'free style' and you can both satisfy your host and produce a good piece of journalism."[6]

One wonders, however, how "good" such journalism could be. Perhaps it depends on whether the reporter wants to get future invitations or how a reporter feels about the host's treatment. In fact, as one writer has noted, the length, content, timing, and placement of a three-warranty report often depend on the reporter's evaluation of the treatment.[7]

The Blurring of Advertising and Editorial Functions

For many years, news organizations directly solicited and contracted advertising. In October 1993, the government introduced the advertising agency system on a trial basis in a number of cities to break the media's monopoly on the production, management, and display of advertising.[8] Under this new system, advertising agencies are supposed to solicit and produce advertising, while the news media are supposed to serve as display vehicles only. To get around the new regulations, news organizations simply turned their advertising departments into advertising firms. Although these firms are supposedly "independent" affiliates, for the most part it is business as usual. On the other hand, although the introduction of the new system has led to the emergence of many advertising agencies outside the media system, due to their lack of expertise and a track record of success they can hardly compete with the news media. Advertisers do not trust these agencies and still prefer to approach news media outlets directly.

Advertising management in many media organizations is often chaotic. Although advertising departments and editorial departments are formally separated, in practice they are often connected and their functions are often blurred. Journalists sometimes solicit advertising while gathering news. In some news organizations, not only the advertising department but each programming or editorial department can also place advertising in a particular program or on a specific page.

Since sponsorships are usually managed by individual editorial departments, it is even more common for journalists to solicit sponsorships, especially since they can receive commissions for them. A journalist revealed that the commission in his national news organization is 3 percent; it can be 5, 10, even 20 percent in other organizations. Whatever the amount, the possible income from one deal is very large compared with a journalist's salary. One writer explained, "I have a friend working for a major newspaper in Beijing. He solicited 400,000 yuan's worth of sponsorship at once and received 80,000 yuan for himself."[9] That is at least fifteen years of salary in 1992 yuan. It is hardly surprising that journalists write favorably of potential advertisers. Indeed, news and features are sometimes offered as "bonuses" for netting an advertising or sponsorship deal.

While some journalists gather both news and advertising/sponsorships on their own initiative (of course, with the implicit permission of their organizations, which give them commissions), others obviously are assigned this dual task. One radio reporter told how he and a colleague took on two tasks during an out-of-town assignment. One was to solicit a sponsor for a program; the other was to write an analytical piece about a new personnel management system in a factory. When they met the factory director, they easily solicited a five-digit sponsorship. In return, they changed their reporting angle and turned an intended analytical piece into a puff piece.[10]

The blurring of editorial and advertising functions often goes all the way to the top of management. Wang Fang, a doctoral candidate from Fudan University's School of Journalism, for example, remarked without any critical reflection that at some newspapers in Guangdong Province the editor-in-chief is also the general manager of the newspaper's advertising firm.[11]

At the same time, advertising sales representatives often pose as journalists because invoking the authority of the press apparently increases the effectiveness of advertising solicitation. As one writer put it, "Everybody in the news organization can carry a press card to solicit advertising and sponsors. A certain television station has more than thirty vehicles, each has a 'news gathering vehicle' sticker on it."[12]

Journalists and Secondary Occupations

As in other sectors of the economy, moonlighting—particularly, working in the private sector while on the government payroll—is not unusual among journalists, although as government employees they are forbidden to run their own businesses. One common secondary occupation of journalists is public relations. Some journalists not only attend news briefings but also organize such activities, which have become fashionable since the mid-1980s. They act as "freelance" public relations agents for business organizations. Journalists and news organizations, because of their good connections and their access to the media, are favored by businesses as public relations experts and collect handsome fees.[13]

When journalism and public relations overlap and when both are the subject of abuse, the consequences are often beyond imagination. The following is an astonishing case that shocked the media and business communities of Beijing and Tianjin in 1993. Ms. Gu, the deputy editor of a magazine, held a briefing for a number of companies to promote their products. The Tianjin-based Huaqi manufacturing company failed to pay the 8,000 yuan participation fee. As a result, Gu charged in the news briefing that its product, a fruit drink, had quality problems. As a result, the factory suffered 80 million yuan in losses. More than one thousand workers lost their jobs. Gu insisted on payment of the fee immediately and said to the factory director afterward: "As a remedy, I can hold a news conference with the same people attending; I can even bring CCTV reporters to your factory to make a feature report."[14]

It is also common for journalists to hold second jobs as reporters and editors of other journals and magazines, especially those published by business organizations, and as consultants and advisers to business firms. In some cases, journalists actually have to work at these jobs, but more often business firms do not require much of them. They can get paid simply by writing positively about their business employers in their primary jobs and by providing business information. Journalism is sacrificed at the altar of business.

From Bribery to Extortion

The most talked-about form of corruption in journalism, of course, is "paid journalism," i.e., journalists or media units receiving material benefits for publishing promotional material disguised as news or features. It is, as one writer suggests, "the biggest news" about the Chinese media in the 1990s.[15] The reward for paid journalism can be cash and negotiable securities; gifts; reimbursement of receipts for personal expenses; personal favors such as job, housing, day-care, and educational arrangements for family members and relatives; free travel, house renovation, telephone installation, air-conditioning, and other services; money for the mini-treasury of editorial departments,[16] and advertising and sponsorship contracts—in short, anything that brings material benefits to an individual journalist or a news organization. Payments are made "legitimate" under such listings as "transportation fee," "meal subsidy" (it does not matter whether reporters spent anything on either) and "trial uses" of various commodities. Although "paid journalism" is the standard phrase used by both official and unofficial sources to describe this phenomenon, in essence it is bribery. As Ding Guan'gen, the Party's propaganda chief, pointed out, it is "an abuse of power for private gain."[17] "Mercenary journalism" is perhaps a more appropriate term.

Since the late 1980s, paid journalism as a systemic phenomenon has developed as follows. First, bribery has grown from small to big and from material gifts to cash and negotiable securities. At the beginning, journalists were known to receive free meals and small gifts that related to their work and carried a symbolic meaning, such as a pen, a notebook, a folder, a towel, a tea cup, or other local product. Gradually, the gifts became more valuable and unconnected to any event or locality; they included electronics and household goods, jewelry, and cosmetics. Eventually, donors exhausted their ideas for novel gifts and journalists had more gifts than they knew what to do with. Also, gifts were inconvenient to carry, especially with the proliferation of news conferences and publicity events in the early 1990s. A red envelope containing cash is becoming preferred. With cash, the trade in news space and air time is more efficient and more direct. Delivery of a ready-to-publish news or feature article together with cash to an editorial office becomes possible. The amount of cash has increased over the years, perhaps corresponding to inflation and increasing demand for publicity. Although it began with only fifty yuan, by 1992 the regular amount was around two hundred yuan and by late

1994 the "market price" was, according to an insider, three hundred yuan for a news story and five hundred yuan for a feature. For a particularly long feature story of three to four thousand words, the price could be as high as ten thousand yuan. When stocks and negotiable securities became popular in 1992, journalists began to receive bribes in these fashionable forms as well.

Second, paid journalism has expanded from business clients to government clients. Previously, most gift-givers were businesses. Lacking governmental clout, they rely on the power of money. Gradually, however, social organizations and even government departments have felt the need for publicity. During my research in late 1994 in Beijing, two stories illustrating this were circulating in journalism circles. In one case, red envelopes were issued to reporters attending a social event organized by educational authorities in which a vice-chairman of the National People's Congress participated. According to insiders, an activity involving an official at this level would usually warrant news reporting on its own merits. Perhaps, because the giving of red envelopes has become so common, the people organizing the event felt obliged to do it. Or perhaps, under the current context of "no money, no reporting," the organizers realized that red envelopes were necessary to ensure coverage. Or perhaps it was intended as insurance or an incentive for more elaborate reporting than usual. In another case, red envelopes were presented to journalists covering a ceremony celebrating the publication of a book by a senior Party leader. Just as factory directors and business managers buy reporters' services, some government officials have allegedly also paid reporters for feature stories boosting their images.[18]

Third, paid journalism has grown from an individual practice to a collective custom. Over the years, journalists have developed a system of cooperation and benefit-sharing with colleagues in the same editorial department. When they get a gift or receive a red envelope, they will share with one or two colleagues, especially superiors and editors. Naturally, some beats and assignments are more "lucrative" than others and editors who are confined to newsrooms have little opportunity to receive payoffs. This leads to tension. Editors could delay or even refuse publication of a story for which a reporter had entailed an obligation. Occasionally a client has paid but the story remains unpublished.[19] This, of course, embarrasses the reporter and affects credibility with clients. Even the shortening or delaying of a piece can cause considerable distress because clients may complain that they have not been adequately compensated in the reporter's work.

Such newsroom politics makes collective corruption necessary, not to mention safer. There is a net of mutual protection. In the Great Wall Machinery and Electronics Corporation scandal, for example, the *People's Daily* reporter divided his 100,000 yuan bribe into three portions. The smallest, 20,000, went into his own pocket; 50,000 was turned in to his department; and 30,000 was given to the director of the department.[20]

The progression from individual corruption to collective corruption has another dimension. As Wang Shuang writes, paid journalism has evolved from "a guerrilla warfare" of individual journalists to a "battle of the whole press corps."[21] Once, individual bits of bribery journalism were inserted into different pages of newspapers or news broadcasts. Later, whole pages or blocks of time were sold to individual clients with the money, in many cases, going to the mini-treasury of the editorial team responsible for the page or time block. These pages are called "special pages" (*zhuan ye*) and they usually contain favorable reports about specific cities, counties, towns, or enterprises.[22] Such pages are similar to the paid information columns and programs discussed in chapter 3, with the content of the pages either written by journalists or provided by the clients. The difference is that these special pages are more specifically designed to meet the advertising and publicity needs of a particular client.[23]

Fourth, paid journalism has progressed from "unorganized" to "organized" bribery. As in bribery anywhere and in any context, people usually will not take a bribe from someone they do not know or trust. But the direct giving and taking of bribes between individuals who know one another is too limited for many businesses and individuals who want to publish paid journalism. Within journalism circles, a special group of intermediaries known as "news brokers," comparable in some sense to stock brokers, have emerged. These people, however, are not full-time brokers in the open marketplace but rather work behind the scenes in their spare time—or, more likely, in their working hours because they usually hold easy government jobs. Some even work in the media or related areas.

Articles in journalism trade journals and personal observations provide a profile of this group. They are usually very good at socializing and making connections, they have close relationships with the authorities in the media, and they are familiar with the situation at the grass-roots level. They also have a good understanding of the "news market," knowing what kind of news is in demand and suitable for publication. They make connections between news sources and the media by organizing briefings, trade fairs, and other publicity opportunities and by organizing three-warranty reporting on a client's behalf and asking for favors on journalists' behalf. In the process, of course, they make considerable money.[24]

Finally, rather than passively accepting bribes, some reporters have reportedly engaged in active negotiation for a better deal and even extortion. The following are some of the stories told in trade journals.[25]

At a grand opening banquet for a new business, four tables of journalists showed up instead of just one. A stunned host had to increase the number of gifts and add dishes.[26]

Four reporters refused to attend a company's news briefing because they knew that the company's directors were to get more expensive gifts than they. They covered the briefing only after they got the more expensive gifts. Similarly, a refrigerator factory invited two reporters from the provincial Party newspaper to write promotional pieces. Three-warranty reporting and gifts produced a series of positive reports in the Party organ. At a farewell banquet, the journalists suggested that they visit the factory's customers in the scenic cities of Hangzhou and Suzhou. They received all-expenses-paid vacations in the two cities. The factory director ordered his sales office in the provincial capital to send a hotel room refrigerator to each reporter for "trial use," and the factory gave each one a receipt for ten days of accommodations at thirty yuan per night.[27] Supposedly, they could turn in these receipts to their own organization or other clients for reimbursement.[28]

A reporter from *Henan Daily* (Henan ribao) extorted a well-known personality by threatening to expose his tax evasion. Another reporter threatened to write negative pieces and "internal reference" material to get "publicity fees" from businesses. He asked for a five thousand yuan "newspaper page fee" from five business enterprises he visited. Three of the five enterprises gave him the amount and were rewarded with positive reports.[29]

Not just reporters have reportedly engaged in extortion. Editors have their own targets. Letter-page editors, for example, allegedly have collected from organizations and individuals by informing them of a critical letter. A bribe may prevent publication or soften a potentially damaging letter.[30] Editors who handle pieces from amateur correspondents may demand gifts or "sponsorship" from a correspondent's unit. These amateur correspondents, of course, are publicists for their own institutions. Some have been allocated funds by their units for bribing editors. Even if they have to pay themselves, they may find the expense worthwhile. Their reward from their unit for getting a piece published is often larger than their expense.

From Advertising-as-News to News-as-Fabrication

Bribery in journalism not only produces an abundance of advertising-as-news but also, in some cases, leads to false reports and deliberate distortion. During the Cultural Revolution, political needs were met with false and fabricated news reports. In the current atmosphere of promoting getting rich by any means, pursuit of money has also turned black into white. In 1987, the media exposed the case of Zhao Guangji, a reporter with *Shaanxi Workers' News* (Shaanxi gongren bao) who accepted a ten thousand yuan bribe and turned a swindler into a hero in his stories. In April 1994, the national media were forced by the Party to expose another scandal about themselves. This time it involved not just one reporter from a small non-Party organ in a remote province but many journalists from a number of major national media organizations in Beijing. It involved not a single swindler but the illegal fund-raising activity of a big company that affected tens of thousands of people. The scope and the details of the case of the Great Wall Machinery and Electronics Corporation (GWMEC) reveal how serious the problem of bribery has become.

The story begins with an unexpected meeting between Shen Taifu, the general manager of GWMEC, and Cai Yuanjiang, a reporter from CPR. Cai later assumed a second job as editor of a magazine published by Shen's company and received a monthly salary of a few hundred yuan. The two became very close. In June 1992, when Shen began his illegal fund-raising activity, Cai, at the suggestion of Shen, invited his college friend, *Science and Technology Daily* (Keji ribao) reporter Sun Shuxing, and two other reporters from two of Beijing's major newspapers to accompany Shen's fund-raising tour in Hainan Province in a typical case of three-warranty reporting. Shen gave each reporter two thousand yuan and an expensive suitcase. On June 27, Sun published a long feature story on the tour in *Science and Technology Daily,* the organ of the State Science and Technology Commission that was on the forefront in the 1989 struggle for press freedom and even praised by students for telling the truth during the democracy movement. It was the leading story of the day and was highlighted with an editorial note. The story not only did not question the legality of Shen's fund-raising but also praised him and his venture. According to the headline Shen raised "twenty million in twenty days." With this report, Shen's fund-raising attracted more and more people.

In July, Sun phoned Shen from Guangzhou and told him that he and Cai were accompanying Li Xiaoshi, deputy chairman of the State Science and Technology Commission, on a tour that would include the Shenzhen Special Economic Zone and Hainan Province. Shen flew to Guangzhou and stayed in the same hotel with the journalists and the official. He gave each journalist five thousand yuan for information. At the suggestion of the two journalists, Li visited Shen's business branch in Hainan and gave a speech praising his operations. The speech was widely reported and further legitimized Shen's activities.

Promotional reporting and bribes continued between the reporters and Shen. More journalists became involved, more articles were published, and more bribes were handed out. The amounts grew from two thousand yuan each in the beginning to ten thousand yuan each in the end. Cai, for example, received a total of forty thousand yuan. With the help of journalists, Shen and his company made many sensational news headlines. In January 1993, with the publication of another long feature article praising Shen in *Science and Technology Daily* and more than twenty other newspapers, the propaganda campaign waged on Shen's behalf reached a peak. In typical Party journalism tradition, the media set up Shen and his company as role models in economic reform, Shen as an entrepreneur, and his firm as a pioneer utilizing science and technology to benefit the people and society. He fit the Party and government agenda of promoting the private sector and developing technology. By the end, Cai became so closely identified with Shen and his interest that he bribed Li, the official of the State Science and Technology Commission, on behalf of Shen's company.

Shen and the journalists had gone too far. One of the sensational headlines Shen and the reporters created was that Shen's company was going to sue Li Guixian, state councilor and director of the People's Bank of China, who had criticized the company's activities. The case was exposed by the government and so were the journalists. In addition to Sun and Cai, many other reporters were arrested or investigated, including some from *People's Daily*. In eight months, the fraud created more than one hundred thousand angry investors, who could recover at most 30 percent of their investment. Of the more than 1 billion yuan raised by Shen, only half was retrievable.[31]

Government Regulations, Ethical Codes, and Anticorruption Campaigns

It is not that there are no rules. Since the economic reforms, the Party and the government have issued numerous regulations and guidelines intended to prevent malpractice. The "Provisional Regulations for Advertising Management" promulgated by the State Council in 1982 decreed that news and advertising should be separated. On October 15, 1982, the State Council's General Office issued a circular on strengthening advertising management. The general office "strictly prohibits journalists from soliciting advertising in the name of news reporting; strictly prohibits the publication of advertising in news formats for a fee."[32] The same principle was emphasized again and again in subsequent government regulations.[33] Some contained more specific provisions, such as "non-advertising departments in television stations should not undertake advertising business,"[34] "the advertising business of a newspaper should be undertaken by its advertising department and specialized advertising personnel; no other departments and individuals should be involved in advertising," and that the government "strictly prohibits 'paid journalism.'"[35] In February 1995, the Advertising Law of the People's Republic of China was enacted, which codified these rules.

There were further regulations aimed at tightening control in related areas, such as news bureaus, press cards, and news briefings. For example, in August 1993, the State Council General Office issued a circular asserting that "units that hold news briefings should strictly observe the principle of truthful journalism. . . . No cash gifts or negotiable securities should be given to reporters and press units under any pretext."[36]

Furthermore, after seventy years of journalism under the Party, the Chinese Journalists Association finally established a code of ethics on January 19, 1991.

According to the code, journalists "should not publish any forms of 'paid journalism,'" "should not put news and editorial spaces up for sale, nor accept nor extort money and gifts nor obtain private gain." It also pronounced that "journalism activities and business activities should be strictly separated. Reporters and editors should not engage in advertising and other business activities nor obtain private gain."[37] In 1994 this section was expanded to include the statement that journalists "should not accept money or negotiable securities in any form from units and individuals they report on."[38]

While it is perhaps an overstatement to say that government regulations and codes of ethics have had no effect, unquestionably journalists and the media have continued all forms of illegal and unethical practices despite them. "Orders without implementation, prohibitions without stopping" (*youling buxing, youjin buzhi*) is a common phenomenon in government. The saying "policies from the top are countered by strategies from below" (*shangyou zhengce, xiayou duice*) is not only popular but also accurate. In the words of a well-known Chinese jurist, "the problem doesn't lie in the allegation that we have no law to abide by, but in that we have not abided by the law."[39] Enforcement of regulations is weak, not to mention the loopholes in them and that most of them come too late. Codes of ethics are not binding at all. In particular, when administrative bodies are corrupt, it is hard to enforce administrative orders effectively. If a bribe to officials at the State Press and Publications Administration can lead to issuing a newspaper publication license to a unit that does not have the necessary funds and personnel, how can one expect such a body to assure the legality and morality of media practices?

With the exception of a few pieces exposing extreme cases and some trade journal articles, the media have not been active "watchdogs" of themselves. In May 1993, ten senior journalists from the revolutionary era presented a petition to the Party warning that journalism was "sliding into the muddle of money worship."[40] The petition received little attention from the media.

In 1993, the Party finally decided to launch a campaign against paid journalism. On August 4, the Propaganda Department of the Party's Central Committee and the State Press and Publications Administration issued a joint circular prohibiting it. The circular calls for press units and journalists to adhere to the principle of serving the people and socialism, hold to the Party principle and the principle of truth, abide by the law and professional ethics, be honest in performing their duties, and defend the reputation and image of the media.[41]

On the same day, the Party's Propaganda Department lectured top officials from major national media organizations at a forum in Beijing. For a short period, the media waged a campaign against paid journalism. Meetings were called at all levels of government in charge of media organizations. Editorials and public notices were published. More specific ethical codes and disciplines were established by news organizations. Telephone hot lines were set up for the public to report cases of paid journalism.

While the campaign yielded some results, and some news organizations seemed to take the issue seriously (at least for a short time), like many other anticorruption campaigns waged by the Party in recent years, it was another case of "loud thunder, small raindrops." In some instances paid journalism was simply temporarily suspended, with units telling journalists at news briefings, "Sorry, the wind is blowing hard at the moment, so we did not bring a gift for you, but next time . . ."[42] In other cases, the practice simply went underground. In still others, it goes on as usual. When a public relations agent asked journalists about the impact of the campaign, the response was, "You hear the noise of somebody coming upstairs, but nobody ever shows up."[43] Thus, it is not even a case of "loud thunder, small raindrops," there are no raindrops at all. One of the major national newspapers, *Farmers' Daily* (Nongmin ribao), for example, organized a news briefing on behalf of a private company in Beijing during the height of the campaign and gave out 150 yuan to each attending journalist.[44] In April 1994, eight months after the initial circular was issued, the Party's Propaganda Department issued another, urging the media to continue to strengthen ethics.[45] This circular did not receive much attention in the media.

On the other hand, as Xia Shangzhou observes, the Party is not at all tough on this issue. The 1993 circular, like all the government regulations before it, did not deal with such issues as three-warranty reporting or essay and news reporting competitions sponsored by government units and businesses. And while the circular prohibits units from giving cash and negotiable securities to journalists, it does not prohibit material gifts.[46] Moreover, neither government regulations nor ethical codes nor the Party's circular prohibits journalists from moonlighting. Compared with regulations and codes around the world, Chinese requirements are extremely soft. Indeed, the Party's campaign against paid journalism may have spread the practice. As one radio news producer suggested to me during an interview, the campaign made many businesses and individuals realize its possibilities.[47]

Roots of Corruption

Unethical practices in journalism are not confined to China, but the degree and scope is perhaps China's unique contribution to world journalism. The journalism historian Li Shiyi concluded from his study of Chinese newspapers over the past one hundred years, as well as newspapers in Hong Kong, Taiwan, and Western countries, that the particular connection between news and business in the Chinese media is rare elsewhere.[48] The extent of corruption suggests that the problem is systemic. Neither Party circulars nor campaigns are enough to eliminate corruption in Chinese journalism. Although some of these practices are transitional phenomena, the problem appears to be worsening.

Corruption is not just a moral issue. Journalists are no more corrupt than any other occupational group in China. Corruption is a structural problem, rooted in the contradictions between the Party's old ways of conceptualizing and organizing journalism and the new commercialized environment under which journalism operates. It is one manifestation of the contradictions of the current form of "socialism with Chinese characteristics." Party journalism has not been replaced by commercial journalism in China, as was the case in nineteenth-century America where the new penny press challenged the dominance and logic of the partisan press and gradually replaced it.[49] In China, it is the Party media system itself that is being commercialized. The media simultaneously operate with two different logics—the Party's and the market's. The contradictions between them provide fertile ground for paid journalism. One media official interviewed for this study provided a vivid metaphor: paid journalism is the disfigured offspring of two incompatible organisms.[50]

Old Concepts, New Contexts

Party journalism has always emphasized positive reporting, especially the achievements of government departments, businesses, and individuals. It has created model enterprises, model government units, and model workers. Under a planned economy, when enterprises need not advertise, this type of reporting is of little immediate economic consequence. But in a market economy, it becomes a form of covert advertising and a public relations exercise for the reported subjects. Reports of a product's winning a prize or of a hotel's receiving an award for service is advertising. Nothing is more effective for private doctors than feature stories about how capable they are or how selflessly they serve patients.

Compare the concepts and effects of "news" in the pre- and post-reform eras. Earlier, news was openly identified as propaganda: Factory X undertakes Y measures with result Z. Government department X follows policy instruction Y and does a good job in Z. In the reform era, Party and government have promoted the concept of the news media as instruments of economic construction and encouraged their involvement in the micro-economic stimulation of market demand for products and services. The typical news-writing formula is not significantly different: Factory X boldly carries out management reform and, as a result, productivity soars, quality improves. Firm Y invests in advanced technology with excellent returns on its investment.

In both the pre-reform and the reform era, "news" writing is a public relations exercise. Rather than transforming the old system, the new system reinforces its essential character. For example, Shen Taifu and GWMEC were portrayed as positive models by the media. Had they not been exposed, the media's campaign waged on his behalf would have been taken as a good example of the media's effort in promoting the Party and government policy of developing high-tech industries and promoting economic prosperity.

Because news reports bring benefits to businesses, many feel obligated to provide journalists and news organizations with gifts, advertising contracts, and sponsorships. Many journalists and news organizations think this mutual assistance is reasonable and justified. The definition of "news" in the Party tradition provides plenty of opportunities for doing public relations and advertising in this way. Compared with advertisements, news stories, features, and editorials are more credible and therefore more effective. Moreover, the cost is much less than buying advertising time or space. Paid journalism has become the most cost-effective means of advertising.[51] This remains true even though some clients have indeed invested a lot in media organizations and journalists.[52] There are enormous numbers of willing buyers. Journalists and the news media are well-positioned to sell what clients want. The Party may blame business and journalists for this unethical and illegal market exchange, but its own definition of what is news makes such an exchange not only possible but also beneficial to both seller and buyer in a commercialized environment.

Economic Realities and Occupational Disorientation

Journalists and the media are willing partners in this exchange for a number of reasons. Declining government subsidies mean that the media have to find their own financing. In this drive for money, some media organizations inappropriately apply the contract responsibility system to each department.[53] Reporters and editors are given individual incentives and quotas. One television station, for example, signed a financial responsibility contract with its news department that required it to bring in one hundred thousand yuan a year. The news department thereupon offered staff members 30 percent of what they solicited for the station. Business openings, anniversary celebrations, release of new products, or like opportunities found the news staff soliciting publicity pieces for the paid information program and also offering free promotional pieces on the regular news program.[54]

In some organizations, even individuals are assigned quotas. Li Jie, a writer with Beijing People's Radio, for example, reported that a Beijing news organization stipulated that units would get bonuses if their income surpassed a contracted amount. If not, directors, reporters, and editors would be penalized financially. The quota for the ten reporters and editors responsible for business reporting was 3 million yuan a year. A message was soon posted: "Three million a year, 300,000 per person. Everybody must work hard, if not, get out of here!"[55] Li also noted that many journalists began to write positive stories about units before asking for "sponsorship."[56] Journalists, in a way, are thus forced to practice paid journalism by their organizations' inappropriate financing.

Indeed, with the drive to raise money and the prevailing glorification of getting rich, journalists have experienced a dramatic occupational dislocation. One version of a popular ditty circulating among journalists since 1992 captures the situation:

> The first class of journalists run their own businesses.
> The second class of journalists trade stocks.
> The third class of journalists solicit advertising.
> The fourth class of journalists receive red envelopes.
> The fifth class of journalists write for other papers.
> The last class of journalists write for their own papers.

Another version ranks the first class of journalists as those who sell State secrets. The underlying message of them all is that the best journalists are those who make the most money. There is an intended sarcasm, but the importance of money-making as a standard is underscored nonetheless. As Li Jie observes:

> In news organizations, the standard that evaluates journalists has become multi-dimensional. A journalist should first be able to write and, second, be able to create income. Those who are unable to solicit money feel inadequate, especially when receiving bonuses derived from income created by others. Conversely, those who are poor in news reporting can still feel good about themselves if they are able to make money. . . . There are dual standards even in the evaluation of media officials. . . . A responsible person from a Beijing media outlet openly declared in a meeting: "A departmental head who is incapable of creating income is not a good one!"[57]

Under such circumstances, those journalists who concentrate on their investigative and writing skills find themselves out of fashion, out of place. Zhang Jianxing expresses their dismay: "After being a journalist for so many years and after winning so many journalism awards, I woke up one morning and found myself in the last class of journalists. Knowing that I am still writing, a friend praises me for being pure and innocent. Looking at the strange smile on his face, I have no tears in my eyes, but there is bitterness in my heart."[58]

Peer pressure and the imperative to get along can mean that paid journalism becomes a survival necessity rather than an ethical choice. When the majority of reporters pick up red envelopes, the few who do not may cause discomfort among their colleagues and upset the host.

The loss of subsidies and, in some cases, the get-rich-fast mentality push news organizations to go after money by any means. Smaller, specialized newspapers are particularly aggressive. Many of these were established during the reform years, and they usually do not get much support from their sponsoring units. Specialized newspapers are disadvantaged in the advertising market. Unlike major Party organs, they usually have only a loose affiliation with their sponsoring institutions, be it a government department or nonprofit organization, and they are not closely supervised. All these factors make them most likely to practice extreme forms of commercialism. In addition to publishing advertising as news and selling whole pages, some sell press cards, seats on their boards of directors, even the newspaper itself—its registration number.

Journalists' low income also augments the temptation to sell journalism for money. Because journalists are government employees, their salaries are set by the state in accordance with professional ranks, of which there are four. In 1993, the base monthly salary for each was 180, 140, 113, and 82 yuan. When bonuses and subsidies were added, the monthly income was between 300 and 400 yuan, which, under the market economy, was just enough to buy two pairs of Nike shoes. Government efforts in increasing salaries can hardly keep up with high inflation rates. Surrounded by intensive lifestyle advertising, few people are willing to maintain a minimum standard of living, particularly not journalists, who are in a position to see the lavish consumption of China's nouveau riche. Moonlighting, dining at public expense, and accepting gifts and cash bribes are a way of life for most officials. Indeed, the regular salary of some is so negligible that payday does not generate much excitement. Few journalists can resist the temptation offered by one paid news report that can bring in a red envelope with as much as a whole month's salary, not to mention an advertising deal worth years of salary.

The Double Burden of Overpoliticization and Political Repression

The old mechanism of control is at least partly responsible for the growth of unethical practices. In the tradition of Party journalism, the only standard of discipline is political correctness. Journalists and media officials are evaluated on political standards alone; they are criticized or fired only because they have made a political mistake. Such limited criteria have affected virtually all journalists and media officials, from reporters to the Party's Propaganda Department. The political standard is the only standard of both self-discipline and control from above. Because political loyalty takes precedence and even replaces professional integrity, professionalism and ethics are not stressed. When ethics are promoted at all, they are often highly abstract and politicized, as in the principle of "serving the people." Journalism organizations and media officials are preoccupied with the political management of journalists, not their ethical behavior.[59]

With the exception of a few slogan-like Party instructions, such as serving socialism, serving the people, observing the Party principle, and specific instructions about how to produce politically correct reporting, neither the Party nor the media had concrete ethical guidelines. The first code of journalism ethics was not drafted until 1991. Thus, when the market economy—and with it, people holding out red envelopes—suddenly appeared, neither journalists as individuals nor journalism as an institution was prepared to deal with it appropriately.

Although the Party blames money worship and moral corruption by journalists for paid journalism, there are important political and morale reasons for it as well. Journalism in China is a repressive institution, especially since 1989. Journalists' creativity and investigative initiatives are often squashed. With little professional autonomy and few prospects for an aspiring journalist to develop professionally, to do enterprising, investigative reporting, morale is generally low. The practice of the usual Party journalism, with endless reports of meetings, achievements, and role models, makes journalism dull and unchallenging. As a result, journalists' talents are being diverted into businesses, either the new ones within the media, independent enterprises, or their own businesses.[60]

In addition to more money and more benefits, journalists find fewer restrictions and more opportunities to develop themselves and use their creativity in the business sector. Award-winning journalist Zhang Jianxing tells how a very capable colleague of his quit journalism and took an "untenured" position in a stock firm. On the surface, the reason was that the firm provided housing, but the underlying reason was that "journalism is dull!" according to Zhang.[61] In Guangdong, the best news bureau chief of *Nanfang Daily* switched to manager of the newspaper's advertising firm. The "number one pen" of *Shenzhen Special Economic Zone News* (Shenzhen tequ bao) also became manager of an advertising firm. "It is a creative and stimulating job; it fascinates me," she said.[62] Few journalists would describe their jobs in the same way.

Many journalists have admirable professional and political aspirations but end up practicing paid journalism because there is no opportunity to realize them.[63] Indeed, it is perhaps not surprising that paid journalism became widespread after 1989. There is, in a way, an element of passive political resistance in the practice.

Commercialization without Independence

The simultaneous operation of the Party logic and the market logic is the most important structural reason for corruption in the media. In the United States the nineteenth-century commercial penny press emerged as an independent capitalist business from the beginning with no formal ties to political parties and state institutions. Media in China, however, whether completely or partially dependent on commercial revenue, all have institutional affiliations with the Party, the government, or quasi-official institutions. Their monopoly status and their role as parts of Party and government apparatuses mean that they are not really independent business entities, even though most of them are managed financially as if they were. Because of this media "commercialization without independence," as Joseph

M. Chan has put it, the market principle is not completely applicable.[64] There is no media market where survival depends completely on ability to compete. CCTV, for example, is a state monopoly. Although it relies heavily on advertising, its survival does not depend on its market success. Even if it failed to attract any advertising, the Party still could not afford to close it. The same is true of Party organs at all levels.

Party and government bodies often use their administrative powers to promote sales of their affiliated newspapers. Compulsory subscriptions are possible because most are institutional rather than individual. In fact, subscription to Party newspapers is still a strictly enforced political duty. To increase subscriptions, Party propaganda departments issue orders, organize meetings, and rely on quotas, responsibility contracts, permission to use public funds, and moral sanctions.[65]

Government departments have their own specialized newspapers and often organize similar mobilization meetings, issue circulars, and assign compulsory subscription quotas to maintain sales. In Sichuan Province, eighty provincial departments published 186 newspapers and journals in 1991, all for sale.[66] A poor county in Hebei Province had to subscribe to thirty-two newspapers not distributed through the post office.[67] If national Party and specialized newspapers distributed through the post office are included, the total number is even larger. One township government in Sichuan Province, after using up all its operating budget on subscriptions, docked salaries to meet its quotas.[68] In a middle school in a remote mountainous area in a poor county in Zhejiang Province, all grade nine students were forced to subscribe to the county's Party newspaper.[69] Compulsory subscriptions, like many forms of extralegal fines and charges, forced "contributions," and purchases of unneeded goods levied on peasants, has become another means by which authorities extract funds from institutions and individuals.

Administrative measures used to be the only means by which Party newspapers obtained compulsory subscriptions during the pre-reform years. Now administrative orders are supplemented with material incentives. Newspapers often award rich commissions to units and individuals who help them in subscription drives. Some newspapers even offer free advertising and the publication of favorable news and feature items in exchange for a unit's subscriptions.

In short, although media financing has been fully, or at least partially, marketized, media organizations are not yet fully independent economic entities and their survival is not determined by the market. The "sale" of newspapers is also far from being marketized. The papers with the largest circulation are not necessarily the ones favored by readers. A middle school with a limited budget for newspaper subscriptions, for example, is obligated to subscribe to national, provincial, and county Party organs as well as the specialized papers published by government education authorities. If it does not meet these requirements, it risks, among other things, compromising its status as a "good" or "model" school. In a society that is still extremely centralized and hierarchical, few institutions want to take such a risk. But after subscription obligations are met, there is little money left to purchase what teachers and students actually want. Young teachers and students, for example, would find *China Youth News* or *China Sports News* (Zhongguo tiyu bao) much more interesting and meaningful than the dull, poorly edited local Party paper.

The absence of a genuine media market means that Party and government newspapers do not have to be accountable to readers. Television stations are notorious for not keeping to their publicized schedules, which in a way is a contract of trust between the stations and their audiences. The failure to follow schedules reflects a lack of commitment toward their audience. As Wang Shuang writes:

> Newspapers, radio stations, and television stations all hold iron rice bowls. Circulation numbers and audience rates do not affect their survival. So long as they do not commit serious political mistakes, they can continue their operation year after year despite "paid journalism" all over the newspaper and the station. Under the current situation in our country, a news media outlet is often the "single child," the only shop on the block. Nobody competes with it, no matter whether it is good or bad. Even if a newspaper's subscriptions decrease at an annual rate of 20 percent, it will still not close its doors. Such a situation provides a hotbed for the growth of paid journalism.[70]

Despite increased dependence on commercial revenue and rhetoric by media scholars and even government bureaucrats about introducing market mechanisms, Party/state apparatuses are not willing to give up their control over the media. They will not allow independent broadcasting stations and newspapers. Nor will they allow institutions to stop subscribing to major Party and government organs. This is media commercialization with "special Chinese characteristics."

Consequences of Corruption in Journalism

An important demand of journalists in the 1989 struggle for press freedom and the debate about press reform was promotion of the media's watchdog role. For a long time, Party control has been the principle reason for lack of critical political reporting. Now submission to the power of money means that it is even less possible for journalists to fill the watchdog role. If they engange in false advertising, false news reporting, and paid journalism, How can they expose official corruption? While the Party and the government are struggling to establish order for the proper functioning of a market economy, mercenary journalism actually helps to promote unfair competition and illegal economic activities. Indeed, some media organizations are directly and indirectly involved in fraud and profiteering, among others.

Critical economic reporting is so lacking in the regular media that a special reporting campaign had to be organized from above in typical propaganda campaign fashion. In 1992, under the initiative of the Chinese Journalism Culture Promotion Committee and the Economic Department of *People's Daily,* and with the support of the State Council and other government agencies, twenty major national media launched a news reporting campaign for product quality—the Ten Thousand Li Journey for Product Quality in China (*Zhongguo zhiliang wanli xing*). A special organizing committee was set up to determine topics, to assign them to different organizations, and to finalize reports.[71] To maintain the campaign's integrity, CCTV provided a special budget for journalists involved to ensure that no paid journalism occurred.[72] Perhaps because the media regularly lack critical scrutiny of product quality, and also because of the orchestrated effort, the campaign was widely applauded.[73] Ironically, even this high-profile campaign was abused by other journalists or individuals claiming to be journalists. There were seven cases in which the name of the campaign was used for blackmail. One group was able to extort 1 million yuan from businesses in Tianjin.[74]

With widespread paid journalism, many journalists have benefited from economic reform and official corruption and are thus even less likely to reflect the problems and concerns of ordinary people. Further, few journalists are willing to conduct investigations in poor areas. The media are so busy reporting on rising business stars and the lifestyles of the rich and famous that the plight of millions of peasants traveling across the country in search of jobs remains largely untold. When they do make it into the news, it is often in a negative light, as symbolized by the word *mangliu,* a massive flow of human beings in an undirected, blind fashion, implying disorder and a threat to society.

The following example is illustrative. During the Spring Festival holidays in 1993, after a year of hard work in the sweatshops of the coastal cities, many young women returned to their hometowns for a break. It was reported that many went by air rather than less expensive rail. The national media claimed that these workers had become so rich and enjoyed such a comfortable lifestyle that they could fly home. What a great achievement of the economic reforms. In fact, most of these women were quite unhappy about spending their earnings and would have preferred to help their poor families. They flew only because they were unable to buy train tickets, which were difficult to get because of increased demand and inadequate investment in railway transportation. Chaotic management and corruption—with ticket agents selling on the black market—also account for the difficulties. With huge investments in airlines, airplane tickets are easy to get, although much more expensive. Instead of exploring the rail ticket shortage and the real reasons for "choosing" to travel by air, journalists reported what fit the Party's propaganda needs in accordance with their own limited understanding caused by their insulated, elitist lifestyle.

Under the tradition of Party journalism, reporters are used to taking orders from the Party and the government. Now, they also "take orders" from those with money. In both cases, they do not have to take initiative and develop investigative skills and with the current situation there is not much incentive for them to do so. When the president of a television station asked journalists to come up with their own topics and go to the grass-roots to find news, the response was that without an invitation, where could they find news?[75] Indeed, because invitation journalism and other unethical practices are becoming the norm, some educators worry that a whole generation of journalists has been affected. Journalism professors are still teaching ethics and investigative techniques, but with the following attitude: "I know they are not practical in the real world of journalism, but at least I want my students to know what is right and what is not."[76]

The inflated image of prosperity and the lack of critical reporting about economic reforms seem to serve the Party's purpose of political control well, at least for the short term. Advertising-as-news is politically safe not only for journalists but also for the Party. When journalists are preoccupied with meals, gifts, and chasing after advertising contracts and sponsorships and writing promotional pieces, they have less time for critical reporting that might touch a sensitive political nerve. But there is the other side of the coin. The abundance of reporting on newly established businesses, successful entrepreneurs, and prosperity in general has fueled both the general public's and news workers' own rising expectations and, with it, frustrations with their jobs and unexciting daily routines. This has been destabilizing.

Most importantly, journalistic corruption has meant a loss of credibility among the people. An opinion survey in Beijing in 1988 revealed that journalists were at the top of groups with bad images. Twenty to 35 percent of those surveyed did not trust the news.[77] No more recent figures are available, but it is likely that the image of journalists is worse. Following are some common perceptions I collected during my research in Beijing in late 1994:

— Forget about "the voice of the Party and the people." The media are mouthpieces of whoever gives them money.

— Who cares about a laudatory piece in the paper? Spend a few bucks and you can buy one.

— The stuff in the media has nothing to do with news at all; it's all about money.

— When journalists come, they take the gifts, grab the material that has been prepared for them, and go.

Journalism is losing credibility not only among the general public but also among the business community. Journalists involved in three-warranty reporting, for example, have been dubbed "high-class beggars." With the growth of extortion, many businesses, especially smaller ones with limited coffers and those victimized by the media, have begun to avoid them. Enterprises are now plagued with demands for fees and taxes from many government officials. Business people complain loudly about incessant demands and harassment.[78] Journalists are now viewed similarly because when they visit a business, they often ask for money, and enterprises cannot afford to let them leave with an empty hand.[79]

Finally, the degradation of journalism hurts the struggle to democratize the media system. While this cause is perhaps still alive in the hearts of many journalists, corruption provides a good pretext for the Party to put journalists on the defensive and to defuse the pressure for media reform. Moreover, the Party might use a campaign against corruption as an excuse to punish politically rebellious journalists. During the theoretical ferment on media reform in the late 1980s, liberal reformers were able to use such concepts as "factuality" and "objectivity" to convey their critique of Party journalism for twisting news for propaganda purposes. But after journalists became known for twisting news for money, such arguments were perceived as hypocritical. It is the Party whose campaign against journalists now looks legitimate. As Ding Guan'gen, the Party's ideological chief, has argued, the practice of news writing for illicit payment and describing a bad thing as good in return for bribes is "totally against the principle that news reporting must be based on facts, objectivity and fairness."[80] Against such a charge, Chinese journalists currently have no defense.

5

Broadcasting Reform amidst Commercialization

Although the dominant institutional arrangements and conceptual frameworks of the news media have remained largely unchanged under commercialization, new institutions, new formats, and new practices have emerged *within* the news media system, gradually gaining momentum and expanding their range. More specifically, while the overall situation remains commercialization without independence, commercialization has created some opportunities for relative autonomy at least in some areas where the intertwining of Party control and market-oriented journalism has taken different forms and created a different set of tensions and accommodations. In this chapter I will examine three different sites of relatively autonomous innovation in broadcasting, the Pearl River Economic Radio (PRER), Shanghai East Radio, and CCTV's News Commentary Department. In the next chapter I will look at similar developments in newspapers.

Broadcasting, the best illustration of the hierarchic and monopolistic structure of the Chinese media, has for decades been organized on the basis of national and local monopolies, with one radio and one television station under each level of government administration. Expansion can occur in only two ways: by the establishment of new stations by government administrations that have not had their own stations, usually municipalities and counties, or by the addition of new channels to existing stations.

By the mid-1980s, a provincial radio station commonly had at least two channels with different schedules and content. The traditional "people's radio station" was in fact a multichannel radio network that provided a wide range of informational, entertainment, and educational programming. The main channel usually carried general interest news, educational, and arts programming. The secondary channels transmitted some of the same general interest programming but at different times and provided some original programming in specialized areas, such as music and business news.

Although piecemeal reforms increasing entertainment and news about the society at large (in contrast to Party and government activities) made programming more attractive, broadcasting by and large remained essentially unchanged until the mid-1980s. The following description, drawn from broadcasting researcher

Luo Hongdao's characterization of the "official model" of broadcasting, is a useful recapitulation of the main characteristics of traditional broadcasting:[1]

1. The broadcast system emphasizes the media's mouthpiece role for the Party and the government and stresses the transmission of policy directives and education of the public. It neglects the role of broadcasting as simultaneously the voice of the people and the means by which the people exercise supervision over Party and government. It neglects direct participation by the public.

2. Programs stress propagandistic, educational, inspirational, and guidance roles and overlook the function of broadcasting as a means of social communication. In other words, political and ideological functions are fully exploited, but the personal, social, and psychological dimensions of communication remain unexplored.

3. There is an unequal power relationship between the broadcaster and the audience. One is at the top, the educator, the guide; the other is at the bottom, the one to be educated and to be guided. One is an active agent, the other is a passive subject. There is no equal, reciprocal exchange. This relationship is characterized by the authoritative, serious-sounding, impersonal, standard Mandarin delivery of the announcer.

4. To allow direct coordination with their work, the organizational structure of the media corresponds to that of Party and government departments. Programs cater to the needs of government officials and elite audiences.

5. The reporting and editing process is separated from the broadcast process. Reporters, editors, and announcers have distinct functions; one is not to be mixed with the other. Announcers, for example, merely read what has been prepared by others and approved by news directors or someone even higher in a station's administrative hierarchy.

This "official model" of broadcasting became increasingly unpopular with audiences under economic reform and a new openness. With the popularization of television by the mid-1980s, radio had a difficult time attracting audiences and—as a result—advertising. However, any sense of urgency for change was repressed by uncertainty and the fear of political risks.

PRER: From Official Model to Popular Support

By the mid-1980s, with reform and opening up, listening to outside broadcasts was no longer considered counterrevolutionary. While many university students throughout the country listened to the Voice of America and the BBC, the mass audience in Guangzhou tuned in to commercial stations from neighboring Hong Kong. As commercial links between Hong Kong and Guangdong Province increased, Hong Kong stations actively sought audiences in the Guangzhou area with special programs, hoping to add to their advertising revenue. A February 1985 survey by three young Guangdong People's Radio journalists found that in the core of Guangzhou City, Hong Kong stations held an 84.6 percent share of the audience. On the streets, almost all taxis were tuned to Hong Kong stations.[2]

Out of professional pride and the need to lure back its audience, on December 15, 1986, Guangdong People's Radio turned its Cantonese-language channel into Pearl River Economic Radio (PRER). The more liberal reform environment of Guangdong and the relative political openness in Beijing at the time made it possible to obtain approval for this from provincial and national authorities. Moreover, the Guangdong broadcast authority had a good case. If the Party's media could not attract audiences, its propaganda could have no effect. Guangdong People's Radio emphasized that the reform was to be a "change in form but not in nature" and framed the logic behind the move as upholding "laws" of mass communication that are universally applicable.[3]

PRER was an immediate success. Within three months, the station commanded 54.9 percent of the audience while the Hong Kong share dropped to 22 percent.[4] During the next five years, the PRER share remained above 50 percent in Guangzhou and nearby areas.[5]

Operational Concepts, Format, and Content

The success of PRER can be attributed to its modification of the "official model." The imperative to lure back audiences forced it to take audience preferences rather than Party and government propaganda objectives as its primary consideration in programming. Yu Tonghao, vice president of the station, went so far as to say that "if there is a single most important line governing PRER programming . . . [it is] that audiences are the masters."[6]

In contrast to the "official model," PRER has established itself as a "popular, informational, service and entertainment model" of radio.[7] It defines its audience as the majority of the people, those with middle to low levels of education. Instead of trying to indoctrinate its audience from the top and designing programs around the propaganda goals of leaders, it tries to "meet audiences' needs, cater to their tastes, communicate with them, solicit their participation, serve them and accept their supervision."[8]

PRER largely "depoliticizes" its content and emphasizes light entertainment, information about daily life, and, as is reflected in its name, economic issues. In its broadcast day of nineteen hours and ten minutes, business news airs at the top of each hour and includes a wide range of paid information about specific operations. General news is broadcast on the half hour, with emphasis again on business as well as social issues. Noncontroversial social, sports, and personal affairs; light entertainment, such as popular music and game shows; and service-oriented information on such topics as food, clothing, traffic, and weather comprise the bulk of programming. Following the format and style of its Hong Kong competitors, PRER devotes large blocks of time to magazine style programs, scheduling eight a day with news, general information, and entertainment. Phone-ins, live broadcasts, studio-audience participation, and naturalistic modes of presentation have also been adopted.

Live broadcasts have replaced recorded programs for the most part. Program hosts with distinct personalities have replaced conventional announcers. Instead of simply reading from preedited and precensored material, program hosts participate in gathering, editing, and finalizing their material. They broadcast live based on preapproved program outlines and material and are allowed to make impromptu remarks to elaborate on the prepared material. Such a "personality" may be the head of a program's production team and thus assume more responsibility and enjoy more autonomy than conventional announcers.

The arrangement of programs fits the daily rhythm of the audiences. While Sunday programming is mostly entertainment, the Monday-to-Saturday schedules accommodate the patterns of the six-day work week.[9] The early morning show is of general interest for an audience getting up, washing, exercising, and eating breakfast. It is fast-paced. At the earliest hours, for example, it offers music to accompany exercises; during breakfast time, it provides news and business information in preparation for work and conversations with colleagues. The 8:30 to 11:30 morning show is aimed at the elderly, housewives, private entrepreneurs doing business on the streets, and taxi drivers. Lunch hour provides commentaries on economic and social issues for a working audience as well as families. In the afternoon, programs feature topics for farmers and children. Supper-time and evening prime-time programming is meant for relaxation and entertainment. The station affirms its audience's "right to entertainment": "The masses have the right to receive legitimate entertainment during their time after work. . . . Entertainment is absolutely not just a means, it is at the same time the very content by which broadcasting serves the people. Therefore, PRER breaks with convention by not arranging propagandistic and educational programming during the prime time before and after supper. Instead, it offers mainly entertainment."[10]

Audiences are encouraged to participate in phone-in programs and can even request particular songs as "gifts" to others for a fee. During talk shows, they can discuss their problems and seek advice regarding jobs, relationships, home decoration, personal appearance, and consumer choices. They can also complain about public services, like poor road maintenance, late garbage pickups, and shortages or interruptions in water, gas, or electricity services. They can comment on the quality or price of housing or goods for sale. PRER also literally brings radio closer to the people with live broadcasts from the streets. Approximately three hundred thousand persons participated in PRER's on-site broadcasts in the first year.[11]

Radio hosts use everyday language in an intimate, warm, soft tone, and present themselves as friends. The traditional dense and serious propaganda material is diluted by skillful use of small talk, "nonsense," and music.[12]

The Structure and Political Nature of PRER

PRER, however, is not an independent radio station. Although its programming and format borrow heavily from Hong Kong commercial radio, it is not a copy. It presents itself as a new station, but it really is only one of six channels operated by Guangdong People's Radio. PRER is in fact a subsidiary, with its personnel, financing, and resources controlled by Guangdong People's Radio. The president and one vice president of Guangdong People's Radio hold similar titles in PRER. An editorial department under Guangdong People's Radio is responsible for most of the magazine programs. PRER's hourly newscasts are provided by the news department of Guangdong People's Radio. Some arts programming is also handled by the arts programming department of the parent station. Such a setup obviously does not challenge the one government, one radio station principle.

The word "economic" in its title is an obvious attempt to be politically correct, to play it safe, a choice made "to reduce the risks and any resistance to reform."[13] Further, its specialization in economic and business affairs fits well with the Party's and government's priorities and the new role of the media as instruments of economic construction. In this sense, the station does seem to be an "economic" station. But otherwise the commercials, the audience orientation, and the heavy emphasis on entertainment are similar to those of Hong Kong stations. The vague and neutral term "economic" is safer than "commercial," to which the Party and the government still object.[14]

PRER is no political threat. It does its ideological job in its own specific way. As Zeng Guangsheng, Director of the PRER Editorial Department, explains in an article summarizing the station's success:

> In our program design, we include considerable service-oriented and entertainment content. We try to avoid straightforward and undisguised propaganda as much as possible. We want our audience to be educated through joyful laughter, lovely music and the cordial language of our hosts without knowing it. We do not reject positive, straightforward propaganda in commentary programs, but more often, we want our programs to bring the Party's lines, programs, policies, and correct ideas to the audience in a clever and natural way, just as spring winds bring rains.[15]

Political conformity is strictly observed by the station: "Hosts and reporters do not articulate views that are inconsistent with those of the Party Central Committee."[16] The station's self-acknowledgment of its role during political unrest is especially telling. During the 1987 student demonstrations, PRER claimed that it kept the attention of youth, and particularly university students, and as a result the majority of them did not listen to the "incorrect propaganda of Hong Kong stations." Vice President Yu Tonghao praised the station because it "effectively stabilized the thoughts of youth and maintained a stable and unified situation."[17] The ideological effect of this diversion was, as Zeng Guangsheng argued, "no less than straightforward and positive propaganda."[18]

While many traditional Party organs in Beijing became active in the struggle for press freedom in early 1989, disrupting their regular routines and supporting student demonstrations, PRER continued to offer business and entertainment fare as usual. During that crucial period, according to Zhu Yan, a policy researcher with the Ministry of Radio, Film, and Television, the station "said nothing that was inconsistent with the Party Central Committee. It did not say anything about which it was unsure. Nor did it inject personal feelings into broadcasts." Moreover, the station "followed the directions of the [Guangdong] provincial Party Committee, actively and effectively provided correct guidance to public opinion, and played a good role in suppressing turmoil and unifying the thoughts of people in the whole province."[19] These claims are made in official publications by the station's own leaders and approving researchers. While it is likely that they exaggerate, they indicate intentions and possible effects.

Following suppression of the pro-democracy movement, the political atmosphere was stifling; many people were depressed, and business activity declined as policies were readjusted. The cultural and entertainment industries suffered major setbacks as a result of a campaign against "peaceful evolution" to capitalism. In this context, PRER and the Guangdong branch of the China Trade Promotion Committee cosponsored a large culture and trade fair in Guangzhou between December 23, 1989, and February 11, 1990, to provide a diversion during the New Year and Spring Festival holidays. Through its upbeat tone, the fair strove to "create a stable, prosperous, and joyful social atmosphere to greet the arrival of the 1990s."[20] In staging the fair, the station shouldered its responsibility as the Party's ideological apparatus and shared the concerns of the Party and the government for political stability. In short, the fair was organized "mainly for its political and social effects."[21]

Thus, by responding to the economic, personal, and psychological needs of its audience, PRER expanded the reach of the Party media from a narrowly defined political and ideological function into areas ignored by traditional Party organs, thus performing an important service. By providing an outlet for discussion of and, in some instances, solving of individual and personal problems, it increased social cohesion. While some Party ideologues were initially wary of the station's approach to reform, its success suggests that the Party's propaganda work is expanding from an elitist and reductionist view of ideology. The station is, in a way, an effective instrument of the Party's bread-and-circus policy even as the public's need for entertainment and popular culture is being acknowledged.

PRER also plays an important economic function in sustaining the traditional radio network. Because of its popularity, its simpler production procedures, and its various sources of income, especially advertising, PRER provides the bulk of the commercial revenue of the whole provincial radio network. In its first two years, PRER's information service alone generated close to 1 million yuan in net profit.[22] The total advertising income for Guangdong People's Radio network doubled in its first year and doubled again in the second. In 1990, PRER accounted for 70 percent of Guangdong People's Radio's total advertising income of 6.38 million yuan.[23] As a "cash cow," PRER provides much needed funds for the other channels of the provincial radio network.

Broadcasting Reform in Shanghai

PRER was the product of its proximity to Hong Kong as well as the liberal reform policy of Guangdong Province and the relative political openness of China in the mid-1980s. The establishment of Shanghai's East Radio on October 28, 1992, resulted from similar elements: the special status of Pudong, where the station is officially registered, as a special economic development district in Shanghai, and the liberal economic policy ushered in by Deng's spring 1992 talks on his trip to south China. Geography is important in this case because Pudong is believed to be a potentially independent administrative region. By registering the station there, the authorities made an exception to the "one government administration, one radio station" policy, which was possible in the reform climate created by Deng. As Chen Shenglai, president of East Radio, has said, the station was "a product of the spirit of Comrade Deng Xiaoping's southern tour talks"[24] or, as another writer put it, it is a "major reform measure put forward by the Shanghai Broadcasting Bureau in its effort to implement the spirit of Deng Xiaoping's southern tour talks."[25] The initiative for starting East Radio, as well as East Television, came from the Shanghai Broadcasting Bureau. Gong Xueping, then head of the bureau, took the proposal to Shanghai's deputy Party secretary, who supported the idea and appointed the chief of Shanghai's Party propaganda department and a deputy Shanghai mayor to help with planning. Final approval, of course, had to come from Beijing.[26]

Both Party Organ and Commercial Radio Station

Compared with PRER, East Radio represents an even more radical departure from standard operations. First, its audience is much larger. Unlike PRER, which broadcasts in Cantonese, the dialect understood only in its area, East Radio broadcasts in Mandarin, the official national dialect. Moreover, although East Radio is registered in Shanghai's Pudong District, it seeks a much wider reach. This is reflected in the station's slogan: "Based in Pudong, serving Shanghai, covering the Yangtze Delta, facing the whole country, and spreading overseas."[27]

Although the station is still officially affiliated with the Shanghai Radio and Television Bureau, it has an unusual degree of autonomy. It is organizationally independent from the Shanghai People's Radio with the same rank (provincial level). It is independent financially, receiving no state subsidies and thus completely dependent on commercial revenue. Its start-up fund was borrowed from the Shanghai Broadcasting Bureau. It pays salaries according to a merit-based scale, rather than the official scale set by the state.

Although staffing is still limited by a recruitment quota set by the government (sixty persons initially), the station has exceptional freedom in personnel selection. Limited democratic and competitive mechanisms were introduced into hiring procedures.[28] As a result, a group of young, well-educated, experienced, dedicated, and reform-minded journalists with an average age of thirty-two was hired. The station president was not simply appointed from above, but was selected by open competition in which seven candidates presented their "platforms" to a panel of judges consisting of broadcast administrators, senior journalists, and experts. After their recommendation, the final decision was made by the Shanghai Broadcasting Bureau. Vice presidents were nominated by the president and approved by the bureau. They in turned appointed heads of each department and offered jobs to selected editors and journalists in the Shanghai Broadcasting Bureau.[29]

As a result, the station is much closer to an independent commercial radio station in the West than is PRER, although it is still state-owned and still an official propaganda organ. It is not explicitly stated in any description of the station in academic and trade journals, but in reality the station work is contracted out to its staff. In contrast to PRER, East Radio is on the air live twenty-four hours a day. Its six-hour midnight-to-dawn block "Accompanying You Till Dawn" (Banni dao liming) offers diversion and companionship to the sleepless. Absence of the word "economic" in its name reflects accurately that, unlike PRER, it is a general interest station. In fact, it runs two channels: a twenty-four-hour general interest AM channel and an FM channel specializing in music. Slogan-like euphemistic phrases used by writers in trade journals and station officials in describing the station, such as "to be connected with the world track,"[30] "to operate in accordance with modern management mechanisms," "the first mainland news organization that operates in accordance with international conventions," and "the first mainland news organization that has European and American efficiency," all suggest that the station takes commercial broadcasting as its model.

"East News" and the Experiment with Audience Participation

As with PRER, light entertainment and talk shows, which make up the bulk of the station's programming, serve as diversions. Talk shows, in particular, let people discuss personal issues and feelings and offer counseling and emotional support. As Wang Wei, the host of the nighttime talk show explained, "audiences pour out their hearts and feelings and seek psychological harmony."[31]

The station, like PRER, provides a safety valve, a buffer zone for the release of political, social, and personal tensions in a period of rapid social change. An illustrative case: On November 16, 1992, less than twenty days after the station opened, the nighttime program received a letter from a young man asking help. He had been a contract worker who had been fired three years earlier because of disagreements with factory leaders. He was still jobless and had tried many times to seek revenge and finally attempted suicide. With approval of departmental and station leaders, the program editor and host worked out a plan. The host read the letter on air, asked the audience to keep the phone lines clear, and told the young man to call in. He did, describing his problems and pouring out his frustrations. Afterward, the audience phoned in with assistance and support. Some offered help in finding a job, while others gave psychological and emotional support. The young man was "rescued." Without the program, he might have followed the example of the military officer who vented his frustration over state policy by shooting scores of people in Beijing before taking his own life.

The young man was obviously a victim of political and economic dislocations in the transformation from a planned to a market economy. He was affected by the unaccountable power of factory leaders, inadequate job protection, unequal employment opportunities, and lack of unemployment insurance. This radio program brought forward a political and social problem and solved it on a personal level. Although the problem remains for millions of others, as far as the program and its audience were concerned, something had been done. Such programs defuse political and social tensions and help maintain social order. Indeed, talk show hosts succeed where the Party's professionals in propaganda departments have failed. They have even provided inspiration for the professionals and were invited to help at "rectification camps." Indeed, a Shanghai District Party secretary credited them with being more capable at ideological work than the professionals.[32] Shanghai's Ideological Work Research Society praised East Radio's nighttime talk show as "a new type of ideological work in the new era" and reported it to the Propaganda Department of the Party Central Committee.[33]

But there is more to East Radio. Unlike PRER, which does not have its own news department, East Radio makes news the mainstay of its overall programming. The six-to-nine morning show is devoted to news and current affairs. In 1992, the middle hour of news was the longest and most comprehensive in the country, the next longest being thirty minutes. This one-hour portion comprises six segments: fifteen minutes of "flashes," fifteen minutes of more details about selected subjects prepared by its own staff, five minutes of phone-ins, five minutes of digests of stories and commentaries from newspapers across the nation, five minutes of commentary, and five minutes of background about news personalities. These segments are relatively independent, separated by commercials, but are complementary in content and sequence. A major event might be reported among the flashes in the first fifteen-minute segment and then pursued in depth in the second fifteen minutes, followed by a commentary, and concluded with a description of the persons involved. Such a frame accommodates both the work of reporters and the needs of listeners. For reporters, the diverse format means that their material can find some spot within the program and can be flexibly instead of rigidly constructed. As for the audience, those who have time to listen only to news briefs will not miss the major news of the day, while those who have more time and interest can get details as the program unfolds. This format is also commercially attractive because listeners are hooked to the whole program. Advertising revenue from this one hour accounts for 60 percent of the station's total.[34]

In the trade journals, this program design is referred to as "acting in accordance with the laws" of journalism and radio communication. This means that media practices are based on an appreciation of the technological bias of the medium, respect for the internal logics of news production and news reception, a recognition of the relative autonomy of the medium, and respect for the production and reception of news. This appreciation is something that the tradition of mass-line Party journalism, developed mainly in the remote villages in the revolutionary base areas in the absence of modern communication technologies and in relation to a totally different political and social setting, has not been able to offer. In addition to its conceptual limitations and political bankruptcy, mass-line journalism has failed miserably at modern mass communication. Despite, and perhaps precisely because of, the intention and single-minded stubbornness of the Party's ideologues, the Party has failed in its ideological work. Although the Party has persistently rejected "bourgeois liberalization," it has not rejected the idea of learning Western media practices—but only within its own institutional framework. However, institutional changes are necessary for this learning to be possible. As soon as there is some relative institutional autonomy, young media professionals will eagerly import media formats and practices. Moreover, they are willing to try even more innovative practices than are conventional in the West. In doing so, of course, they pose a real challenge to the Party's model of political communication.

Production values advocated by journalism reformers in the early 1980s, such as brevity, speed, diversity, freshness, and a high percentage of information, have been realized in East Radio's news programming. A survey by journalism students of Fudan University found that the number of items in the first thirty minutes of the morning news program averaged forty-three. Time devoted to an item averaged thirty-five seconds. Sixty-three percent of the reported events had happened in the previous twenty-four hours; on Shanghai People's Radio, 51 percent had.[35] The station's limited news staff (seven reporters, five editors, and three hosts initially) means that it has to have a large and diversified network of sources. Items in its fifteen-minute "East News Flash" (Dongguang kuaixun), for example, come from its own reporters, other newspapers and radio stations, and services provided by Xinhua, Radio Beijing, and Chinese correspondents overseas.

The traditional Chinese concept of news that focuses on Party and government achievements, on activities of leaders, on meetings, and on the work of government departments and production units is replaced by one that emphasizes breaking events and information that is not initiated by official sources but concerns daily life. The news values of Western journalists have been adopted. The news personality feature, for example, is no longer only about positive role models but about newsworthy personalities of all kinds, like Ross Perot or Saddam Hussein. Changed values are also reflected in the arrangement of news. In contrast to the common practice of international news following domestic news, international news is occasionally the lead story. Because of its different concepts and different methods of gathering news, the station carried a number of stories not covered by other media in the early months of its operation. These included a midnight telephone interview with artists going to perform in Taiwan, a story about a former deputy county magistrate who went into business after being released from prison, a series on the new phenomenon of tipping, a telephone report about a helicopter crash, an investigation of why construction of the People's Memorial Monument in Shanghai was so slow, and a report on how an electricity supply department cut power without notice, causing business losses.[36]

Under the new system, Chen Shenglai, president of the station, reported that journalists "have gradually sharpened their eyes for the news. They have gradually said farewell to 'invitation journalism' and 'paid journalism' and pursue the true realization of news values, and at the same time, the true realization of their own self-worth."[37] Chen tells how a reporter for the station scooped the rest of the Shanghai press corps. A group of reporters accompanied a deputy mayor on an inspection tour of an area where the stalls of illegal vendors had been cleared from an intersection. While all the other reporters ground out routine pieces about the tour, the East Radio reporter returned to the site half an hour later and found that the vendors were back. He did an on-site report.

The station's young journalists have gone further than merely adopting Western practices. Their experiments with audience participation have radically changed the orientation of news reporting. Instead of simply offering tips, listeners actually report news and provide commentary. Such public participation, as Chen argues, is like putting readers' letters on the front page.[38] It gives listeners a significant role. Although it has since been modified, the phone-in segment of the morning news show initially accepted calls from listeners with what they thought would be news. Editors would take the calls and ask the caller's name, address, and topic. Those calls editors thought worthwhile would be transferred to the studio for live airing in a conversation with the host announcer.[39] At one point, there were more than four thousand calls waiting during the program's five minutes. Most callers reported problems with utilities, poor product quality, or other personal concerns.[40]

The significance of phone-in news is not limited to the five-minute segment. Reports by listeners sometimes are followed up by staff and treated in depth in subsequent broadcasts or provide topics for commentaries. Because it is broadcast live and because it may lead to further investigation, the program exerts effective public pressure on utilities and businesses. It is an important forum through which listeners exercise some supervision over authorities and businesses. Live broadcasting means that criticism bypasses protective layers of bureaucracy and thus has direct impact on individuals and institutions. As Chen said, the design of the program "provides an essential mechanism that ensures supervision by public opinion. Here such supervision through the media is no longer an ornament that can be added or removed at will. . . . There had been no such mechanism in radio before."[41] The suspense over whether a reported problem will be solved or how a criticized individual or institution will respond draws listeners back day after day.

Gradually, listeners' concerns went beyond the personal to include common ones like worn-out national flags and public transportation, wherein the audience, to use the words of Chen again, displayed "a sense of citizenship and performed a supervisory function over the state and the society in their role as masters [of the country]."[42] The political challenge posed by the station became apparent. Three months later, the program changed from live broadcasts of phoned-in reports to recorded ones. It accepts calls at any hour. Editors select calls for broadcast after checking with individuals and institutions involved, then add comments by the program host. According to Wang Zhiping, deputy director of the station's news department, city Party authorities instructed that the segment be changed "due mainly to political considerations."[43] Wang, however, also cited practical reasons. Because of the number of calls and the short air time available, selectivity was poor and the station could not check the validity of statements. In addition, because most of the callers were involved in what they reported, it was difficult to ensure their "objectivity and impartiality." Although Wang acknowledged that the issues raised by callers were mostly valid and that there had been no apparent mistakes, he added that he thought that the segment "lacked adequate theoretical preparation." After the change, the number of calls broadcast had increased from two or three to five. Furthermore, "if callers do not express their ideas concisely and properly, the editor can help organize their thoughts, ask them to repeat, and make calls clear."[44]

Apparently, political pressure was the main reason for the change. However, Wang's rationalization on professional grounds is also noteworthy because elitist assumptions underlie it. Spontaneity and the authenticity of live conversation has been largely compromised. That editors check with those criticized before broadcasting also reintroduces the possibility of bureaucratic meddling as well as corruption. In short, this intervention by the Party illustrates containment of reform and commercial logic. The democratic potential was clear, and so was the commercial potential. However, the critical potential was restricted even before the station had enough time to experience potential tensions between democratization and commercialization.

The station's talk-show program, "Today's News" (Jinri xin huati), is also extremely popular. It, too, invites listeners to phone in and discuss a wide range of issues. In its first month, topics included transportation safety, marketing and advertising practices, commissions, the new phenomenon of keeping pets, extramarital love, the campaign against poor product quality, citizens' moral standards, factory directors' salaries, and the movement of officials and artists into business.[45]

Thanks to such programs, East Radio's popularity has soared. In its first month, it received an average of four thousand letters per day.[46] A Shanghai journalism trade publication described how shops tune to it to attract customers and commuters listen on their way to work. A hotel manager forbade his staff to have the station on at work. University students complained that their addiction to the station distracted them from their books. Department stores clerks were kept busy selling portable radios because of the station. A warehouse's formerly slow-moving stock of portables sold out because of it.[47]

Experts from all over the country praise East Radio for bringing the news closer to the people, for exercising its watchdog function, and for acting as a voice of the people.[48] The station staff, on the other hand, believe that "what we have done is only to put into practice the standards of journalism put forward by the older generation of broadcasters scores of years ago, such as 'brevity, freshness, speed, liveliness, and breadth,' as well as the requirement that 'the people's radio serves the people.' We have only transformed the wishes of our precursors into reality in a very limited and preliminary way."[49]

Thus, ironically, the ideal of the people's radio serving the people has been partially realized through commercial logic. There are profound contradictions among the notion of "the people" in mass-line journalism, the notion of "citizen" and "citizenship" that reportedly has emerged among the call-in audience, and the notion of "news consumers" in commercial logic. In time, the station will have to make daily decisions that reflect the tensions among the three different types of journalism: mass-line, democratic participatory, and market-driven.

Competition in the Shanghai Broadcasting Market

Following East Radio in October 1992, Shanghai East Television was established in January 1993; it shares the same institutional structure and operational principles. Together they brought the age of competition to Shanghai broadcasting. The two new stations compete equally with Shanghai's preexisting stations. The monopoly of the older stations is gone, and their power is further diminished by many of their young and experienced personnel moving to the new stations. The two new stations are completely dependent on commercial revenue, but the older stations also rely heavily on advertising income. Audience ratings, therefore, are important to them.[50]

As a result of the competitive pressure of East Radio, Shanghai People's Radio shook up its news department and expanded its early morning news program. Decisions over personnel selection, use of funds, and the allocation of bonuses were decentralized within the department. The traditional beat system was reorganized to reflect better the change from a planned economy to a market economy. Previously, beats had been organized primarily around production sectors (heavy industry, light industry, agriculture, and so forth) and government planning departments. Some production beats were dropped, while new beats for trade and commerce were established. At the same time, more reporters were put on general assignment, covering breaking events in all areas. Others were organized around specific programs designed to attract listeners with special interests. In addition, competition was introduced, so that general reporters and those covering specialized subjects may report on any topic and "invade" beat reporters' territory. At the same time, the organizational structure was simplified; a middle level in the traditional five-level bureaucracy of news production was removed. The entire news department staff was given an opportunity to change jobs under a democratic selection process. Reporters filled in job request forms, which were evaluated by colleagues who made their recommendations by secret ballots. Management assigned jobs on the basis of the request forms, of the evaluations, and of the consent of the individuals. Job tenure was removed and job security reduced to an annual renewable contract.

On February 10, 1993, four months after East Radio went on the air, People's Radio expanded its thirty-minute 7:00 A.M. news program to one hour with format and content obviously influenced by "East News." The goal, as set by the station's management, was to bring the program closer to the listeners, closer to daily life, and closer to reality while at the same time maintaining the authoritative character of the news. The new format is similar to that of "East News," but it has its own characteristics and strengths. The lead-in music is still a revolutionary song but with a faster pace. Its general news segment is twenty minutes, five minutes longer than "East News Flash." Although People's Radio has a large staff, it enlarged its news sources. Two editors were sent to Beijing to arrange with Xinhua, Radio Beijing, and other news organizations to send special dispatches. But People's Radio did not pursue such goals as brief and fast-paced stories as absolutes. Its newspaper digest segment covers not only national and local newspapers; it outdoes its competitor with stories from the world's leading newspapers, a breakthrough for China's media. In competition with East Radio, People's Radio has the advantage of its larger labor force. The idea of introducing stories from world newspapers, for example, came from the director of its international department, who once studied in Britain. Similarly, in the sports section, People's Radio added an English-reading editor who translates international sports news, making it available earlier than before. A segment on international stock markets, money exchange rates, and other financial news has been added, reflecting the growing interest of not only the public but also of the political and economic elites.

To bring the news closer to the people, which had been East Radio's main attraction, People's Radio also adopted listener phone-ins. A twenty-four-hour news hot line, staffed by reporters, was instituted. Callers' stories are either broadcast as is or followed up by reporters. For example, a few days after the program was initiated, a caller exposed a joint-venture business that was violating employees' personal rights by searching their handbags when they left work. The practice received three days of continuous reporting in news and talk show programs and discussions with law professors and ordinary citizens. The practice stopped.

People's Radio has another popular program that competes directly with East Radio. The one-hour talk-show "Citizen and Society" (Shimin yu shehui) focuses on "hot topics that concern the general public, and build a bridge of communication and understanding between citizens and mayors, citizens and the government, and citizens and the society."[51] In an obvious attempt to keep the audience from tuning in to the new station, this program was first broadcast on October 26, 1992, two days before East Radio went on the air. Then, nine days after East Radio's start-up, "Citizen and Society" began a path-breaking series in which Shanghai's mayor and four deputy mayors answered phone calls live and discussed issues of public concern. Similar programs had been tried elsewhere. In Tianjin and Beijing, district leaders had an "office hour" on the radio, mainly to take complaints and to solve problems on the spot. The Shanghai series was the first to invite provincial-level leaders to participate.

Although this might be matter of course elsewhere, it was no small step for a Chinese station. Even reports of leaders' speeches typically go through several edits before publication. They are checked by the leader's secretary, officials at the propaganda department, and even the leaders themselves. Radio and television interviews with leaders are all pre-recorded. On "Citizen and Society" and similar programs, these leaders are taking questions from listeners and discussing them live on the air. Previously, the media were in the passive position of transmitting speeches already given, now stations are in the active position of initiating an event.

The events are still controlled, however. Each official deals with only one issue that has been chosen by an editor and telephone calls are carefully screened. One issue on a show during the busy spring season was city transportation. Did the mayor feel the problem? Yes, when he saw his wife's unhappy face after a trying bus ride home from work. The government's emergency response and long-term plans was discussed, as were citizens' suggestions. Also debated was the city's policy of encouraging technological and cultural workers to start up their own businesses or to take jobs in business. Plans for developing the Pudong District were also on the agenda with input from citizens on such concerns as transportation, the environment, education, and wage policy. Shanghai's sponsorship of the Far East Asian Games was another subject. Finally, Mayor Huang Ju talked with citizens about concrete plans to improve citizens' lives in the coming year.

Each show started with a brief discussion between the host and the guest to establish a topic, which was followed by the guest's answering phone calls. Just as the leaders tried to solicit understanding from the listeners, the callers were usually polite, offering suggestions. For example, the show about preparing for the Far East Asian Games was, according to one account, much like a government "internal working conference."[52] In contrast to other media reports about how smoothly the work was proceeding and how Shanghai was ready for the games, on this program a deputy mayor expressed his worries about various areas. His candid sharing of information, according to this account, increased citizens' understanding of what the government was doing and aroused consciousness of their responsibility for participating in dealing with problems. The station had worried that angry callers would complain about difficulties, express negative opinions, and embarrass the leaders, but all went smoothly. In addition to mayors, various other officials have participated.

People's Radio has been highly acclaimed for this program. Shanghai journalists and even national news organizations in Beijing crowded into the studio for firsthand reports. Ding Guan'gen, the Party's propaganda chief, praised it and recommended that media officials in Beijing imitate it. Shanghai's mayor Huang Ju expressed his appreciation for the opportunity to appeal directly to the public. He said that such a dialogue was needed not only by citizens but also by the city government. The station's journalists were exhilarated:

> The producers of "Citizen and Society" are very excited. The mayors and citizens are having a direct dialogue, something totally unimaginable before. Yet it is so simple: Our government serves the people, our government officials are public servants. . . . Why cannot our media create more opportunities for direct communication between citizens and their servants? . . . Once the self-imposed fence is removed, any worries become unnecessary. . . . A "bridge" has been built by means of the airwaves. Its construction is not easy, but it has enormous implications. Officials and citizens talk with each other over the "bridge," a bridge covered by the red carpet of socialist democracy.[53]

While socialist democracy certainly means more than a talk show and one can argue about the extent to which a program like this contributes to democracy, its implications should not be overlooked. At Tiananmen in 1989, students on bended knees before the Great Hall of the People pleaded for a dialogue with government leaders on such political issues as press freedom. Now, in Shanghai, the People's Radio is providing a regular channel for dialogue. Topics might still be limited and nonpolitical, but it is better than no discussion at all.

This movement to bring the media, and through them government leaders, closer to the public was initiated by East Radio and carried further by People's Radio in their competition for professional esteem—but, more importantly, for advertising. There is similar competition between Shanghai Television and East Television. Indeed, competition for audience is sometimes fierce. But since the broadcast authority has the right to approve programming, this competition is regulated. The same is true in the Shanghai newspaper market, where, unlike in other cities, three well-established newspapers compete.[54] To enlarge its readership, the morning paper *Wenhui Bao* planned an afternoon edition. *Xinmin Evening News* (Xinmin wanbao) in return planned a morning edition. Both were stopped by city authorities. This is an example of a regulated market in which political authorities practice "macro adjustment and control"—economic jargon currently in vogue in China.

Although competition is sometimes unfriendly, there is a "socialist" element of friendly market competition. While the old stations have learned much from the new stations, the new stations remain quite modest. Ten days after the reorganization of Shanghai Television's channel 14 programming, East Television's officials visited to learn from it.[55] In writing about media competition in Shanghai, Lu Xiaohuang and Wen Lu argue that cooperation, mutual support, and learning from each other are important:

In Shanghai media circles, studying brother and sister papers and stations has become customary from rank and file reporters and editors to executives. When media officials gather at meetings, they will ask each other about their new strategies, new thoughts and new initiatives. . . . If you have new strategies and methods, I will send people to study and learn; it is even common to take away a complete file and written material for study. . . . For example, personnel reform at *Xinmin Evening News,* reorganization of news production at East Radio and East Television were all mutually studied.[56]

So far, competition and mutual learning have resulted in more attractive programming. But learning from competitors also implies learning how to attract audiences away from them.

CCTV's News Commentary Department: A Special Economic Zone?

Having begun in Guangdong and Shanghai, broadcast reform finally reached Beijing, the heart of the Chinese media system. On May 1, 1993, CCTV, the country's most influential station, launched a magazine program, "East Time and Space" (Dongfang shikong). Almost a year later, on April 1, 1994, it introduced "Focus" (Jiaodian fangtan). Both were products of CCTV's reforms.

"East Time and Space" is a one-hour morning magazine show. In addition to news, the program contains four eight-to-nine-minute segments. One is called "Focus on the Moment" (Jiaodian shike) and is similar to "Focus" in that it is an in-depth look at a single issue. "Sons of the East" (Dongfang zhizi) is a personality profile segment featuring interviews with distinguished individuals.[57] "Television Music" (Dianshi yinyue) introduces MTV style videos, background information, and interviews with singers and musicians. "Living Space" (Shenghuo kongjian) centers on ordinary people and daily living.

Originally, the program was broadcast at 7:00 A.M. on CCTV-1 and was rebroadcast twice on CCTV-1 and CCTV-2 in the morning and the afternoon. It was launched without much publicity and was CCTV's first experiment in morning-hour news and current affairs programming. Most urban Chinese get their news from home radios in the early morning, from newspapers at work, and from television in the evening. The new program changed some people's habits. Some media students claimed it caused a "silent television revolution in the daytime." At the request of viewers, the program, or part of it, is now rebroadcast six times across CCTV's four channels, including in prime time. Important segments are rebroadcast on weekends.

"Focus," a thirteen-minute current affairs program broadcast at prime time (7:38 P.M.), follows the evening news. Because it provides single issue in-depth reports and is hosted by different journalist-hosts, it is similar to "Focus on the Moment." Using television reporting techniques widely used in the West, such as on-the-spot reporting, visual documentation, and in-studio interviews, it provides "follow-ups to current affairs, background analysis, perspectives on hot social issues, and discussions of topics of common concern."[58] The program is rebroadcast three times on CCTV-1 the following day. In 1994, it had the second highest national audience rating (23.8 percent) of all CCTV programs, just behind CCTV's 7:00 P.M. evening news, which had a rating of 45.6 percent.[59]

Compared with those in Guangzhou and Shanghai, CCTV's reforms are timid. Instead of being stationwide, they are confined to individual programs and departments. The idea of a second radio or television station, even a modest one like PRER, not to mention East Radio and East Television, at the national level is still unacceptable to Party leaders. According to one insider of the Ministry of Radio, Film, and Television, CPR once proposed its second channel become one like PRER, but was turned down.[60]

Reform is also timid in that CCTV has not touched the core of its news programming, its 7:00 P.M. evening news show, which remains conventional Party journalism packed with reports of leaders at ceremonial functions and government achievements. One industry insider said that this show affects too many people— its influence is too broad—for it to be reformed easily. Indeed, so many powerful vested interests are involved that any change would have major political implications. Although a survey revealed that many of its news reports are unpopular, they continue to dominate the program.[61] To avoid clashing with vested interests, it was decided to begin reforms with new programs. This reflects the same effort to minimize resistance as when PRER adopted a conservative institutional arrangement with its parent station and described itself as an "economic" station.

There is, however, a bold aspect to CCTV's reform. While PRER focuses on business information and on entertainment, and its programs are oriented toward a mid-to-low-educational-level audience, CCTV's reform is in the most important areas of news and current affairs, and it aims at a mid-to-high-educational-level audience. Central to CCTV's reform is the establishment of the News Commentary Department, which produces both new programs. Just as the two programs are unusual, this department is itself unusual among CCTV's other program-producing departments. As I will describe in some detail in the following section, it is—again to borrow a term from the economic sphere—a "special economic zone" within the CCTV News Center.

Organizational Setup

The CCTV News Commentary Department was established in 1993 as a relatively independent unit under CCTV's News Center specifically to produce the two programs.[62] Yang Weiguang, CCTV chairman and the chief designer of its reform, considers them part of an overall objective of "building CCTV into a world-class television station."[63]

The News Commentary Department replaced the international department of the CCTV News Center. It also drew personnel from an in-depth reporting team that produced the popular current affairs program "Observation and Thinking" (Guancha yu sikao). Like at the Shanghai East stations, the work is contracted out to a group of professionals and CCTV provides only air time. The department is financially independent, relying entirely on revenue from commercials inserted *into* the two programs (not from advertising before or after it; that goes to the station itself). Of the thirteen minutes allotted to "Focus" in evening prime time, there are ten seconds of advertising after the program title. The remaining twelve minutes and fifty seconds have no commercial breaks. The hour-long morning program "East Time and Space" includes about ten minutes of advertising between its four segments. In 1994, the ten-second advertisement in "Focus" brought in 40,000 yuan a day. Approximately one-fourth went to program production, the other three-fourths to equipment, salaries, and other expenditures. The department borrowed 2 million yuan from CCTV for start-up capital.

Unlike other departments under the CCTV News Center, the News Commentary Department has autonomy over personnel and is not restricted by government employment quotas. With the exception of the thirty founding staff members, who were originally on the CCTV official employee list, the majority of its workers (160 in mid-1994) are contract workers hired by the department and not considered part of CCTV's formal staff. Their files, for example, are kept in the Beijing Human Resources Exchange Center. But they enjoy the same benefits as CCTV formal staff except for job tenure. Their contracts are renewed yearly, and they can be fired.[64] Their salaries are based on a merit system, evaluated monthly by producers, with a considerable gap between lowest and highest.

As at the two Shanghai East stations, new practices like hiring at large through exams and the promise of increased autonomy and room to experiment have attracted a well-educated and ambitious work force. Most are in their late twenties and early thirties, with university or even graduate degrees, experienced, and enterprising. Because they received their university education in the reform years of the 1980s, they are open-minded and pro-reform. Their previous experience in the media has given them a good grasp of the problems of the old news structure and concepts. Sun Yusheng, director of the department, for example, was in his early thirties in 1993 and already a star journalist.[65]

The department also has autonomy in the acquisition and use of such resources as editing and recording equipment and means of transportation. This is exceptional among news organizations in China under its centralized system. For example, a news organization usually has a transportation department, which is outside the news department. If reporters need a car, they have to write a request and get it approved by heads of their program unit and generally their department before submitting it to the transportation team. This is, of course, cumbersome and inefficient. At the News Commentary Department, all the necessary means of production are at the immediate disposal of its personnel.

The relative autonomy of the department is signified by its own program logo as well as by its physical location outside the CCTV building.[66] It rents an office floor in a humble old building behind the Military Museum in a western suburb of Beijing, one block from the modern and impressive CCTV tower. Its newsroom is crowded and plain, and the furniture is poor. However, the department's main office in the CCTV building itself, and the completion of final production in the studios inside the CCTV building on a huge twelve-square-meter screen, symbolize its ultimate connection with and control by CCTV.[67]

Program production is organized around a producer-responsibility system. Producer is a new position in China; as in the West, producers have control over finance, personnel, and equipment. In addition to the three production units that put together "Sons of the East," "Television Music," and "Living Space," the entire news staff responsible for the reports on "Focus on the Moment" and "Focus" is divided into four production units, each headed by a producer who is accountable to the director of the department. Each unit consists of approximately ten persons, including editors, reporters, camera operators, and hosts, as well as necessary production equipment. The ten-member unit is further divided into reporting teams of two to three persons, working on different topics or different aspects of a topic. There is a broad division of labor between the one unit that specializes in international topics and the three units specializing in domestic affairs. The four units occasionally join together on a major and urgent topic, but mostly they work independently and compete to have their programs accepted by the director and by the station because the number and quality of programs that get on the air can affect the income and continued employment of a whole unit.

The News Commentary Department has also been innovative in television journalism. As at East Radio, innovations are justified as following so-called "laws of communication."[68] Sun Yusheng, one of the main architects of the new programs, explained that one guiding principle during the designing of "East Time and Space" was that they should "employ notions of modern mass communication, explore the functions of television in accord with the laws of television communication."[69] What that means is that the department wanted to move away from the "picture plus narrative" format typical of television journalism in China and adopt sophisticated techniques that more fully exploit television's potentials as a communication medium. Thus, rather than heavy-handed voiceovers added to prerecorded images, the programs use on-spot reporting, street interviews, synchronous sound recording, naturalistic lighting and camera angles, and other methods that "capture the natural flow of the life process" and "reflect the true state of life."[70] Instead of overt editorializing, according to Zhang Haichao, a producer, the programs try to "provide the audience with multi-dimensional information and give them space to think [for themselves]. Program hosts and reporters never express conclusive opinions. Instead, they try to let viewers draw their own conclusions."[71] In contrast to typical Party journalism, whose archetype is a boring government report, the programs utilize a more attention-grabbing story format. Zhang explained that they try to use a narrative form that has a beginning, a process, and an end. Such practices are considered by both producers and broadcast researchers as following the notions of modern communication. They are common in Western television, whose "codes," "conventions," and ideological implications have been "deconstructed" and analyzed by media scholars.[72] In China, however, pioneers in broadcast reform, producers and researchers alike, have just begun to apply them.

Topic Selection and Framing

The very nature of the institutional setup of the department determines that its two programs have to be both politically correct and commercially viable. CCTV is one of the most tightly controlled media outlets in the country, and news and current affairs programming is particularly so. The programs must speak for the Party. At the same time, they must be popular among the people, as well as of "high quality, high taste, and authoritative, matching the status of CCTV as a national television station."[73] They cannot simply attract audiences with sensationalism or, to use Yang Weiguang's term, with "side bar" news.[74] CCTV cannot go as far in "diluting" political and moral messages as PRER and other local stations.

The effort to please a wide audience is clearly shown in the different components of "East Time and Space." Among its four segments, the first two have a heavy political, social, and "high culture" content that caters to the political and cultural elites; the MTV music segment is designed to attract the young and those less politically oriented; the "Living Space" segment is intended to be of interest to virtually everybody. Within its limits, each segment tries to accommodate as broad an audience as possible. Thus, while "Sons of the East" features mainly political, economic, and cultural elites and focuses on their achievements and their ideas, it also draws attention to another side of them as ordinary members of society, describing their feelings, their personalities, their families, and their personal lives.

The biggest challenge, however, is to please both the leaders and the led at the same time. This is an art that is perhaps best manifested in the selection of "hot topics" for the "Focus" programs. International topics are relatively easy, but those with a domestic focus are sensitive and choosing them is a demanding task. For the program to be popular, the topics must deal with "hot spots," "confusing issues," and "touchy problems" of wide concern. A topic must meet three criteria.

It must be something that the leadership has paid attention to, that the public is generally concerned about, and that is widespread or has some degree of universality. However, a percentage must meet the Party's requirement that propaganda should be "positive." In addition, as a current affairs program, topics must reflect the Party's current propaganda priorities. The following are illustrative:

Topics for "Focus on the Moment" (August 9–14, 1993)[75]

September 9: Who will do basic research in the sciences? This topic reflects a concern about the tendency of middle-aged and young scientists to drift away from basic research into business and applied research, as well as the overall declining interest in basic research.

September 10: A discussion of a recent massive explosion in a Shenzhen factory warehouse.

September 11: Perspectives on university students taking summer jobs, a widely discussed trend.

September 12: A discussion about the problem of upgrading worn-out and dangerous electrical circuits in apartment buildings.

September 13: A discussion of an airplane hijacking to Taiwan. Negative incidents are no longer taboo, and discussions of them contain elements of exposure and commercial appeal. However, the report contained an important political element, the government's stand on Taiwan's treatment of the incident.

Sept. 14: An in-depth report about farmers in Shandong Province paying high salaries to technical personnel. This is a current trend and "positive" in the government's view because use of technology in agriculture is considered important for modernization.

Topics for "Focus" (January 16–20, 1995)[76]

January 16: China has made remarkable achievements in protecting intellectual property. This was an apparent piece of positive propaganda during difficult talks between the United States and China on intellectual property.

January 17: After Shanghai consumers named the best and worst shops, a discussion resulted about whether the worst should be expelled from a busy street and its manager fired.

January 18: A program commemorating the fifth anniversary of the enactment of the national flag law.

January 19: If you cannot finish your food in a restaurant, pack it and bring it home. The discussion addressed the waste caused by extravagance in restaurants.

January. 20: Let us eat in a more scientific way (continuation of the previous day's topic).

Although the above samples are not large enough to be statistically reliable as indicators, it is worth noting that the topics for the morning show are less propagandistic and have more potential for exposing faults and for critical reporting. The propagandist orientation is more apparent in the five topics for the prime-time show. Two, intellectual property and patriotism, are apparently straight political propaganda. The last two provide room for both criticism and education.

How a topic is framed is also significant, especially with analytical pieces that deal with confusing and controversial issues. The "Focus" programs, because of the critical edge of some and because of their national influence, are particularly careful in sustaining political stability, which is the overriding concern of the Party leadership. Sun Yusheng, director of the department, had this to say when asked about the key to doing a good job in reporting: "During the process of previewing the programs, I keep thinking about the following questions: Will this produce negative effects? Will it cause damage to political stability? Will it intensify tensions and be detrimental to solving the problem? After all these possibilities are eliminated, I will say that an item is a good one and should be broadcast."[77]

The following report from *Press and Publications News* suggests the ideological function of the programs in defusing the social tensions resulting from the reforms—to speak positively in the language of official discourse—in providing "correct guidance to public opinion" and "maintaining political stability."[78]

The report concerns the program's treatment of the phenomenon of universities charging increasingly high tuition rates and fees. Because this is a controversial, difficult, and recent development that concerns many people, it fits the selection criteria of "Focus." Until recently, higher education has been completely subsidized by the state, and university students have paid no tuition. The same developments that led to commercialization of the media have meant that the state is increasingly unable to provide sufficient funds for education at all levels. Cost of education is not a concern for those who have become rich during reform, but it is an increasing burden for workers and farmers, who have benefited relatively less from reform. Inequality in access to higher education, therefore, is evident.[79]

This is hard for many people to accept, especially since equality had been promoted as a fundamental socialist principle for so many years. Judging from the *Press and Publications News* report, the televised discussion avoided the issue of inequality and did not pose serious political questions about commitment to fundamental socialist values in an era of reform:

> If the focus were on the question of whether parents can afford to pay [tuition fees], especially on the question of whether a student whose family cannot afford the fees can still go to university, the program would be difficult to handle. Therefore, they adjusted

the angle by focusing on background analysis of the policy for charging tuition fees, describing tuition fees in foreign countries, and explaining our country's difficulties and inability to provide sufficient investment on high education in a short period. At the same time, the program pointed out that one of the solutions to the problem is to encourage students to study hard and win scholarships.[80]

Instead of directly addressing critical questions, the program explained and rationalized by describing similar practices in foreign countries. The reasoning apparently was that if it is an international "convention," it is a "normal" phenomenon. The appeal to the financial difficulties of China solicits acceptance of the status quo, perhaps even sacrifice on the part of those who have been victimized.

No ideological work is complete without offering a solution to a problem. The report suggests one such solution—students can get scholarships. That "solution" is inappropriate considering the size of the problem. Government scholarships are few, and private scholarships in China are even fewer.

On the other hand, it is important to note that compared with conventional Party journalism, the "Focus" programs are democratizing in many aspects. That an issue like increased tuition fees in higher education is raised at all is extraordinary since conventional journalism has largely avoided it. In fact, the "Focus" programs have produced many critical pieces. The programs often speak against official corruption, exposing the damage done to individuals and to society by bureaucraticism, poor government administration, delinquent government officials, and illegal and unethical business practices. They raise issues that concern the common people, speak on behalf of those at the bottom of society, and seek social and economic justice for them. They do this by exploring such topics as the price and quality of consumer products, medical services, the rights and welfare of women and children, even the plight of a peasant working in the city. For this, reporters have to develop their investigative skills and sometimes find themselves in confrontational and even potentially dangerous situations. They may trace a situation for months. For example, they drove across several provinces to visit farmers. They went under cover to record the world of illegal business and trade.[81] They even hid behind a bunker at night to capture live images of a thief stealing a bicycle. There is, indeed, a sea of difference between these practices and three-warranty reporting and invitation journalism.

In addition to "Focus," the democratizing tendency of the programs is also demonstrated in "Living Space," which portrays daily life in what many media scholars have heralded as an "awareness of the common people," or populist sentiment (*pingmin yishi*), that contrasts with the elitism of much conventional Chinese journalism.[82] The program lets people speak for themselves, as symbolized by the segment's motto: "tell ordinary folks' own stories." In contrast to the role-model approach characteristic of conventional Party journalism, this segment depicts the ordinary and the trivial (*fanren shoushi*). It publicizes the pleasures of ordinary people, celebrates their values, their dignity, their feelings, and the beauty in their personalities and their lifestyles. Using a naturalistic documentary style, the program has covered such topics as the routines of women textile workers, postal workers, and street vendors, focusing on their hardships, their endurance, and their dedication; high school students preparing for university entrance exams; the tears and laughter of a reunion of university graduates; the pain of parents losing a son to murderous gangsters; and an old woman who spends her savings to buy turtles destined for food so as to return them to nature. Instead of treating people as objects to be managed and shaped, the reporters treat them as protagonists who speak, laugh, and cry on screen in their everyday environment. Previously, when a camera crew went to shoot factory workers, they would first notify factory leaders, who would put on a good show. Now, "Living Space" camera crews may appear unannounced. Even camera angles are arguably more democratic than is conventional on regular Chinese television news, where viewers look up at elites and down on others.

As a result of the wide use of documentary reporting techniques in the two programs, an interesting reversal of roles has occurred within CCTV News Center. Although "East Time and Space" and "Focus" are produced by the News Commentary Department, they have more respect for factuality and provide a broader range of opinions than regular news programs. They are more likely to "let facts speak for themselves" and "let the audience draw their own conclusions" and are less likely to do symbolic violence to social life.[83] The following analogy offered by Chen Mang, producer of "Living Space," is perhaps overly simplistic, but it does suggest a reduced propagandistic approach to reporting: "This piece of cake [a slice of social life] is very delicious in itself. But you [the journalist] chew it first, and then pass it to the audience. Why not just cut a piece and give it directly to the audience?"[84]

Frequent displays of telephone numbers and messages soliciting news tips reflects the effort to give viewers a role in news collection, a commitment initiated by Shanghai's East Radio. Topics mandated from above account for approximately one-third of those on "Focus," but the rest are either initiated by the journalists or by members of the audience.[85] There is, indeed, a significant and highly visible difference between these programs and the CCTV 7:00 P.M. news, where a majority of domestic items are highly propagandist, with topics apparently assigned from above.[86]

Dancing with Chains

Notwithstanding the department's relative organizational, financial, and editorial autonomy, which, according to one author, is the "envy of many in journalism circles," the programs are kept under close scrutiny.[87] Moreover, while journalists were experimenting with a new brand of television journalism, the authorities tried a new form of control by coaching producers and journalists to automatically reflect the perspectives and standards of the authorities.

Just a few months after the first airing of "Focus," the CCTV hierarchy, as well as a selected number of producers and reporters from the News Commentary Department, were summoned to Party headquarters to hear praise and advice. Most importantly, they received instructions from top officials of the Party Central Committee's Leadership Group for Propaganda and Ideological Work, of the Party's Propaganda Department, and of the Ministry of Radio, Film, and Television. Ding Guan'gen, the Party's ideological chief, presided. One problem with the program, according to a broadcast official, was that there had been too many critical pieces; the department was reminded that "focus" should not necessarily mean exposure and negative reporting.[88]

The instructions from the top Party ideological hierarchy were effective. In a seminar on the "Focus" programs, CCTV President Yang Weiguang spoke both as a transmitter of instructions from above and as the top official of CCTV. In addition to general requirements that the programs be consistent with the Party line and uphold the principle of "correct guidance to public opinion," some of Yang's instructions and comments set specific political and ideological boundaries. They were apparently intended as a precaution and perhaps, more importantly, as a correction to tendencies that had been perceived as going in the opposite direction:

> No matter whether a topic is a positive or negative one . . . programs must give people encouragement, confidence, and strength to march forward, rather than a feeling of hopelessness.
>
> . . . Problems that the government has paid attention to or is trying to solve may be dealt with. . . . Don't deal with problems that are essentially unsolvable. Don't deal with those problems for which there are definitely no immediate solutions.
>
> Exercise caution about controversial issues and personalities . . . don't report on controversial figures in "Sons of the East." The choice of interviewees and sources to quote is very crucial. It is of primary importance to seek the opinions of responsible authorities and to clearly state the position of the government. Such authoritative opinions are what guidance over public opinion means. They take a clear stand on right and wrong. It is not enough just to have the public talk.[89]
>
> Don't induce interviewees to express dissatisfaction toward the Party and the government and to talk about the mistakes committed by the Party in the past. For example, a reporter asked the interviewee this question in one program: "Have you ever said something that was against your own will?" Who forced him to speak against his own will? The Communist Party?[90] Now you are all laughing, but the program has been broadcast.[91]

Critical media scholars in the West have laboriously analyzed the content of television programs and found that the media perform their ideological functions through their selection of topics, their avoidance of controversy, their framing, and their use of those in authority as "primary definers" of an issue.[92] Here, these techniques were being explicitly imparted to journalists. The purpose, of course, as Yang said elsewhere in the speech, is to build consensus among "higher level leaders, station leaders, leaders of the News Center, leaders of the News Commentary Department, producers, reporters, editors, hosts" and to turn overt censorship into self-censorship.

> There is a station decision which requires that reporters present their interview topics to the News Center and a responsible station president for approval before they do the interviews. At the same time, it requires that the preview standard for "Focus on the Moment" and "Focus" be tightened up, i.e. be previewed by a responsible vice-president of the station. But I feel that this is a passive method. . . . The role of the station and News Center leaders is not to "gun down" a program in the final stage. The most positive measure is to make every reporter and editor, every producer his [or her] own gatekeeper, i.e., to make the leaders and the reporters, editors and hosts share completely the same perspective, have the same standards of judgment.[93]

Professionals in the department are indeed very careful. While Sun Yusheng stressed making sure that programs do not cause political instability, producers explained that since a television program is expensive, they take great care in selecting topics. Despite pressures from above and efforts from below, the programs are still previewed at the station president level, and about 10 percent are rejected. As one journalism researcher in Beijing remarked during an interview, the people in the department are dancing with chains on.

The pressure from above is certainly constant. However, the journalists work under competing pressures, which are perhaps best symbolized by the layout of the department's house organ. In the front pages, the director transmits instructions and personal comments as well as those from above. Close to the end, there are letters of appreciation from viewers and, more importantly, their concerns, expectations, and proposals for topics. At the very end are the daily audience ratings that affect professional self-esteem and are a reminder of the bottom line, an important consideration not only for the survival of the department but also for individual income and benefits. The middle pages include the journalists' articles reflecting on how they do their jobs. They seem quite proud of pushing the limits of control. Sun Yusheng's instructions are framed negatively, warning against causing social instability, which one could argue is the minimum requirement of being a Party mouthpiece.

One final note on the political and ideological orientation of the programs: As mentioned earlier, the motto for "Living Space" is "tell the ordinary folk's own stories." The choice of "ordinary folk" (*laobaixing*) here is noteworthy. It is not *renmin* ("the people," as in official Party discourse—"serve the people") or *qunzhong* (the masses, as in "the mass line"). Nor is it *gongmin* ("citizens," as in legal and democratic discourse) or *guanzhong* (audience). *Laobaixing* is folksy, the opposite of official and political. It was used frequently by the Party in the revolutionary years, when it tried to solicit the support of a public not yet under its political domination and attempted to establish its cultural leadership. The word that the program uses for ordinary people is perhaps suggestive of the program's ideological ambiguity. Although the language has moved away from official political discourse and mass-line journalism, it has not embraced an alternative political discourse stressing the democratic rights and responsibilities of citizens to voice their concerns and actively participate in decision-making.

Equally significant, though, is that after a process of trial and readjustment based on audience ratings and the intuition of staff members,[94] the program has moved away from a narrow form of consumerism in which the audience is addressed explicitly as consumers seeking only information about products (market-oriented, "at your service" information and practical advice) to a broader and less explicit form of consumerism. It draws upon the experiences of people themselves. Thus, although it depends on commercial financing, it increases its audience by rejecting a narrowly defined consumerism. "Living Space," in particular, is praised in trade journals as a rare "untainted island" in the sea of commercialism on television. The News Commentary Department has paid special attention to maintain integrity and credibility. "Sons of the East," for example, is extremely careful when reporting on entrepreneurs. The department has also turned down proposals for collaborating in business ventures. Paid journalism is rare in the two programs because of the type of reporting they include. And thanks to the monopolistic status of CCTV and the programs' popularity, direct pressure from advertisers is reportedly not yet a problem.

The Diffusion of the Reforms

As I have argued in the previous chapters, media reforms in the early and mid-1980s were mainly operational and technical. Just as a theoretical ferment was being created to push reform on the conceptual and structural level, the movement suffered a major setback with the suppression of the 1989 democratic movement. I have also argued that despite rapid commercialization, the overall framework of the media system remains largely unchanged. Commercialism is simply superimposed on the Party system. And it is precisely this that has led to massive corruption in journalism.

The analysis of the three cases of broadcast reform in this chapter, however, add some nuances to the broad strokes of the previous chapters. These are cases in which reform and commercialization have brought at least some conceptual and structural changes. With these reforms, new stations and programs introduced a new, though limited, logic of media operation. News and information have been made more attractive. They are geared more to the interests of the people, thus putting some truth into such slogans as "serve the people" and "people's radio serves the people" and the media are the "people's mouthpiece." Although these new stations and programs do not carry the word "people" in their names, they are closer to the people than the old ones that do.

Although the Shanghai East stations and CCTV's News Commentary Department depend completely on commercial revenue, they appear to be less subordinated to business interests than other crass forms of commercialism in established Party organs and traditional broadcast units. Practices of "paid journalism" reportedly are less. Higher salaries, stricter guidelines and the enforcement of them, increased autonomy for journalists to realize their professional aspirations, and, most importantly, the need for credibility and changed concepts of news have all contributed to reducing corruption. Despite tight Party control, the commercial need to attract audiences, combined with an enthusiasm for reform of younger professionals recruited through open competition and working under new institutional mechanisms, have all helped to push the limits of what is politically permissible in news reporting. The progressive and emancipatory potential of the market place have been partially realized. One journalist I interviewed claimed that reporters feel "liberated" and regain a sense of dignity when they have a place to practice critical reporting and not "paid journalism."

These reforms are important developments since the mid-1980s. From the three cases cited and their timing, it is clear that reform has moved from the periphery to the center and from the technical and operational level to the structural level, although this is still limited. Geographically, reform has spread from south to north, and from the local (PRER) to the regional (East Radio and East Television) and finally to the national level (CCTV). It began in radio and moved to the more popular and influential medium of television. In terms of content, it commenced with PRER's focus on business and entertainment and expanded with East Radio and Television's overall programming, finally appearing in one of the most influential areas possible, current affairs on CCTV. To be sure, the overall structure of the CCTV News Center has not been altered, and the centerpiece in CCTV news, its 7:00 P.M. national news, is still being produced under the same organizational control and with the same archaic concepts. But a special zone has been created within the CCTV News Center, with new programs produced under a new arrangement with a new style of journalism.

The significance of the cited cases is not limited to them, however. The establishment of PRER and the two East stations, in particular, has triggered two waves of broadcast reform throughout the country. After shock waves swept through broadcast circles, they were imitated in various degrees. Since 1987, PRER's economic station model has spread to many parts of the country. Although the Ministry of Radio, Film, and Television was slow to approve applications, especially before 1992, by the end of that year there were thirty economic radio stations and nine economic television stations.[95] Since the latter half of 1992, the pace has quickened. As of 1994, there were more than one hundred economic radio and television stations. Although the term "economic" continues to be used by these stations, many of them are actually commercial general interest stations. Some have an institutional setup similar to PRER's, while others have relatively more organizational and editorial autonomy, especially some established since 1992. For example, Shaanxi Economic Radio, which officially started broadcasting in October 1992, has a high degree of autonomy. All its personnel, including the president, are hired in an open competition on a yearly contract basis. Financially, the station is on a responsibility-contract system in which, after handing over a given amount to the parent station, it is responsible for its own profits and losses.[96] Many of these radio stations have achieved wide popularity.

Moreover, formats and presentation styles have slowly spread to conventional stations, although with much reluctance and hesitation at the beginning. Magazine programs, hosts, phone-ins, and live broadcasts have been adopted by some conventional stations, at least in parts of their programming. In March 1993, even CCTV changed all its news broadcasts, with the exception of the 7:00 P.M. national news, from recorded to live programs.

In some provinces and municipalities, the diffusion of the PRER model has led to the breakup of traditional people's radio stations into specialized stations. This transformation usually begins with the separation of an economic station from the parent station, followed by the appearance of an art-and-entertainment or music station and an educational station. Other specialized stations have focused on such areas as traffic, children's programming, and even the stock market. These subsidiary stations enjoy different degrees of autonomy, ranging from PRER's relative lack of it to the complete contracting out of Beijing Music Radio that grew out of the stereo music department of Beijing People's Radio. In this case, the relationship between the music station and the parent station is similar to that between the CCTV News Commentary Department and the CCTV News Center.

Thus, the overall tendency is to decentralize broadcasting. Although there is no specific survey material available, the general pattern seems to be the less political the contents, the more autonomy a subsidiary station may enjoy. The politically sensitive news and current affairs programming, for example, is in most cases still run by the traditional people's radio stations under the old institutional structure. Specialized stations, because of their higher productivity and greater popularity with audiences, usually generate more revenue, part of which goes to the people's station to support news and current affairs programming. In a few cases, such as in Guangdong, Tianjin, and Beijing, the news and current affairs programming departments, like other departments, have also become specialized news stations that take the major responsibility for political propaganda. In these cases, the traditional people's stations no longer run any programs and are instead administrative bodies transmitting policy directives, exercising final editorial and financial control, maintaining broadcast facilities, and administering other aspects of the broadcast network.[97]

This tendency toward decentralization and specialization, however, is still in the early stages, and its diffusion has been uneven across the country and between radio and television. However, advantages and problems are already apparent. On the positive side, the new types of stations counterbalance the lopsided political and propagandist orientation of the "official model" and give fuller play to the economic, cultural, and entertainment functions of broadcasting. First among the problems is a lack of overall planning in the distribution of channels. Second, in an effort to attract audiences and make money, many specialized channels, despite different names, basically offer the same programming, such as human interest stories, game shows, and psychological counseling hot lines. Third, the competition for audiences has induced many stations to cater to vulgar interests. Fourth, because of a lack of well-trained personnel, especially program hosts, and the overstretching of productive capacities, program quality is often poor.[98] There is, therefore, a danger of approaching the other extreme from the Cultural Revolution's "big talk, empty talk, and falsehood"—that is, "small talk" that is similarly empty.

Although PRER has been imitated across the country, so far the institutional setup of the two East stations in Shanghai has not been paralleled in other provinces. The government has not given up its policy of one level of government, one radio and one television station. Because the two Shanghai stations were approved by the central authority as a special case using the geographic status of Pudong as justification, other local governments are effectively prevented from copying the model. However, it is likely that the Shanghai model has influenced the institutional organization of specialized radio stations established since East Radio went on the air in 1992.

In addition, the East stations' example has added energy and scope to the wave of diffusion. Their breakthroughs and the subsequent changes in the two older Shanghai stations as a result of competition have also affected programming elsewhere. Their large news nets and their relative openness have led reporters from other stations to send them sensitive stories that cannot get approval in their own stations. When reporters in the Beijing radio station were prohibited from writing about the September 1994 shooting incident in Beijing, they sent the news to Shanghai East Radio. At the same time, the East stations are becoming a news source for other stations. A radio news director in Hangzhou, for example, told me that his station regularly picks up news from East Radio. Finally, because of their regional reach, the Shanghai East stations have not only introduced competition into Shanghai but also have exerted some pressure on stations in neighboring provinces.

The CCTV News Commentary Department model is still too new to be copied. However, already the Beijing media community has felt its pressure. An article in *Journalism Front* (Xinwen zhanxian), published under an apparent pen name, has attempted to redefine what is important in news after praising the "Focus" programs for addressing the concerns of ordinary people. The article asks: Why do the lead stories in newspapers and on the air not even touch the "focuses" of the "Focus" programs? To be sure, the lead news must emphasize positive propaganda, must publicize excellent political and economic and social situations, report various achievements and important speeches. But aren't the issues that directly affect peoples' lives also important news? Shouldn't they be on the front pages?[99]

The new style of television journalism and the treatment of ordinary people as protagonists in "Living Space" has also caused some in the journalism community to say "This is the way journalism should be done."[100] Eventually, they may influence television news in general.

In short, the reforms analyzed in this chapter represent major steps in the course of broadcast reform. Their novel institutional organizations and their new content and formats all, in one way or another, shape reforms elsewhere.

6

Newspapers for the Market

The monopolistic status of broadcast stations means that it is relatively easy for authorities to exercise control during commercialization. The situation in the newspaper sector, however, is slightly different. To be sure, the government still keeps tight control of newspapers. As stipulated by the 1990 Provisional Regulations on Newspaper Management, all applicants for publishing newspapers must be approved by the State Press and Publications Administration.[1] All newspapers must carry an official registration number. Moreover, with the exception of Party organs, all must have an area of specialization and must have a "responsible department" (*zhuguan bumen*, i.e., an official publisher) that maintains leadership and control. For a national newspaper, this department must have the minimum rank of a central government ministry; for a provincial paper, the minimum of a provincial bureau; and for a county paper, a county-level government entity. This prevents the launching of a second general interest newspaper in an area to compete with the Party organ, unless Party and government authorities themselves set it up. With the exception of Party organs, all newspapers focus on specific subjects, like the economy, the legal system, health, education, or culture, or they target specific readers like intellectuals, workers, women, farmers, or youth. This effectively prevents newspapers from being independent civil institutions outside the Party/state apparatus or the pseudo-civil organizations dominated by the Party.

Nevertheless, the newspaper sector is more pluralistic in its structure than the broadcast sector. Because of the comparatively small technological and financial investments needed and the availability of commercial print shops,[2] it is relatively easy to start a newspaper—with the necessary official connections. Control of official "responsible departments" over specialized and special interest newspapers is usually loose. Unlike Party propaganda departments, which exercise direct control over Party organs and broadcast stations, these responsible departments usually have no direct responsibility for propaganda and ideology. Moreover, while governments at different levels continue to invest in the broadcast sector, they have reduced their investment in newspapers significantly. In 1992, about one-third of newspapers were totally dependent on commercial revenue. For the two-thirds that still received government subsidies, the amounts were generally rather small and growing smaller. Many specialized newspapers have been established not only to carry out propaganda within a particular government department but also to "create income." In short, in comparison with broadcasting, the newspaper sector is structurally more diverse, the commercial imperative is stronger, and, with the exception of Party organs, Party and government control is relatively loose.

The situation is further complicated by the fairly widespread use of the contract system (*chengbao*), which has been limited in scale in the broadcast media. With the exception of Party committees and major government departments, many official publishers have contracted out publication to the newspapers' managements. Typically, a contractor pays the license holder a fixed sum regularly. While the papers are legally owned by the license holder and officially under its editorial supervision, the operative control rests with the contractor, who is responsible for editing, printing, distribution, taxes, and all other expenses.[3] In some cases, individuals or groups have persuaded a qualifying unit to obtain a license on their behalf. This was how the *World Economic Herald* got its license to publish from the Shanghai Academy of Social Sciences and the Chinese World Economists Association.[4]

On the distribution side, the reforms of the early and mid-1980s have led to a diverse distribution system and the creation of a newspaper market literally on the streets. With the end of the post office's monopoly of newspaper distribution in the mid-1980s, alternatives have developed. In addition to office and home delivery, both postal and nonpostal distribution systems find their final outlets on city newsstands.

Indeed, street newspaper sellers are important components of the city landscape in reform-era China. There were approximately twelve hundred individual newspaper vendors in metropolitan Beijing alone in 1992.[5] In contrast to institutional subscriptions, which provide newspapers to offices, street retail outlets provide the major source of newspapers to private homes. These are papers that individuals are willing to spend their own money on, out of personal interest rather than institutional imperatives. The pattern of consumption is completely different between the two. In the office, newspapers are free, and to read one is often considered legitimate political and professional education at work. It is more or less a part of the job. When you first arrive at your office, when you are tired of working, when you are in passive protest against your superior, or when you do not have anything else to do, you read a newspaper. No matter how unattractive it is, you will flip through it anyway (although few people admit that they read *People's Daily*). Newspapers sold on the streets, however, have to compete not only among themselves but with other commodities and forms of popular culture for the passerby's leisure time and cash. A study of these papers, therefore, reveals much about reform and commercialization in the emerging newspaper market in China.

The chapter is divided into two parts. The first is an overall survey of newspapers sold on the streets. The analysis is based on a sample of newspapers gathered in Beijing, Shanghai, and Hangzhou.[6] I collected a total of seventy-nine editions of fifty-four different titles. The dates and locations are rather arbitrary, and the sample is not exactly representative or random. However, the analysis is not limited to the sample, which is mostly used for illustrative purposes. It draws on descriptive and analytical material in the trade journals as well as from interviews.

The second part is a more specific case study. In it I examine the reforms carried out by *Beijing Youth News*, a Communist Youth League organ that has achieved remarkable market success.

Newspapers on the Streets

Most street vendors do not sell major Party organs or the majority of the specialized newspapers published by government departments. Thus, in Beijing, major national Party and government organs, including *People's Daily, Guangming Daily, Economic Daily, Worker's Daily,* and *China Women's News,* are rarely available on the streets. These are "official" papers, subscribed to with public money and for consumption in offices, classrooms, and factory workshops. Similarly, many street vendors do not carry *Beijing Daily,* the official Party organ of the Beijing Municipal Party Committee. The situation is the same in other cities.

Most commonly found on the streets are the local evening paper and local radio and television weeklies. The radio and television weeklies contain schedules, stories about television series, program reviews, features about radio and television personalities, and other entertainment material. They sell well. *China Television News* (Zhongguo dianshi bao), published by CCTV, for example, sells 600,000 copies on Beijing streets alone. It had an average circulation of 2,380,000 per issue in 1992, second highest of all newspapers in the country, just below *People's Daily.*[7] It has the highest private subscription rate of all newspapers.

The Evening Papers

The other best-sellers are the local evening papers, usually general interest dailies. In most cases, they are under the direct control of the municipal Party propaganda committee and are aimed at urban families. Two, Shanghai's *Xinmin Evening News* and Tianjin's *Tonight's News* (Jin wanbao), trace back to progressive commercial evening papers before 1949. In the late 1950s and early 1960s, the Party, perhaps in recognition of the need for newspapers as a form of popular culture for the urban population, created eleven others, most notably *Yangcheng Evening News* (Yangcheng wanbao) in Guangzhou and *Beijing Evening News.*[8] With contents more diversified and closer to everyday urban life, the evening dailies carry more soft news than morning Party organs and are more entertainment oriented.

Although they are also responsible for propagating Party policies and directives, they are less straightforward in their approach.[9] During the Cultural Revolution, all thirteen evening papers were forced to close because their human interest stories and their entertainment and family orientation were viewed as incompatible with the revolutionary fervor of the time.

Since 1979, all have resumed publication and many new ones have been established. By the end of 1992, there were forty-two.[10] By the end of 1994, the total was 128.[11] The wave of newspaper expansion following Deng's talks has particularly favored evening newspapers, which have become the fastest growing sector in the industry. In major cities like Beijing, Tianjin, Shanghai, and Guangzhou, the daily circulation of evening papers is higher than that for the morning Party organs.[12]

In contrast to the main Party organs, evening papers rely on street sales for most of their circulation. *Beijing Evening News,* for example, sold more than 400,000 copies a day on the streets in 1992, or more than 60 percent of its total. Nanjing's *Yangtze Evening News* (Yangzi wanbao), a more recent arrival, sold more than 90 percent of its total circulation on the streets that same year.[13] This heavy dependence on the market compels these newspapers to cater to the interests of readers and be responsive to their sensibilities. As the title of an article written by the editorial committee of *Yangtze Evening News* put it, the newspaper must "Think Highly of Readers, Understand Readers, and Be Close to Readers."[14] The paper carries out annual readership surveys and adjusts its contents accordingly.

Evening papers try to write political and economic news from a personal angle and to soften hard news reports. Indeed, the motto of the most successful evening paper in the country, Shanghai's *Xinmin Evening News,* is "shorter, shorter, even shorter; softer, softer, even softer" (*duanxie, duanxie, zai duanxie; ruanxie, ruanxie, zai ruanxie*).

The wide popularity of evening newspapers can also be attributed to their attempts to address the concerns of city residents and to voice their complaints against bureaucracies, particularly public utilities. Like the phone-in broadcast news and talk shows, they exercise some form of public opinion supervision over government and business.

In 1994, the most talked about evening newspaper in journalism circles was *Qianjiang Evening News* (Qianjiang wanbao) published in Hangzhou. It gained reader popularity and received high evaluations in media circles for its policy of "encouraging the newspaper to participate in community life and inviting readers to participate in running the newspaper."[15] Since the mid-1990s it has become an active originator of community events, adding a new twist to the Leninist notion of the newspaper as a collective organizer and propagandist. It sought medical treatments for sick children, created voluntary service teams to restore public utilities following a major storm, invited government officials to hold office hours in the newsroom to solve problems for concerned citizens on the spot, exposed illegal business activities, and sought social justice for the powerless. In a practice reminiscent of the best tradition of mass-line journalism, in which journalists are encouraged to learn from the people and participate in their activities, the newspaper reported on individuals and institutions at the grass roots. Its reporters have taken temporary jobs to understand better the experiences, perspectives, and feelings of workers. Instead of upholding mainstream American journalism's notion of detachment, reporters have assumed the roles of shop attendants, sanitary workers, public utility employees, and neighborhood committee cadres. All these, of course, generate news not only about others but also about the newspaper itself and the journalists involved.

At the same time, the paper asks readers to participate as amateur journalists by providing tips and writing stories. Readers can become "reporter for a day," even plan story assignments. Neighborhood committees reportedly often phone the paper with advice on how to organize reporting activities and how to better meet the needs of its readers.[16] Through this active participation in community affairs, the newspaper publicizes itself and stages events that attract a large readership while successfully blending propaganda with commercial success.

The official press circle celebrates the "*Qianjiang Evening News* phenomenon" as an example of "carrying forward the Party press's fine tradition of closely connecting to the people."[17] It is clear, however, that mass-line journalism has been effectively commercialized, or to put it in another way, the commercial potential of mass-line journalism has been exploited by the paper. On the other hand, the commercial imperative has been domesticated, contained, and incorporated into mass-line journalism. The commercial logic, therefore, provides a mechanism for the (partial) fulfillment of the promises of mass-line journalism.

Tabloids and Crime Stories

Many street vendors also sell dozens of tabloids. There are two meanings for this word, both of which apply in China. First, a tabloid is a newspaper that is half the size (a quarto, i.e., a sheet folded into quarters) of a regular paper (broadsheet or folio, that is, folded once). Most of the papers sold on Chinese streets are quartos. Second, tabloid means sensational, because the first papers in the West to adopt this smaller size tended to emphasize crime, gossip, and entertainment.[18] Indeed, the term "small papers on the streets" (*jietou xiaobao*) is almost a synonym for sensationalism, fabrication, and vulgarity.

The first wave of tabloids appeared in 1984–85.[19] Because of their concentration on sex, murder, and gossip, they came under Party attack during the campaign against "Spiritual Pollution" during this period. However, since most of these papers did not carry explicit pornographic and "counterrevolutionary" material, they did not violate any laws or regulations. The government could not simply ban them. But local Party propaganda departments issued circulars demanding more supervision and editorial control by "responsible departments" and tightened registration procedures.[20] However, tabloids continued to flourish, particularly after Deng's trip south in the spring of 1992.

Of the seventy-nine editions of fifty-four papers I sampled in three cities, some are from faraway places.[21] Most are weeklies, published by a diversity of government departments and institutions, including legal departments, public security bureaus, courts, local people's political consultative conferences, research institutes, and professional associations. Major Party and government newspapers also publish tabloids, many of which are news digests.

The tendency for businesses to become involved in the media industry is also evident in the samples. While the January 10, 1995, issue of the *Hainan Legal News* (Hainan fazhi bao) named the Hainan Provincial Legal Bureau as its principle publisher (*zhuban*), it also listed under its masthead six business enterprises as "co-sponsors" (*xieban*), with one as "chief co-sponsor." Presumably, these enterprises provided funds, and the chief co-sponsor probably provided the most. Similarly, *Global Digest* (Huanqiu wencui, January 22, 1995) listed *People's Daily*'s International Department as its main publisher and included under its masthead two business co-sponsors. On page 4 the paper named eleven business enterprises as its "board of directors." It is unusual for a newspaper to have a board of directors in China, and calling enterprises a newspaper's "board" is certainly not conventional elsewhere. The only explanation, of course, is that these enterprises put up money and got publicity in return.

These papers are generally more expensive than Party organs (especially when size is counted in), and they carry less advertising. The paper in the sample with the most advertising is *Nanfang Weekend* (Nanfang zhoumo), with approximately 20 percent of its space devoted to advertising. Many papers have only about 5 percent advertising. Because they are mostly weeklies distributed nationally and because they mainly cater to poorer city residents and the mobile population, especially migrants from the countryside, they are not ideal vehicles for paid journalism, which mainly promotes businesses and consumer goods and services. Moreover, they do not share a Party organ's responsibility for promoting the economy. Nevertheless, these papers have found their own market niche for paid journalism—for example, in publicizing doctors with treatments for conditions such as cancer, diabetes, and infertility. A feature about a doctor who "serves the people with his whole heart," published in *Xi'an Public Security News* (Xi'an gong'an bao, January 20, 1995), even managed to incorporate the doctor's phone number, address, and the bus route to the doctor's clinic into the story. The January 29, 1995, issue of the *Weekly Digest* (Meizhou wenzhai), published by *Anhui Daily*, also included a publicity piece for a local liquor manufacturer, an apparent violation of the paper's editorial principle.[22] Such examples suggest the pervasiveness of paid journalism even in street tabloids.

The majority of the papers in my sample, forty out of seventy-five, are "law and order papers"—published by government legal departments and public security bureaus. The front page usually carries stories about the sponsoring department with headlines like "Public Security Departments in Xi'an Create a Series of 'Loving the People' Activities," which reflect typical Party journalism conventions. The commercial appeal of these papers does not lie with such conventional news, however. The long, detailed descriptions of crimes and the pursuit of criminals on the inside sell the papers. Of course, legal departments and public security bureaus can provide much privileged information to their own newspapers and are thus well positioned to profit from these stories. Gruesome crimes and distorted human relationships, not reported in the mainstream papers, receive full and extensive treatment. My sample included the following: baby-sitters kill the baby's mother; a father rapes his four daughters; three brothers share one brother's wife and sell their babies; an aunt kills her niece, chops up the body, and stores the parts in refrigerator; a former prisoner makes money by offering training courses in criminal activities and his students commit scores of robberies and rapes, including those of little girls; gangsters battle police with automatic weapons in Beijing suburbs; the gory crimes of a serial killer; prostitution and the underground market for pornographic material; and robbery, murder, and fraud involving fabrication of State Council documents and the seal of the State Council. In contrast to crime news in the Western news media, these stories are written from an insider's view, with detailed descriptions and narratives, even dialogues between criminals and victims and investigators. The stories are related from beginning to end, often after imposition of the death penalty.

Some of these stories celebrate the bravery and efficiency of law enforcement officers. Others end with a moral lesson and thus supposedly educate readers. However, they are clearly written primarily to tell a good story and sell papers. They expose the dark world of crime, but exposure and social critique are not the main purpose. Moreover, most are about crimes perpetrated by those in the lower classes.

Weekend Editions

The tabloids, however, do not have a monopoly on crime stories. Many other papers also seek a share of the market despite a conceptual barrier. Party dailies, in the best tradition of mass-line journalism, are supposed to educate rather than entertain and to cultivate socialist "spiritual civilization." Other newspapers justify their existence by serving special interest groups with specialized contents. To get around these official limitations, the "weekend edition" (*zhoumo ban*) was created.[23]

There has been a flurry of these editions since the early 1990s. In the past, since major newspapers were mainly for official consumption in the workplace, few paid much attention to weekends, when readers would be at home. In 1981, *China Youth News,* the official organ of the Central Committee of the Chinese Communist Youth League, published its first weekend edition in an attempt to increase readership. With more colorful and attractive page layouts and, more importantly, with more critical news and features, news about popular culture stars, as well as interesting short essays and poems, the paper was an instant success.

The rapid development of weekend editions, however, did not begin until the early 1990s with the rise of commercialism. Between 1981 and 1990, there were fewer than 20 newspapers with weekend editions. By early 1994, however, there were more than 400, approximately one-fifth of the 2,040 papers in China at the time.[24] By the end of 1994, the number had jumped to 500, or one-fourth the total.[25] The years between 1992 and 1994 were not only a period of expansion, in which newspapers added more pages to increase both editorial and advertising space, but also the years of weekend editions. "Page expansion fever" and "weekend edition fever" were the terms frequently used by trade journals to describe this period. In early 1992 alone, at least 55 provincial and central Party and government organs added weekend editions.[26]

Except for a few like *Nanfang Daily*'s *Nanfang Weekend* and *Nanjing Daily*'s *Weekend* (Zhoumo), which have separate registration numbers and are therefore independent papers, although under the control of the main Party organ, the majority of weekend editions are not independent because of government licensing restrictions. However, their parent papers cultivate weekend editions as "special economic zones," often with separate editorial teams, more flexible editorial policies, and a contracting out arrangement. For a Party paper, a weekend edition offers an opportunity to avoid news of speeches, meetings, and the activities of leaders. Here it has more autonomy in topic selection and contents. It is the only edition of the week that is published for readers rather than for leaders. For many specialized newspapers, a weekend edition lets them go beyond the confines of their special area and cover whatever sells. Weekend editions are the "unofficial papers" of the official Party and government organs. Even for tabloids, whose official control is more remote, a weekend edition means even more freedom.

The weekend edition provides a special space created by the official Party and government newspapers to experiment with journalism for the market. Although the financing of these newspapers has largely been marketized, the bulk of their content on weekdays is not geared to market expansion. What is in the newspaper is not what the readers are interested in and will spend money on. The readers know it, and the newspapers know it. In Beijing, a journalist from a major newspaper conducted a random survey, asking readers to list ten of their favorite newspapers. The majority of respondents named the major national and provincial newspapers only after listing five or six small papers, such as evening papers and the *Reference News*.[27]

Nevertheless, tight political control and the official nature of newspapers, as well as long entrenched habits, all mean that newspapers cannot simply change their contents to attract readers. Just as CCTV dare not reform its 7:00 P.M. news, major Party and government organs cannot undertake large-scale reforms on their front pages during the weekdays. This is precisely the dilemma of reform and marketization of the press in China.

Official subscriptions still account for the main portion of newspaper consumption. On the other hand, as more papers enter the market and subscription prices go up even as government budgets shrink, most publishing enterprises have begun to realize that they must make their products more attractive. Weekend editions, therefore, are a way to experiment on a limited scale, to avoid straightforward confrontation with conventional Party journalism, and to reduce political risks. As Deng Xinxin puts it, "journalists have long been thinking and exploring ways and methods to improve news reporting in the main newspaper. However, because there are many problems and difficulties in this area, people turn to the weekend editions."[28] Thus, for some newspapers, especially major Party and government organs, the purpose of a weekend edition is not only to keep readers loyal to the main paper or to increase revenue but also to set up a pilot project for market-oriented reform.[29]

For this reason, many newspapers invest a lot of effort in their weekend editions. Those of major national papers like *Economic Daily, Guangming Daily,* and *Workers' Daily* are usually more interesting than their daily editions, with more critical and analytical pieces focusing on controversial social issues similar to those on CCTV's "Focus" programs. Although many of these popular papers are not independent at all, they are often sold on the street separately. *Beijing Daily*'s weekend supplement, named *Jinghua Weekend* (Jinghua zhoumo), for example, is only one part of the paper's Saturday edition. Street sellers reportedly pull out the pages of the weekend insert, throw away the rest, and sell the weekend insert for the price of the whole paper.[30] In short, "weekend edition" has become a synonym for "readability" and market-oriented journalism.

In my sample, there are twenty-nine weekend editions, accounting for approximately 39 percent of the total sample. This percentage, of course, is considerably higher than the 25 percent of total newspapers with weekend editions. A few of the weekend editions are indeed not only highly readable but also contain occasional critical material. The three issues of *Nanfang Weekend,* in particular, contain some thoughtful feature stories and political and social commentaries. The October 28, 1994, issue, for example, had a story exposing the chaotic and lawless aspects of life on the streets of Nanchang, capital city of Jiangxi Province. Reflecting on the lack of fear in the eyes of a criminal receiving a death penalty, Wang Meng, a well-known writer, commented on the prevalence of violence, the failure of the death penalty to intimidate criminals, and the willingness to sacrifice lives in the political culture as a whole. The paper, considered one of the best "quality" weekend editions in the country, enjoys a readership in intellectual and cultural circles and has an average circulation of 1.2 million copies, one of the few with a circulation above 1 million.[31]

Of the two samples of *Chinese News Clippings* (Zhongguo jianbao), a successful newspaper published by young people under the joint sponsorship of the State Council's Information Center and the Changzhou City Economic Planning Commission, the end-of-the-month edition (January 28, 1995) had more analytical and better edited material than the regular issue. In addition to pieces on such topics as health and culture, it brought together many thoughtful, informative, and critical stories from the press on political, economic, and social issues, including well-researched and well-written stories from numerous new special interest papers. The four stories on the front page, for example, were about official corruption, the relationship between money and power, and bureaucratism.[32] Other stories were about massive public spending for private residential telephone bills; the number of police officers killed on the job in 1993 (2,500); illegal weapons; urban poverty; unemployment; forced retirement; rural poverty attributable to government policies, unequal distribution of land, and other economic and social reasons; and tax evasion by many high-income persons.[33]

Most weekend editions, and most of those in my sample, however, are rather different. Since political control is still tight and few papers are willing to touch sensitive political issues, many eschew serious political topics, offering only entertainment. Their sensational material has been categorized by the Chinese press as "red secrets," "golden temptations," "pink sweets," and "black horror." "Red secrets" (*hongse jiemi*) are human interest stories about past Party and government leaders, particularly Mao and Jiang Qing. "Golden temptations" (*jinse youhuo*) are about the pursuit of wealth and the lifestyles of the rich and famous, both domestic and international, but especially about China's rising stars in business, entertainment, and sports. "Pink sweets" (*fengse tianmi*) are sentimental love stories. "Black horrors" (*heise kongbu*) are sensational crime stories, particularly murder cases involving sex and money, similar to those in crime tabloids.[34] All kinds of human interest stories describing the unusual and the extraordinary find a place in the weekend editions. For many years, the famous "man bites dog" story line was criticized as the worst manifestation of bourgeois commercial journalism. Now, some weekend editions fill their pages with nothing but such stories.

Weekend editions of specialized papers have little or nothing to do with their area of specialization. There is no clear editorial policy. The governing principle appears to be to print whatever sells. If weekend editions are experimental sites for reform, then perhaps it is fair to say that while there are some examples of analytical and informative journalism, what has been flourishing is extreme commercialism beyond the recognition of any conventional definition of journalism. The following are some examples from my sample.

The end-of-the-month edition of the organ of the Hunan People's Political Consultative Conference, *Xiangsheng News* (Xiangsheng bao), is a case in point. Everything, including the format, is organized to be sensational and marketable. There is no nameplate across the top of page one. Instead, two huge headlines run across the top separated by a skull: "A Person Who Deciphers Death Codes" and "Unidentified Female Corpse behind Neon Lights." These cover almost the entire top half of the page. "Death codes" and "person" are bigger than other words on the page. At the top left corner, running up and down, is what might be called the paper's nickname, "Revelations of Secret News," printed in white on a red background. This, however, is not the official nameplate. The real name, "Xiangsheng News: End-of-the-Month Edition," appears next to "Revelations of Secret News" in much smaller black type. A kind of masthead, again identifying the paper as "Xiangsheng News: End-of-Month Edition," in red and in somewhat larger type, is at the bottom right corner. It includes the date (only the year, 1995, no month or day), serial number, registration number, and publisher. A buyer would not see it on the newsstand.

At the top right of the front page is a small square keyed to articles inside: "Pornographic Movies Shake Taiwan Families," "Criminal Records of Young Women behind Bars," "The Four Death Valleys of the World," and "Qiu Chuji: The Grandfather of Eunuchs." Inside, in addition to those listed, are all kinds of "man bites dog" stories (some not at all new) from all over the world. One is "a collection of strange pigs." Another is a compilation of other unusual animals: a cat with a human face, a dog that delivers her owner's baby. A third contains such stories as a four-year-old boy who recognizes the family dog as his mother and a person mistakenly diagnosed as having cancer who wins a lottery.[35]

Some weekend editors have asked newspaper vendors to read their proofs before publication. Vendors, knowing what sells, suggest changes, particularly in pictures and headlines.[36] Journalism in China thus exhibits two extremes. On the one hand, Party authorities are expected to preview Party organs to ensure political "correctness" and moral purity. On the other hand, vendors are requested to preview newspapers to ensure their marketability (although this is not yet widespread). For some papers, Party censors do the previewing during the week, newspaper dealers on weekends. On May 14, 1993, the official China News Service reported one such example, provided by Liang Heng, director of the Newspaper Department under the State Press and Publications Administration, at a news briefing. Liang announced that *Jiangxi Daily* (Jiangxi ribao), organ of the Jiangxi Provincial Party Committee, transferred final preview power of its end-of-the-month edition to a private bookstore and had since published pornographic articles under such headlines as "A Golden Sex Dream under a Coconut Tree" and "A Whore and Her Thirty-Eight Men."[37]

Like economic radio stations, many weekend editions have become the cash cows of official Party and government organs. Government organs in particular have faced financial difficulties because of inadequate subsidies and limited advertising caused by their specialization and lack of readership. To increase income, some have contracted out part of their publication permit to entrepreneurs to run weekend editions. The Ministry of Culture's *China Culture News,* for example, was 360,000 yuan in debt in 1992.[38] It contracted with Zhang Zoumin, an editor, to launch *Weekend Culture* (Wenhua zhoumo) on January 1, 1993. According to the agreement, Zhang was to pay the newspaper 200,000 yuan a year. Should the operation fail, he would have to pay a penalty of 20,000 yuan.[39]

In its inaugural issue, the paper featured a front-page interview by Zhang with superstar actress Liu Xiaoqing on the prospects for nudity and sex in Chinese films. Accompanying it was a picture of a Western model with her breasts partially exposed; the Chinese character for "naked" was superimposed on one side. Inside were two more nude pictures, one of a black woman. The paper sold well in Beijing, but it attracted foreign media coverage and shocked Party authorities. Because it was seen as having tarnished the image of the Ministry of Culture, it was closed temporarily. Zhang tendered his resignation, but it was turned down. In fact, although Ma Wei'an, the editor-in-chief of *China Culture News,* is well known as a conservative ideologue, he was protective of the weekend edition, apparently for economic reasons. Ma reportedly threatened to resign if the authorities did not allow his paper to "go to the market." He defended it in a television interview by insisting that the material was meant to suit the taste of readers.[40]

Shifting Boundaries of Party Control

The flourishing of tabloids and weekend editions and their distribution through private networks poses a serious challenge to the political and moral codes of Party journalism. Politically, even though some of these papers are published by major Party organs, journalists and writers can express views and report stories unacceptable to the more tightly controlled main Party organs themselves. *Nanfang Weekend,* for example, has become an outlet for expressing what one journalism researcher has called "high-class complaints" (*gaoji laosao*), i.e., well-written and highly implicit political and social critiques, such as Wang Meng's piece on violence. Articles that cannot be published in Beijing under the watchful eyes of central Party authorities may find a place in this paper. Party authorities in Beijing have reportedly threatened to close it, but it has been able to continue because of its popularity and the protection of the more liberal Guangdong provincial Party authorities.[41]

In mid-1993, Wu Hao, deputy director of the Domestic Politics Department of *People's Daily*, published two articles in the department's subsidiary magazine *Tide of the Times*, of which he was the chief editor. The first proposed avoiding the use of the phrase "everyone's thoughts and efforts directed toward one goal" under the market economic system because it was a product of compatible planned economy. In the other, he urged higher authorities to "minimize their interference" and called on "leaders at all levels" to change their mind-set and avoid making irresponsible remarks as they had been accustomed under the planned economy. The articles were published at the height of the introduction of macro-economic regulations and control measures by the government and were thus considered by Party authorities as having "misled readers" and "incited discontent." Wu was removed from his posts for "singing a different tune" from that of the Party.[42]

The tabloids' appetite for gossip has also caused the Party political embarrassment. As "red secrets" have become staples, stories about events and personalities in Party history have not only been interesting reading but also have challenged the Party's official interpretation.[43] More often, however, the tabloids and weekend editions challenged the Party's moral code and taboos, as *Weekend Culture* did with its nude pictures. In my sample, for example, stories cover such topics as homosexuality, sexual harassment of women, and the phenomenon of young women becoming concubines of wealthy businessmen.

In short, the tabloids, especially some of the weekend editions, have violated many aspects of Party journalism in their pursuit of market success. Principles of Party journalism such as positive propaganda, "correct" guidance of public opinion, as well as conventional Party definitions of news have been disregarded or subverted. With many cases of false reporting and pure fabrication, basic journalistic principles such as factuality have clearly been violated. Even respectable weekend editions like *Nanfang Weekend* have printed fiction disguised as feature stories. Because editorial staffs for tabloids and weekend editions are usually small and competition is fierce, gossip and sensational stories are recycled again and again. Reportedly, some buy hundreds of different papers and reorganize and repackage the stories by changing names and addresses and playing with the different story lines and then submit them for publication. In fact, even in my small sample, several similar stories appear in different papers under different titles and bylines.

Except for extraordinary cases, the Party has exercised little control and has been ineffective in checking extreme commercialism. Behind these humble tabloids and weekend editions are powerful government departments and other organizations who are usually more interested in profits than in politics and ideology. In early 1993, the State Press and Publications Administration issued the "Circular on Newspapers Observing the Purpose of Running Newspapers and Strictly Following the Rules for Publication." It stipulates that "newspapers should carry articles based on their areas of specialization" and that they "should not use large space to report details of criminal cases and play up the horrors of murder."[44] The circular also forbids the publication of unregistered papers and states that the type, size, and position of nameplates should be fixed and that the names of special columns and special editions and headlines should not be put in the nameplate position, nor should they be larger than the nameplate. It even says that all violations will be promptly investigated and punished.[45]

In January 1994, the Party's Propaganda Department and the State Press and Publications Administration jointly held a national forum on weekend editions and attempted to bring them into the orbit of Party journalism. On March 15, 1994, these two departments jointly issued a circular on strengthening control of weekend editions. Among other restrictions, the circular stated that weekend editions "should not reprint news and articles from foreign media outlets" and that the editor-in-chief of the main newspaper should exercise final editorial control and that editorial rights should not be transferred to newspaper dealers or contracted to individual editors.[46]

From my sample of newspapers in late 1994 and early 1995, it is clear that these regulations have had little impact, particularly on newspapers not published by major Party organs.[47] These papers continue to "act in accordance with the rules of the marketplace," a favorite defense often voiced by these papers. In response to the Party's argument that if the Party does not win the ideological war, somebody else will (i.e., liberals and liberal ideology), Ma Wei'an, editor-in-chief of *China Culture News,* claims that only after newspapers have conquered the market can they talk about guiding the market and winning the ideological war.

In fact, Party and government authorities have been lax. As one media scholar interviewed for this study puts it, the flourishing of tabloids might be both unintentional and intentional.[48] It is unintentional because the Party does not have the strategy or resources to exercise control. On the other hand, while it keeps a close eye out for serious political challenges, it may simply not want to exercise much control over nonpolitical matters. It appears that so long as these papers do not make serious political "mistakes," they can continue to flourish by feeding on sensationalism. The very different outcomes for the two innovative editors, Wu Hao and Zhang Zoumin, supports this conclusion.

Beijing Youth News

Despite their market success, tabloids are presently confined to the periphery of Chinese journalism. Major national newspapers and provincial Party organs are still caught in a strange dualism, mustering their energy and creativity to publish weekend editions then returning to traditional Party journalism during the rest of the week.[49] Although there is an increasing tendency for "big papers to learn from small papers," and even *People's Daily*'s overseas edition has established the Societal News Department, overall journalism is still characterized by two extremes. The main newspapers still closely follow the Party line; the majority of those on the streets, while not opposing the Party line, aggressively pursue the bottom line.

One newspaper, however, seems to have made a successful leap from weekly tabloid to daily broadsheet by expanding the market success of its weekend edition to the main paper. It has managed to combine successfully market values and the values of Party journalism. It has also managed to achieve a balance between being the Party's mouthpiece and being a reader-oriented, popular, and general interest newspaper. It has been successful both in soliciting office subscriptions and street sales, something few others have done. The paper is *Beijing Youth News* (Beijing qingnian bao). In media circles, its rise is known as "the *Beijing Youth News* phenomenon."

The Rise of *Beijing Youth News*

Beijing Youth News began as an official organ of the Beijing Communist Youth League on March 21, 1949. Its publication was disrupted three times in its history. It most recently resumed publication on March 7, 1981. At that time, it was a weekly four-page tabloid with a circulation of 29,000 copies and an official subsidy of 260,000 yuan. Its official rank was one of the lowest (division level, or *chuji*) in Beijing. Moreover, its affiliation with the Youth League meant that it had less status and political influence than others of the same rank.[50] The initial location of its office, a basement warehouse behind the garage of Beijing's city hall, was indicative of its humble status.

Perhaps precisely because of its obscure status, relative lack of direct control from authorities, and relative lack of vested interest in the Party media system the paper has been able to make the most of opportunities created by reform and commercialization. And while its status as a Youth League organ was a disadvantage in getting major national news,[51] it also meant that it was run mostly by and for the most energetic and reform-minded segment of the population. While other official organs were still talking about reforms but unable to implement them, it was able to experiment with measures to a large extent based on self-determination, self-development, self-financing, and self-restraint.

Beijing Youth News has introduced a series of management reforms since the early 1980s. Although they are common in China, the paper refused to accept any "back door" job placements and pioneered the system of recruiting staff through open competition.[52] It eliminated lifetime tenure, introduced open competition for department heads, and strengthened newsroom democracy. It disregarded the official wage system and introduced a complicated internal wage and bonus allocation scheme that combines basic salary, seniority, productivity, and other standards that led to high salaries, among the highest for Beijing journalists, and good working conditions for its staff. In addition to the regular equipment for newsgathering, each staff member is given a home computer. The paper even provides free meals.[53]

More importantly, as Zhao Xiaofeng observes, the paper's rapid development can also be attributed to the paper's "macro-management perspective." The core of this perspective, according to Zhao, is a clear understanding of the commodity nature of a newspaper, the management of the newspaper as a business enterprise, and an insistence on the primacy of social responsibility while at the same time stressing financial efficiency, the development of subsidiary business operations, and use of other business operations to support the paper.[54] When many official Party and government organs were still unwilling to cut the umbilical cord of government subsidies, *Beijing Youth News* voluntarily gave them up. It signed a four-year contract (1991–94) stipulating that it would not receive any subsidy from the city, while the city would allow it to keep all its profits.[55]

Within those four years, it changed from a four-page weekly tabloid to a daily broadsheet with eight pages on most days. The growth of advertising income was astonishing: 200,000 yuan in 1990, 350,000 in 1991, 5,070,000 in 1992, and 22,000,000 in 1993.[56] From 1990 to 1993, the average income of the staff jumped from 3,000 yuan to 10,000 yuan. Within a decade, the newspaper has grown from a small weekly into a conglomerate that publishes four papers and runs twelve business in a wide range of areas.[57] In 1993, it had fixed assets worth 43,650,000 yuan, and it built a 14,000,000-yuan office building in east Beijing.

The newspaper has an average circulation of 180,000, but based on a readership survey by the Journalism School of Chinese People's University, each issue is read by nearly eight people, with the average reader spending about 72 minutes on it. This is much longer than the less than 30 minutes on average spent on other papers.[58] Street sales and private subscriptions account for 63.4 percent of its circulation, while office subscriptions account for 33.7 percent, much lower than for other official organs.[59]

The composition of its readers says a lot about the paper too. The majority, 83.1 percent, are under thirty-five.[60] Unlike tabloids on the streets, however, it attracts well-educated urban youth; 87.9 percent of its readers have an education level of high school or above (52.2 percent above). This is higher even than for *People's Daily*, whose comparable figure was 72.7 percent in 1993.[61] Five major groups account for 78.6 percent of readership—business employees (23.2 percent), government employees and office workers (20.3 percent), university students (13.3 percent), educational, cultural, scientific, and health workers (11.4 percent), and secondary school students (10.4 percent). This readership composition suggests the "unofficial" nature of the paper. In fact, only 1.8 percent of its readers are leading cadres, compared with 13.4 percent of *People's Daily* readers.[62] However, the paper has the attention of the elite media in Beijing; even *People's Daily* has cited its reports.[63] It has also the attention of foreign media.[64]

"Make the Most out of News Values"

As with many other newspapers, the most popular part of *Beijing Youth News* is its entertainment-oriented weekend edition, the Friday *Youth Weekend* (Qingnian zhoumo), launched in early 1992. Like other weekend editions, *Youth Weekend* sells soft features and entertainment. But while other major newspapers have been unable to transfer the market success of the weekend edition to the weekdays, *Beijing Youth News* put forward the motto: "use news values to push the main paper to the market." As a concept imported from the West, news values imply a different set of standards in news selection from that of Party journalism.[65] Although "news values" has many connotations, marketability is certainly an important component, and this is precisely how the term is being applied.

The newspaper set out to accomplish this objective piecemeal by starting *News Weekly* (Xinwen zhoukan), an eight-page Wednesday edition, in January 1993. "Provide One Thing Only—News," proclaims the paper's logo. *News Weekly* emphasizes nonofficial news, breaking stories, and exclusive reports. It not only *sells* news to readers; it *buys* news from readers. One of its first steps was to establish a news hot line. Any news tip that leads to a published story is awarded a thirty-yuan "information fee." There is a monthly competition for the best tips with prizes ranging between one hundred and one thousand yuan. Telephone numbers of the hot line are printed on almost every page. With its wide network of unofficial reporters, *News Weekly* has become the primary source for breaking news in Beijing.

Another of its specialities is repackaging reports from other media outlets. These are rewritten and presented in special columns such as "most important news of the past week" or "leading stories in world newspapers." Given the tight Party control of major national political news as well as the paper's low official status, it is not yet in a position to sell firsthand hard political news.

News Weekly divides news into categories. Each page contains a different type. On the front page are attention-grabbing major stories, exclusive features, and court cases. There is usually a quarter-page news photo at the top left corner and a smaller picture of a news personality and a news cartoon at the bottom left. Page two has in-depth news, focusing on background, analysis, and personalities. Pages three and four contain "theme news," or features, focusing on one or several topics of general concern. Page five is usually "visual news," that is, photo reports. Page six provides news shorts, items from all over the world classified by topics. Page seven presents social news, mainly human-interest stories, and page eight summarizes opinion polls, quasi-scientific surveys on various, often trivial, topics and with a motto claiming to "give readers a statistical description of reality." These page arrangements have changed over time, and columns on inside pages are constantly being created and recreated. But the editorial orientation remains the same: market success within the permissible political boundaries or, to use the words of the newspaper's editorial committee, "make the most out of news values within the confines of policies and disciplines."[66]

Large and sensational headlines, huge photos, clever, stylish, and sometimes humorous language—even in bylines and column names—and innovative page makeup, including sharp black-and-white contrasts, all contribute to making the paper stand out among its Beijing competitors. Sensationalism is well demonstrated by the front-page headlines of four samples gathered between October 5 and November 2, 1994: "Can One Drive Home a Car for about Ten Thousand Yuan? How Much Is the Price Cut on Cars?" "The Last Moment of a Nine-Year-Old Girl: A Little Bit of Beauty before Death," "Birthday Cake for the Republic: Two Hundred Million Yuan!" "Love inside a Funeral Home." Question marks and exclamation points add to the sensational effect.

Like *Youth Weekend*, *News Weekly* was an instant success on the streets. *Beijing Youth News* applied to the rest of the week the lessons it had learned from its two special editions. The paper is a good example of the effort to find a balance between the Party line and the bottom line, between commercial success and political correctness.

Balancing Party Journalism with Independent Journalism

The paper is full of ideological contradictions, which in a way reflect the ideological contradictions of reform-era China. For example, it celebrates increased consumerism in one story and praises a simple lifestyle in another; it introduces "sustainable development," a theme imported from the West, and tries to convince readers that they can help keep it "sustainable," while on the same page it prints advertising for disposable diapers, another import. It expresses concern for the lower classes in some stories, but others seem aimed at an urban yuppie population and an emerging urban small-business class.

The paper has elements of the nineteenth-century American penny press, particularly in seeking street sales, in breaking away from an elite readership, in down-playing narrow political news, in emphasizing entertainment and news outside the Party/state apparatus, in its sensationalism, in its concern for common people and defense of their interests against corrupt officials and businesses, in its social critique, and in its crusading journalism. It also has elements of twentieth-century consumer journalism, exemplified by its interests in fashionable consumer items such as private automobiles and leather jackets.[67] At the same time, its visual appeal is obviously an imitation of the *U.S.A Today* style of newspaper journalism in a television age.

Like *Qianjiang Evening News*, it exploits the commercial potentials of mass-line journalism. In August 1994, it organized a large-scale invitation to readers to be "reporters for a day" in an attempt to increase readership and bring journalism closer to the people. As part of its circulation drive in the 1994–95 season, it sent postcards inviting readers to "just come to visit us in the office or give us a call." In October 1994, the paper printed front page pictures of and interviews with those who responded. In addition to repeated requests for news tips, the November 2, 1994, issue printed the pager numbers of individual *News Weekly* reporters so that readers could choose who would report on stories based on their tips.

Despite all this, the paper serves as an official organ rather well. Although its news is often sensationalist and its status is minorly official, its politics and editorial policy are comparable to CCTV's News Commentary Department and Shanghai's East Radio and East Television: to make both the leaders and the led happy, to observe the Party line on major issues, and to be constructive in critical reporting.[68]

To be sure, the typical stories of Party journalism—the reports of meetings, activities of Party and government institutions, achievements, or role models—no longer dominate the front page. However, they are still on the front page, although with more innovative treatment. An analysis of stories and their treatment in different editions in October 1994 reveal the paper's orientation and news values and can be compared with traditional Party journalism.[69]

On October 15, the lead story focused on three security guards at the Capital Iron and Steel Corporation who were badly injured in a struggle with thieves. The incident itself, however, serves as a lead-in to more background and analysis about widespread theft of state property. It calls for comprehensive measures to protect state property and for those who guard state property. It features a huge picture of the impressive front gate of the factory at the top, with headlines and summaries superimposed on the photo. The main headline: "Shedding Blood in Protecting Factory" is both attention-grabbing and event oriented. It does not preach, but it utilizes the traditional Party journalism theme of bravery and sacrifice for the state. However, the summary in the corner of the picture in much smaller type carries the disturbing message that the problem is quite serious and the criminals are very aggressive. Based on the style of writing and the information in the story, it is obviously not an official news release but rather a story initiated by a news tip and developed through interviews and research. Throughout its factual report, the story carries a powerful argument for a policy to deal with the problem.[70]

The second story, on the right side of the front page, is a typical official one: the awarding of role-model titles to ten instructors of the Young Pioneers at a ceremony jointly sponsored by the Beijing Municipal Communist Youth League, the Beijing Education Bureau, and related municipal organizations. As the organ of the Youth League, this would have been the lead story if Party journalism were practiced as usual. Furthermore, rather than a picture of the leaders handing out awards or a group picture of the instructors with government and Youth League officials, the story is illustrated by ten small portraits of the instructors that run from top to bottom of the far right column. This gives the models more weight than either the leaders or the ceremony itself. Arguably, such treatment is closer to the original ideal of Party journalism, which claimed that the people themselves are the protagonists of history and should be the focal point. At the same time, it also creates a commercially attractive visual effect.

The subject and treatment of the stories on the front page of the October 23, 1994, issue follow a similar pattern. The lead story, again, is a nonofficial report initiated by a phone tip from a high school in Beijing's Pinggu County. Authorities had asked each graduating student for fifty yuan to organize a dinner for their parents to meet with county officials in charge of university admissions. The report followed the whole process, with detailed descriptions of how the teachers wrote the names, addresses, and relatives of the officials on the blackboard. Pressure was put on students. Classes were canceled so students could persuade parents to contribute the money. The story described the get-together before dinner and the dinner itself. Reporters covered all sides, interviewing students, parents, teachers, and administrators. They quoted the Beijing Municipal Education Bureau as stating such practices were inappropriate. They went beyond the dinner to look at the problem of unwarranted school fees. With vivid descriptions and dialogues, the story is an exclusive and convincing exposure of widespread corruption. Although it concerns a specific incident, it addresses a more general tendency and thus is a good example of investigative journalism within permissible limits and constructive criticism. It may offend those in the middle—the teachers, school administrators, and education officials involved—but it pleases both the leaders at the top and the led at the bottom. And of course, it is a story that sells newspapers. Four other stories on the front page are from official sources and cover government meetings and reports. However, instead of reporting the meetings themselves from the official perspective, these writers extract relevant information and report from the readers' perspective. For example, "Businesses Can Sue Banks" is the headline of a story on the annual working conference of the city's banks. "Be Careful when Shopping" advises the headline over a summary of a report from a state agency responsible for monitoring product quality.

All the sampled issues of *News Weekly* exhibit a similar pattern of topic selection and editorial treatment. While stressing its own exclusive exposés and analytical reports, it also gives due coverage to official stories and themes but enlivens them.

Repackaging the Official Ideology and Selling It with a Profit

Clearly, the paper has perfected the "art of propaganda," sometimes even using sensationalism to convey typical propaganda messages. The front page of the November 11, 1995, issue provides a dramatic illustration. The headline, "Love inside a Funeral Home," is characteristic of the street tabloids, but the story itself reflects the Party line of promoting "socialist spiritual civilization." It tells of a young man raised in a state-funded orphanage who loves his job as an undertaker and has a warm and selfless heart. Owing his life to the state, he believes that he must contribute to society in return. He is engaged to a young country girl, who insists on marrying him despite her parents' objections. The fact that the man is a dwarf adds to the story's sensationalist appeal. A huge picture of the man occupies almost a quarter of the page. While both the headline and the picture are uncharacteristic, the content is typical of conventional Party journalism.

In fact, reporting on role models, a staple of Party journalism, is common in *Beijing Youth News*. Chen Ji, former editor-in-chief of the newspaper, has an elaborate rationale for positive propaganda, of which role-model reporting is an essential component. The following passages from a talk by Chen at a seminar on the Party's media policy of "giving primacy to positive propaganda" clearly demonstrates the "official" side of *Beijing Youth News*.

Positive propaganda means taking a controlling and guiding role on the ideological front. Currently, there is a paradoxical phenomenon in our society. On the one hand, our ideological work promotes hard work and sacrifice; on the other, social phenomena are far from these ideals. What is worshipped is money. Thus, we are confused. Isn't our propaganda too far removed from social reality? . . . But if our media follow these phenomena and even promote them, then how will society turn out? . . . We do not understand and appreciate the workers and peasants, who are the pivotal forces of our society. We regard them as backward, out of step with the time. If they are backward, then, where do our food, our houses, our roads come from? We must solve this epistemological problem.

Strengthening positive propaganda at the present time is not only not out of date, but precisely very timely. Otherwise, our dominant ideology will collapse. No rulers of a society will support those who destroy its dominant ideology. This is the class nature of the dominant ideology. In China, we also will not allow the destruction of the dominant ideology, especially not by the media themselves![71]

Beijing Youth News directly promotes the official ideology by initiating large-scale ideological education campaigns. Such a task appears inconsistent with the soft side of the sensationalist news headlines and the light entertainment orientation of *Youth Weekend,* but it is precisely the hard side of the paper. During the early 1990s, when the paper gained its popularity, it organized large-scale education campaigns each year. Themes were "I Love My Country" (1990), "The Party in My Heart" (1991), "Socialism Is Good" and "National Defense" (1992), "The Tide of Reform" (1993), "Traditional Chinese Virtues" (1994), and "The Quality of Individuals for the Next Century" (1995).

These campaigns were organized around core principles of the official ideology. The political and ideological role of the newspaper was given full play. These campaigns started soon after the crushing of the 1989 democracy movement, which had been spearheaded by Beijing youth. As discussed in the previous chapter, the PRER claimed that its soft entertainment programs distracted the youth in the Guangzhou area and helped to forestall further student disruptions. The radio station also performed its ideological function by sponsoring a large trade fair to distract the people of Guangzhou in a repressive period. Perhaps because of differences in the political culture of Beijing and Guangzhou, *Beijing Youth News* was more direct, providing serious ideological education aimed at Beijing youth.

Cui Enqing, publisher of *Beijing Youth News,* believed that in their political enthusiasm, in their worship of liberal political ideals and Western models of government, in their condemnation of the backwardness of their country, and in their admiration of Western countries, young people failed to understand the historical, political, and social realities of Chinese society. They did not know why China chose socialism. They did not understand the historical and contemporary conditions for the prosperity of developed capitalist countries.[72]

So, in September 1989 the paper began an education campaign. This preceded a call by Jiang Zemin, the Party's general secretary, for strengthened education on patriotism, national conditions, and modern Chinese history among youth on the eve of the October 1 National Day celebrations. Soon after that, Cui reported to the Beijing Party leadership and received the cooperation of the Beijing Education Bureau to carry the campaign into the schools. Editor-in-chief Chen Ji set up a writing team to prepare material.[73]

The campaign was organized around a televised quiz show on the paper's education material among its readers. In addition to school authorities, the Youth Leagues organized newspaper reading in factories and in the military. The newspaper went far beyond its regular function and became an organizer of ideological education in society at large. Chen and a reporter turned the material into a textbook that became the only one of its kind recommended by the State Education Commission for the whole country. In four subsequent years, more than 10 million copies were published—an unprecedented number for a text of this nature. At the same time, the newspaper sponsored a national seminar of education officials and scholars to discuss ideological education. Like the campaign itself, the seminar has become an annual event and a venue for the newspaper to promote its education materials.

If the theme in 1990 was a direct response to the 1989 student movement, other campaigns have been similarly timely. The 1991 campaign, "The Party in My Heart," coincided with the seventieth anniversary of the Party's founding. The 1992 "Socialism Is Good" theme was in response to the collapse of socialist regimes in eastern Europe and the dissolution of the Soviet Union. The 1993 "The Tide of Reform" capitalized on the reform wave brought about by Deng's 1992 talks. The 1994 theme on traditional Chinese values and ethics addressed changes and conflicts resulting from rapid modernization.

These campaigns have not only fulfilled the ideological role of the newspaper but also have became successful commercially. The newspaper's skillful manipulation of material, innovative approaches, and attractive writing style make hard ideological propaganda gentler, softer, and much more appealing. Textbook sales alone have brought in considerable revenue. Indeed, customer loyalty has developed. In 1994, when textbooks on traditional Chinese values were being chosen, some local school authorities reportedly said they wanted nothing but the one published by *Beijing Youth News*.[74]

What is significant is that these campaigns were initiated by the newspaper's management instead of a result of passively implementing Party orders. This paper may have more political freedom than other official organs because of its relatively low official status; however, it has not become a bastion of ideological liberalization. It has used its relative freedom to promote the official ideology, possibly more effectively than others. As Cui Enqing, its publisher, has said, "Marketization and political orientation of the news are not incompatible. The key lies in the perspectives of news workers."[75]

A Tolerable Gadfly

While it may be true that there is no overall contradiction between marketization and promoting the official ideology, in daily operation there are contradictions between trying to attract readers and being an official organ. Indeed, one aspect of the *Beijing Youth News* phenomenon is that the paper often "gets into trouble."[76] When it criticized another city's handling of a sports event, for example, the other city thought the criticism was coming from Beijing's authorities and protested. It also got into hot water when it broke with the convention of Party journalism that local news outlets do not report or comment independently on foreign affairs.[77] But to establish its political influence and the authoritativeness of its reports, especially now that it is a daily, it will have to continue to expand the political boundaries, particularly in the areas of hard news and commentaries on major political and social issues.

In addition to political boundaries, there are also ethical and moral boundaries, and here again the paper has put itself at the forefront in exploring what is permissible. Despite increasing interest in news about court cases and the lives of the rich and famous, there is a lack of laws, regulations, and ethical codes in these areas. How far can the media go in reporting ongoing court cases without affecting an individual's right to a fair trial? How far can the media go in describing the personal life of an individual without violating the right to privacy? What is the difference between legitimate criticism and libel? These are emerging questions. And being on the forefront of media reform, these questions are particularly relevant and urgent for a paper like *Beijing Youth News*.

The paper's pursuit of market success, especially given that street sales account for half of its circulation, also means that it must struggle constantly against total subordination to the market. Indeed, some of its sensational headlines do not match the actual content of articles. Twisting a story line to create a sensational effect has been another problem.[78]

Overall, while the newspaper's challenges against the authorities are big enough to attract readers' attention and increase sales, they are small enough and inconsistent enough not to cause authorities to close it down. Yes, it is often praised, but it has also often been forced to apologize and make "self-criticisms" (a formalized Party tradition in China). One aspect of the job of Chen Ji, former editor-in-chief of the newspaper, is to write self-criticisms each time the newspaper gets into trouble.[79] But like his newspaper, which was on the list of the ten best youth newspapers in the country in 1992, Chen himself carries the title "Excellent Journalist at the National Level" (*quanguo youxiu xinwen gongzuozhe*). The following comment, made by Zhang Baifa, deputy mayor of Beijing City, is worth quoting: "*Beijing Youth News* has been criticized by me many times. But strangely enough, it becomes better and better. . . . I often read this paper. It is very sharp. It makes money, while some other newspapers depend on me to solicit sponsorships. Strangely enough, it is not afraid of making mistakes. It continues to publish despite criticisms."[80]

The paper is unique, a hybrid of an official organ and a popular commercial newspaper. It is still an official organ but makes its readers feel it is not.[81]

7

Toward a Propagandist/Commercial Model of Journalism?

In an unusual exhibition of post-1989 Chinese avant-garde art held in Vancouver in early 1995, Chinese political pop artists presented such striking images as the superimposition of Mao's portrait on a huge Nintendo game board and the juxtaposition of the icon of the Cultural Revolution (a portrait of a man and a woman in Mao suits with raised fists) with the Coca-Cola logo.[1] Inside China, a small cafe in the southern tourist town of Yangshou calls itself Mickey Mao's and features as its logo Mao sporting a pair of Mickey Mouse ears.[2] In journalism, the interlocking of Party domination and market forces has created a scene characterized in large part by the dominance of political and commercial propaganda and a growing tendency toward news as entertainment. While the iron fist of the Party has led to "a thousand papers with one voice," the invisible hand of the market has at the same time created what some critics in China have called "a thousand papers with one star"—a movie star, a pop music star, or whoever is hot in popular culture.

The current news media scene in China can be explained neither by the Party principle nor by market forces alone. To return to the two-fold question posed by Mark Levy in the summer 1994 issue of the *Journal of Communication,* it is clear that news media in China have undergone significant changes over the past decade. The system has been partially commercialized; market forces have penetrated virtually every corner. Many news organizations have achieved financial independence and turned into profitable business enterprises. Commercialism has been carried to extremes in many instances.

Equally significant, some of the defining characteristics of the Chinese news media system remain unchanged. The Party still maintains overt political control of the news media. Indeed, rapid commercialization has occurred during a period when the Party's political control has been the tightest. As Xu Yu notes, "the precondition that the power of the Party may not be threatened in the least" remains "unchanged, or even strengthened" in the context of commercialization.[3] There is still no editorial independence, and no independent ownership of the news media is allowed. As a result, the news media have not emerged as an independent public sphere outside the Party/state apparatus proper. If "a Western, liberal model of the press" is defined by such characteristics as independent news media ownership, legally sanctioned press freedom, and formal institutional independence from the state, it is clear that current developments have not given much promise for the emergence of such a model in China. It seems that for the most part the worst aspects of Party journalism and commercialism have simultaneously been amplified in the major Party organs and broadcasting stations.

During the pre-reform era, the media were freed from private ownership and the profit motive but were under the authority of the Party. While the Party's power over the media has yet to be democratized, and control has even been tightened since 1989, with the increasing penetration of the media by market forces Party journalism is now for sale. From newspaper pages and broadcast time blocks to individual news items and features, there is literally a price tag on each piece of the news media. Before, access to the system was determined almost exclusively by those with political power. Now, it is available to those with economic power, a power the majority of workers and peasants do not possess. As one Chinese media scholar contended bitterly in an interview, journalism in China is currently being sold in two parts: one to the Party's Propaganda Department, another to businesses.[4]

The Party still claims that the media are the voice of the Party and of the people. One journalism educator claimed that since there are no fundamental conflicts of interest among the people, the dominance of commercialism in the media is not a problem. What is good for business is good for the people.[5] But such a view clearly overlooks the increasing class divisions in China. In addition to a rising industrialist and merchant class, a bureaucratic class controls the allocation of key state-owned economic, social, and communication resources. They are unaccountable to the public and often trade their power for private gain.

The media are not only unable to be watchdogs over the Party and the government, but they are also unable to be critical of business interests. Efforts by the Party and the media to protect consumer interests have been undermined by corruption and increasingly powerful private interests. The media's annual Ten Thousand Li Journey for Product Quality in China campaign, for example, has been undermined by corruption within journalism and terrorized. A CCTV team involved in the campaign reportedly received threats from an underground "black society" to drop investigation of a certain issue.[6] Critical reports in such areas as the environment are almost nonexistent. A 1996 survey of 52 major national and local newspapers, for example, revealed that only 0.46 percent of press coverage in 1995 was devoted to environmental issues, and this figure was already a 19 percent increase over that for 1994. Moreover, the survey found that of the limited number of environmental reports, nearly 90 percent were bland or laudatory pieces, while only 10.3 percent were critical stories.[7] Thus, even the official *Beijing*

Review has concluded that "the press is not playing its role as an environmental watchdog. Newspapers have failed to meet public expectations in this regard."[8]

Aside from positive stories about economic growth, the "socialist" feature of the media has been virtually reduced to a few success stories about poverty reduction and a report on the Party's honoring model workers on May Day, accompanied by the Party General Secretary's hypocritical reaffirmation that workers are still "the leading class."[9] Meanwhile, many workers are unemployed or underemployed and fearing the loss of basic necessities. Others are heavily exploited in sweat shops and sometimes strike. While the Party boasts achievements in poverty reduction in remote rural areas, a new form of poverty, urban poverty, has emerged in the centers of economic prosperity. But the media has paid little attention to the unemployed and none at all to striking workers.

At the same time, peasants' lands are increasingly being encroached on by industries and by golf courses and other playgrounds of the newly rich. For example, there were fifty-one golf course development projects in Guangdong Province alone in June 1995. Among the total 1,191 acres of land used by these projects, 118 acres were prime farming land, a large portion of which were illegally appropriated by developers. Moreover, although only twenty-four, or 47.1 percent, of these projects were approved by provincial authorities, the provincial government suspended only seven.[10] Instead of carrying critical stories about these developments, the news media have joined the celebrations of the grand openings of exclusive golf clubs, while portraying peasants hunting jobs in cities mostly in a negative light.

But the newly rich are not satisfied. Would-be investors were so upset with the treatment of the stock riot in August 1992 by the *Shenzhen Special Economic Zone News* that members of the Party's Propaganda Department went to Shenzhen to investigate "media bias."[11] Lacking political information and control over the political process and seeing increasing economic disparity and social injustices, many people are frustrated, even though they are better off now than in the prereform era.[12] A 1996 State Statistics Bureau survey revealed that more than 51 percent of the residents in four of the country's major urban centers are unhappy with their levels of income. Expectations are very high. The desired income level of these residents are, on average, three times greater than the current average income.[13] Another survey of Beijing residents, on the other hand, revealed that corruption and the lack of public order are chief sources of dissatisfaction.[14]

The Newly Commercialized Media Sector: A Critical Assessment

Party journalism as usual is increasingly unpopular among practitioners and targets. Morbid and parasitic mercantile journalism is equally unpopular. The journalism practiced by the Shanghai East stations, by CCTV's News Commentary

Department, and by evening papers and *Beijing Youth News,* however, indicates that a different form of journalism is emerging in a commercialized popular media sector *within* the Party-controlled system. Its practitioners have gained more organizational, financial, and editorial autonomy either by the authorities' efforts to reform the system or by virtue of their less central positions in the existing system. The market logic, in short, functions more or less "normally" (in comparison with mercantile journalism) in this sector. How, then, to evaluate this sector vis-à-vis mass-line journalism and the ideals of media reform in the mid-1980s? To what extent do they represent a possible alternative?

The "People" as Consumers?

The commercialized popular media exemplify some of the reform ideas put forward in the early and mid-1980s. They have imported production values from commercial media in the West and Hong Kong, such as brevity, speed, closeness to readers and audiences and their daily lives, and being more informative and less didactic. At the same time, to attract audiences this sector has to give more consideration to their needs and interests. The people principle and supervision by public opinion, two important ideas suggested during the theoretical ferment leading to the 1989 democracy movement, seem to have found some realization.

But there is a significant difference. Although the people principle is underdeveloped and vague, it was articulated by some reformers as an *anti*-thesis to the Party principle. It was a political concept within an emerging discourse on media democratization, although still colored by the paternalism and elitism of the Party's dominant political discourse. With commercialization, the people principle finds some reflection in a consumerist discourse; and the generalized political entity "the people" find its image in the commercialized media's "audience" approached as individual consumers.[15] The consumerist conception of the audience is apparent in the "service" mentality first articulated by PRER; the audience is to be *served* by informational and entertainment programming. Thus, there is the danger that the Party's most important political slogan, "to serve the people," will find a convenient and reductionist expression in the service mentality of a commercialized system. There is, indeed, a fit between the Party's paternalism and the consumerist discourse of the commercialized media.

Meanwhile, in the context of tight political control, the media's role as voice of the people and as the means by which the people exercise public opinion supervision over the Party and the government has largely been confined to protecting consumers and overseeing public utilities. Moreover, this is limited to the defense of individual welfare on a small scale, primarily specific cases against small businesses and low-level government officials without the protection of a powerful political network. There are still no substantial reports on key decision-making processes inside the Party and the government. There are no open debates on important policies. There is virtually no critical evaluation of reform, for example. Of course, the media are still prohibited from criticizing a Party committee on their same or a higher jurisdictional level and thus are unable to exercise any form of supervision over high-level officials.

I pointed out in chapter 1 that there is no mechanism in mass-line journalism whereby the media would not be detached from the people. Now with commercialization, market logic has partially become such a mechanism. Publications and broadcasters in the commercialized sector, being totally dependent on advertising in a competitive environment, can no longer afford to ignore their audiences.[16] To attract them is an imperative independent of either the teaching of the Party or the intention of journalists. In their pursuit of market success, the newly commercialized media have revived a tradition of mass-line journalism to some extent by adopting a robust rubric of "serving the people." Theories and practices of mass-line journalism have been employed to rationalize marketing strategies.

Thus, the political concept of "the people" is being transformed into "the audience"—indeed, into fragmented audiences as radio and television channels become increasingly specialized. "The people" as the "masters" of society in the rhetoric of Party journalism is being fused with the audience as "a god" with consumer sovereignty. While these developments are still in an early stage, and it is clear that China's media have not finally settled into such a transformation, it is likely that the undistinguished "masses" and "the people" of the Party's mass-line journalism may eventually become the advertisers' targeted middle-class consumers, a group with whom journalists largely identify.

While there is a convenient fit between propaganda and commercialism— *Beijing Youth News* can even make a profit out of its education campaigns—this media sector is operating with profound contradictions and tensions. Any substantial political challenge, and with it greater commercial success, is contained by the Party. CCTV's "Sons of the East" is explicitly prohibited from interviewing controversial figures. East Radio was forced to change its live phone-ins to recorded ones. *Beijing Youth News* has often run into trouble in its attempt to assert more independence in news and commentaries. There is also a tension between mass-line journalism's ideal of educating and enlightening the masses and market-driven journalism's tendency to cater to whatever attitudes and preferences are prevalent regardless of how vulgar or questionable.

It is clear that little progress has been made on the most critical issue of the 1989 democratic movement—press freedom. To be sure, the newly emerged commercial sector has more editorial autonomy, but mostly it does not deal with hard news. Party control of hard political news is as strong with the new programs as it was with the old. Central Party authorities keep CCTV's two "Focus" programs under close scrutiny and their preview procedures are extremely rigid. The two Shanghai East stations are closely monitored by central authorities as well. Similarly, although recorded broadcasts have given way to live news and reporters and hosts have gained a little more autonomy, control is still tight. Previously, the news was aired after previewing by a responsible station leader (usually the president or a designated vice president). Now the president or vice president usually stands behind the newscaster and keeps a watchful eye and ear during live broadcasts.

Despite their limitations, journalism practices in the popular commercial sector have made some important contributions toward democratization. Despite its democratic thrust, the people principle of the mid-1980s contained a strong bias toward elitism. The assumption was that a group of professional journalists, presumably capable of perceiving the Party's wrong course, could correct it by representing the people, speaking on their behalf, and exercising a watchdog function over the Party. Now, with the popularity of telephone participation, first in entertainment, then with experiments in news and current affairs, the elitism of some media professionals and reformers has been at least partially modified. According to Chen Shenglai, president of East Radio: "I used to have a one-sided understanding of supervision by public opinion. For me, it seemed to be supervision of the government by the media. But in fact, the media are ultimately only the means of communication. It is the people who exercise supervision over the government. The media, including radio stations, are merely channels for the expression of such supervision. Therefore, if the media want to play a true role in opinion supervision, they must invite the audience to participate in programming."[17]

This comment contains a regained appreciation of the importance of public participation and the dethroning of the self-important, self-appointed media and media professionals who speak on behalf of the people. I use "regained" here because the tension between the elitism of professionals and grass-roots participation has been at the heart of policy struggles in the past, including within the media. Mao, for example, often rejected the exercise of power by professionals in favor of mass participation. The Cultural Revolution, for example, despite its disastrous outcomes, was known in the West, particularly in left circles, for its critique of elitism and technocracy. As discussed in chapter 1, one aspect of Mao's press theory was that newspapers should be run by the whole Party and the whole people rather than by a few professionals behind closed doors. The amateur correspondents system was a legacy of this participatory perspective.

Now, in a different context, public participation has taken a new, and arguably more effective, meaningful and substantial form. Unlike the amateur local correspondents, who must have some professional qualifications, are appointed by the media, and usually serve as propagandists of grass-roots Party organizations (and now more often as publicists of businesses), phone-in audiences need no qualifications or institutional recognition. They are simply individuals who act on their own behalf without approval of their Party propaganda departments. Thus, there is some truth in the observation that while PRER brought the first wave of reform by making broadcasting content more relevant to the audience, the wide use of telephone participation first in East Radio and then in radio broadcasting throughout the country marked another significant development. Now programs are designed not only to attract audiences but also to give audience members a chance to participate.[18] Similarly, CCTV's News Commentary Department, *Qianjiang Evening News,* and *Beijing Youth News* have all solicited audience input.

To be sure, such participation is still very limited, both in content and in access. A home phone is still a luxury even in urban centers, and phone-in programs are almost exclusively aimed at the urban population.[19] But the democratizing potential is clear and the political challenge is real. As discussed previously, three months after East Radio's experiment with live phone-ins, a sense of citizenship had been aroused among the audience and some callers had already moved away from complaints about poor goods and services to more substantial issues and less individualistic concerns.[20]

At the same time, the elitism of media professionals is also being challenged by a growing populist sensibility (or at least an awareness of the importance of the average citizen) in this commercialized sector, particularly in "Living Space," if discussions in trade journals about the program and the pressure it put on the elite Beijing media are any indication. However, the fate of East Radio's live phone-in news reveals that substantial audience participation is not only politically threatening to the Party but is also something professional journalists are not willing to fight for. Public participation will be mediated by media professionals so as to dissipate any potential threat to the Party's hegemony.

Overall, the emergence of a commercialized sector has been democratizing in that it is closer to ordinary people, addresses at least some of their concerns, speaks their language, treats them as protagonists, and provides them with some access to participation through phone-ins and news tips. While the contributions of CCTV's two programs and the two East stations, as well as the more respectable evening papers and *Beijing Youth News,* are noteworthy, the crime tabloids and weekend editions also have a progressive side. Crime stories, in particular, have exposed the dark side of social relationships, the chaotic social order, and the collapse of traditional and socialist value systems in a society rapidly changing to a market economy. The tabloids and weekend editions have also broken political and moral taboos by occasionally providing space for political and social criticism. At the same time, they have broadened the newspaper readership by catering to a wide range of people, particularly those who do not generally read the main Party and government organs, such as homemakers, the urban unemployed, and the increasingly large number of mobile peasant workers in the cities.

On the other hand, the controlled nature of reform has thus far prevented the new commercial sector from posing any fundamental challenge to the dominant model of political communication. The public's need for entertainment, microeconomic, and business information and, more generally, its participation in economic and cultural life through the media are acknowledged and at least partially fulfilled. However, its rights to political information, to meaningful participation in political life, and to a role in making key economic decisions are still being negated.

Commercialized Media as "Alternative Media"?

One temptation of scholars who are critical of the Party's ideological control is to exaggerate the oppositional nature of the newly emerged commercial sector. Leonard L. Chu, for example, has grouped local television and radio stations, cable and satellite television, profit-making tabloids, evening papers, weekend editions, and other recent arrivals together with foreign broadcasts such as the BBC and the Voice of America and argued that they together "have formed China's alternative media, which the Party has found to be disturbing but impossible to curb."[21] Similarly, Minxin Pei has characterized the new financially independent radio and television stations like Shanghai's East stations as fierce rivals of "the government-funded and controlled stations" with broadcasts that contain material that "had been largely kept out of the official electronic media."[22]

These characterizations, without specific analysis of their actual orientations as well as clear definitions of what such terms as "alternative" and "official" mean, tend to exaggerate the oppositional nature of commercialized media outlets. The relationship between commercialized news outlets and Party ideological control is more complicated than that. If "alternative" means presenting a substantially different political perspective, it is important to note that much commercialization happens *within* the existing media structure. New formats and content based on commercial logic do not generally indicate a revolution from outside the existing media structure but rather an organized reform from within. The adoption of popular commercial broadcast formats and content orientations by PRER, one of the earliest steps toward commercialization, for example, was not so much a commercial imperative as a political and propagandist maneuver. It was an attempt on the part of the Guangdong People's Radio to use commercial formats and content to improve its own performance and lure back the audience lost to Hong Kong commercial stations. Similarly, PRER was intended to be supplementary to the main channel but instead became a popular model copied first by radio then by television across the country, leading to other specialized, financially self-sustaining, and entertainment-oriented broadcasting stations. Nevertheless, these specialized stations are all under the editorial control of either the parent people's radio station or the government broadcasting bureau.

Similarly, the introduction of commercial logic by the Shanghai East stations and CCTV's News Commentary Department are deliberate reform initiatives put forward by the Shanghai Broadcasting Bureau and the CCTV administration with the approval and close supervision of high-level authorities. These are attempts by media reformers inside the system to increase popularity, to enhance responsiveness to audiences, and to make ideological work more effective. They are all top-down reforms.

Further, it is important to note that there are significant differences in terms of organizational affiliation and content among the different commercialized media outlets. Although many evening dailies are official Party organs, some profit-seeking tabloids are only remotely related to the Party's propaganda departments. In the broadcast sector, there is also a sea of difference between a county-level cable station and East Television or the programs of CCTV's News Commentary Department, although these are all commercialized. Although it is true that control is more indirect in some outlets, especially in the tabloids and local cable stations, in the case of provincial-level economic stations, editorial controls are as tight as at their rival people's stations. Whatever relative editorial freedom they enjoy is permitted by the Party and the government, and it can be taken away at the will of the Party, as the Shanghai-based *World Economic Herald* discovered in 1989.

Although some commercialized outlets have challenged the ideological control of the Party, most of these challenges were not fundamental. Moreover, there are far more instances of accommodation. The critical capacities of journalists have for the most part been contained. Commercialized outlets survive and flourish not by directly challenging the Party principle and discarding political propaganda but by softening the tones of political propaganda, moving beyond narrow political propaganda, and broadening content to include social and personal issues. Their contents are supplementary rather than oppositional to the more conventional Party organs. While the readers of Hangzhou's *Qianjiang Evening News* praised the newspaper for what it did for them, the mayor of Hangzhou City also praised it for what it did for the government. While the audiences in Shanghai were excited by their limited opportunity for dialogue with government officials afforded by broadcasting stations, Ding Guan'gen, the Party's ideological chief, praised them and recommended their approach to the Beijing media. Moreover, the stations' methods were analyzed by the Party's ideological workers and found to have contributed a more effective ideological work style. The commercialized media sector has expanded the ideological process to include sociological, personal, and psychological domains.

To be sure, politically controversial and dissenting material sells. There is profit to be made by selling controversial ideas, particularly ideas that are critical of the Party. Indeed, as Minxin Pei has observed, commercialization of the book publishing sector has been largely responsible for the appearance of a number of books that otherwise would not have been available.[23] When a book successfully passes through the loopholes in the Party's censorship system, the Party's criticisms and recall efforts often further publicize it and make people want to read it. But in the news media, not only is control much tighter, but no single newspaper or broadcast station can make a huge profit from one critical piece on one day. While live radio and television formats and call-in programs have made censorship more difficult for the Party, Pei's assertion that these formats have "rendered government censorship useless" is an overstatement.[24] Such an observation totally disregards self-censorship, the more routine and effective mechanism of control everywhere. Moreover, when a television station's censors are standing by, how far can a newscaster or a talk show host go in expressing dissenting views? When everyone knows individuals have lost their jobs for not following the Party line, how many (from program hosts to producers to station presidents) are willing to endanger themselves? In fact, the ideological role of major commercialized media outlets is demonstrated by PRER's effort to organize an uplifting trade fair during the depressing holiday season of 1989–90, by the framing of a discussion on "Focus" about rising tuition fees, by East Radio's "rescuing" of a young worker who had been victimized by the system, as well as by *Beijing Youth News*'s sensational role model stories and its ideological education campaigns.

The less tightly controlled tabloids and some weekend editions are in a slightly different situation, but their relationship with the Party system's ideological hegemony is also contradictory rather than simply oppositional. Their excursions into formerly taboo areas such as homosexuality help to liberalize attitudes and bring social issues to light. But their treatment of these issues is typically superficial, more descriptive then analytical. Their reporting of crime cases is totally different from the muckraking in the Pulitzer and Hearst era in American journalism. Crimes are almost always reported after the cases have been closed and it can be shown that justice has been done. These stories are not crusading for justice on behalf of victims but are instead exposing criminal elements. Indeed, authoritarianism and sensationalism fuse effectively to increase the market appeal of these stories. The description of the crime itself and the process of crime investigation is often implicitly and explicitly linked with the celebration of the bravery and efficiency of the law enforcement apparatus. And of course, in newspapers published by law enforcement agencies, there is no report of the repressive side of these State apparatus and no exposure of police brutality, of violations of human rights, or of massive corruption.

Prospects for a Propagandist/Commercial Model of Journalism

The popular evening papers, the East stations, the CCTV News Commentary Department, and *Beijing Youth News* point to the possible emergence of a propagandist/commercial model of journalism within the framework of an emerging authoritarian market society in China. Although these are all commercially oriented media, they are still under the ideological leadership of the Party. Unlike traditional Party organs, which depend on subsidies, operate as bureaucracies rather than businesses, and do not have to be popular to survive, these are managed as business enterprises and must depend on markets. They follow a logic similar to that of the commercial media in the West.

But unlike Western media, which are first and foremost commercial enterprises, these in China are first and foremost political organs. They need to be self-sustaining, but profit is not their primary objective. In other words, while they are commercial in nature, they are not necessarily profit-driven and they receive preferential treatment in taxation. *Beijing Youth News*, for example, has reinvested most of its profits in itself. If it had been required to hand over its profits to the government's finance department (as other state enterprises are supposed to do) it could not have improved as rapidly as it did. If it were a shareholding public company, it is doubtful that shareholders would have supported nonprofitable endeavors like its specialized papers for students. Although it is now a conglomerate owning other businesses, it uses income from them to support the newspaper operation. There is no evidence it uses the paper as a cash cow to buy other businesses, a common practice of such media conglomerates as the Canadian-based Thomson group.

While this emergent propagandist/commercial model of journalism has to be responsive to its audience, it will cater first to the propaganda needs of the Party, attempting to establish a common ground between the Party and the people by the issues it discusses. It is precisely for this reason that these commercialized outlets are more popular than Party organs, which respond only to the needs of the Party. Their degree of success depends on their ability to put on a good show while "dancing with chains."

Thus, these new commercialized outlets of the 1990s are different from the *World Economic Herald* of the 1980s. Although the *Herald* was financially independent and relatively free from formal links with the government, it maintained informal relationships with at least one faction of the political establishment. These new outlets, however, do not have such specific political linkages. The *Herald* was primarily a political journal, winning its reputation not by its news reporting but by its political commentaries, contributions by prominent intellectuals, and interviews with political and technological elites. By contrast, the new commercialized sector's main staple is news and entertainment.[25]

While the *Herald*'s heroic fight for press freedom made it a martyr of the democracy movement, the political orientation of the paper was far from democratic. Indeed, as Li Cheng and Lynn T. White have argued, the paper had a strong tendency toward elitism. As the organ of China's emerging technocratic movement, it showed "obvious bias for the interests of technocratic elites." "Social welfare, environment, labor, and domestic trade were rare among its domestic coverage. Women, the elderly, urban housing, and other important issues received little attention."[26] By contrast, the new commercialized outlets of the 1990s present themselves as champions of the common people by catering to a mass audience. Instead of centering on government affairs and advising the government, they address the concerns of daily life. Instead of being elitist, they espouse populist sensibilities.

The popular commercial sector represents a model of journalism that is different from either the traditional Party organs or the *World Economic Herald* of the 1980s. Within such a model, there is the possibility that the role of the media will be modified from a narrow and didactic expression of ideology to a more subtle exercise of ideological control in expanded subject areas. The Party ideologues will have to accept accommodation and containment rather than demand complete compliance. The new media will constantly make small troubles for the authorities, but they will not fundamentally challenge the existing political and social order.

For such a new model to be stable, however, there must be readjustments, if not a complete redefinition, of the relationship between the Party and the media. The effort to transform overt censorship into greater reliance on self-censorship is seen in CCTV President Yang Weiguang's coaching of journalists and in his attempt to establish consensus about news criteria among Party leaders and rank-and-file news workers. The exercise of journalism's responsibility to the Party is seen in the preoccupation with political stability by the director of the CCTV News Commentary Department,[27] in selection of topics for "Focus," and in ideological education campaigns run by *Beijing Youth News*.

The key element for the success of such a model lies in a recognition of the relative autonomy of news discourse by the Party. Indeed, many of the reform arguments in the mid-1980s for "separating news from propaganda," for learning "international conventions" of news production, and for respecting "laws of journalism and communication" revolved around the relative autonomy of journalism. Journalists at East Radio and CCTV's News Commentary Department have demonstrated the importance of such a relative autonomy.

I have already noted in chapter 6 how, commenting on the success of *Beijing Youth News*, Cui Enqing argued that commercialization of the media is not incompatible with its political orientation as an official organ. Similarly, Gong Xueping, former director of Shanghai Broadcasting Bureau, who played a crucial role in establishing East Radio and East Television, argued that there is no necessary contradiction between political and commercial goals in broadcasting. According to him, "to effectively run the broadcast media as an industry will not only not undermine their propaganda functions, it will even positively promote their role as mouthpiece of the Party and the people."[28] It is worth noting that Gong, one of the deputy mayors of Shanghai, obviously was promoted for his success in transforming Shanghai's broadcast establishment into an expanding industry while maintaining its ideological function. Many articles in trade journals argue the same point. The initial popularity of commercialized news outlets seems to substantiate these arguments.

But to perpetuate themselves as a stable model, they must continue to enjoy relative autonomy and be able to be critical on concrete political and social issues, to address at least partially the concerns of ordinary people, and to provide audiences with some form of access. The viability of the current popular media outlets in many ways hinges on their ability to articulate popular concerns. "Being critical on small matters and being supportive on major issues" (*xiaoma da bangmang*) is a phrase often used by official Party media theorists to describe the relationship between the commercial media and government in the West as well as the relationship between independent commercial newspapers in the pre-1949 era and the Nationalist government in China. Although present-day commercialized outlets still lack the political and institutional independence of commercial newspapers in the West, they seem increasingly to pursue such an editorial orientation.

The new commercialized outlets face many problems. The absence of legally sanctioned press freedom means that there is always the danger that the Party may tighten up control even further and revoke the limited autonomy. There is also the danger that they may surrender to the pressures of an overall system that remains unchanged. Shanghai's East Television, for example, has suffered from the efforts of its leaders to boost their standing with their government boss—the Shanghai Broadcasting Bureau—by handing in so much profit that it put itself under difficult financial pressures. The continued existence of all forms of paid journalism in other media outlets means that it is difficult for the few journalists in the new organizations to remain untainted. And even if they want to explore some sensitive social issues within the boundaries permitted by Party authorities, they might not get cooperation from nervous local officials afraid of making public statements in live broadcasts. For example, on International Women's Day in 1995 the talk show "Live from East Television" (Dongfang zhibo shi) was supposed to explore the problem of women workers being forced into early retirement. City officials and Women's Federation representatives were supposed to take part. But when the officials retreated at the last minute for fear of making political mistakes, an alternate panel was hastily assembled. What was interesting, however, was that precisely because of the absence of officials, the discussion was more lively and the program was praised by the city's Party authorities.[29]

Indeed, the fate of "Live from East Television" is perhaps symbolic of the dynamics of being both a Party organ and a market-oriented news operation. Seeing propaganda potential in its popularity, Shanghai authorities began to assign mandatory topics like "spiritual civilization." These drove away the audience. Fierce competition from the Shanghai television station added to its problems. It aired less frequently and, according to an insider, it may eventually be moved to a less desirable time slot.[30] However, given that the station generates important revenue, the producers may be able to use the commercial imperative to bargain with propaganda officials to assert some autonomy in programming.

There is an often-noted tradition of distinguishing between "quality papers" and "popular papers" in Britain and, to a lesser extent, in the United States and Canada. "Quality papers" specialize in hard political and business news and cater to elites. They consider news to be information. "Popular papers" cater to a mass audience with soft news and human interest stories and consider news to be entertainment.[31] China's rising evening papers and weekend editions and *Beijing Youth News* seem to have established themselves as China's popular commercial news media and gained status and influence both within the media system and in public discourse.

The reforms and innovations in the newly commercialized sector have been widely reported in trade journals and analyzed by government and academic researchers. The reforms at *Beijing Youth News*, for example, have been studied by the School of Journalism at the Chinese People's University and even recommended by a top official at the State Press and Publications Administration to other newspapers in the country.[32] Will Party organs follow suit and establish themselves as "quality papers" able to survive in the market while at the same time adhering to the Party principle? Although some trade journal articles have pointed in that direction, and there is indeed a market for serious news, there are many obstacles to this transformation. Tight political control and the need for positive economic propaganda mean that these papers will continue to sell themselves in two parts, one to the Party, the other to businesses. Unable to produce hard political news that is attractive, they have chosen to soften their content and move away from politics in a trend of "big papers learning from small papers." Yet what distinguishes a quality paper is precisely hard political news—news about concrete political and social developments delivered with at least some objectivity and opinion columns that provide at least some forum for debates among elites. But this is precisely what is lacking in the main Party organs.

If the Party organs want to go commercial by attempting to be China's "quality papers," the Party itself must first be democratized. It must allow reporting of decision-making processes, allow some critical reporting, and allow reports on differences within the Party. After all, it is this that makes political news interesting.

8

Challenges and Responses

The emerging commercialized sector is the result of the system's accommodation to and containment of various challenges. PRER was a direct response to the challenge of Hong Kong commercial radio, while CCTV's News Commentary Department was a response to the challenge of local television stations as well as to satellite, cable, and commercial interests moving into the national market. The Shanghai East stations were also partly the result of accommodation between national and regional interests. According to one industry insider, the Shanghai Broadcasting Bureau was allowed to establish the two East stations as a trade-off for not putting Shanghai Television programs on a satellite, which would have posed a greater threat to the national monopoly of CCTV than any other provincial station.

So far, all this has been accomplished without substantial change in either the system of control or the system of political decision-making. Indeed, much of this occurred after 1989, when political reform came to a virtual standstill. The stability of the current media arrangement depends on the ability of the system to continue to respond to the challenges outlined below, particularly on how much longer the Party can promote economic reform and "deliver the goods" to the satisfaction of the majority of the population without substantial political reform—and in journalism, continue to contain the pressures of market forces and suppress journalists' desire for more autonomy.

The Resurgence of Press Freedom

Since the 1989 crackdown, even though press reform has taken a sharp turn toward commercialization, the struggle for reform in the political realm has not been abandoned. Whenever there is a chance, press reform resurfaces as a political issue. In July 1992, the Shanghai press seized the opportunity of a lawsuit to raise calls for the "speedy formulation of a press law."[1] Shanghai's *Liberation Daily* published an opinion piece in which Qian Bocheng, a publisher and National People's Congress deputy, wrote: "If we really want to become an open China in the eyes of the world, we must first have an open press or must open up the press. Journalists have the right to interview, the media have the right to report, and the public has the right to know."[2]

In the press reform literature, two post-1992 publications stand out. Instead of arguing for commercialization, they raise press freedom as a political issue, a continuation of the main thrust of press reform discourse just before 1989.

In his three-page polemic published in February 1993, Gan Xifen criticized the Party's tight information control, the phenomenon of "a thousand papers with one voice," and the Party's overemphasis on positive propaganda and suppression of critical reporting.[3] Gan noted that currently journalism is worse than in some other periods, such as the performance of *Liberation Daily* in Yan'an and that of the media just after 1978. He argued: "Newspapers in the West can express different opinions on an issue. . . . They at least pool the wisdom of the ruling classes. But we only allow one voice, which claims to represent all the people. Is this normal in a socialist country during a period of peaceful construction? How long is a policy from the war years going to continue?"[4]

Gan pointed out that journalism's problems rest with the media system, which is beyond the capacity of the average journalist to change. Many want to, but they fear being charged with "liberalism" and experiment only with minor reforms such as publishing weekend editions. Gan observes that journalists are working under stress, waiting for something to happen. Their only hope, Gan argued, lies with the Party Central Committee.

Gan appealed to the Party to declare clearly that it intends to carry out press reform. He urged the Party to enlist journalists in a discussion of what kind of reform would be most suitable for China. He proposed that it should help develop socialist democracy and should not blindly copy Western models: "We must explore our own unique road."[5] At the same time, he asked the Party to make a clear distinction between Party newspapers and non-Party newspapers and allow non-Party newspapers to publish independent news and commentaries on major domestic and international affairs.

Gan suggested that he had been mulling over his ideas for three years and finally decided to put them into print in light of the economic openness created by Deng's spring 1992 talks and Deng's call for combating leftist extremism. He presented his ideas for "judgment by perceptive individuals in journalism circles," intending to open up discussion of press reform. But the Party responded by criticizing Gan.[6] Although Gan claimed that his ideas were shared by many, nobody dared to agree. Obviously he had wrongly judged the political climate. Despite the economic openness following Deng's talks, there had been no political openness. On the other hand, the criticism of the Party's Propaganda Department was not made in public, and any punishment of Gan was carefully avoided.

In 1994, the call for press reform as a political issue resurfaced in *New Theories of Journalism* (Xinwen xue xinlun), a collection of essays by Sun Xupei, then director of the Journalism Research Institute of the Chinese Academy of Social Sciences. Among other criticisms of the media system and proposals for reform, Sun elaborated a notion of "socialist press freedom" and proposed "a multi-structured, multi-tiered socialist media system," including independent newspapers. Similar to Gan's proposal, Sun suggested that only Party organs need to propagate Party policies, while other newspapers should be allowed to report and comment independently within the boundaries of the law. The Party did not like Sun's ideas either. A dispute over the publication process of the book provided the Party with an excuse to remove Sun from his position.[7]

Commercial Imperatives, Local Interests, and Technological Developments

Although the Party may still be able to silence most intellectuals and journalists, the media structure itself has been diversified and thus is more complex. In a decade of liberalization and decentralization, the commercial imperative and local interests have grown much stronger. New communications technologies mean that it is increasingly difficult for the Party to disseminate propaganda centrally. Enforcement of policies on the local level has become a formidable task in such a big country. Although the principle of Party control has not been challenged, the monopoly of national media like CCTV is.

As noted in chapter 6, the Party has adopted a policy of differentiation in the exercise of ideological control. While it still maintains tight control over hard political news, policies for soft news and nonpolitical topics are more relaxed. Indeed, so long as there is no overt political challenge, it seems that anything goes. While such control may be effective in the short run, it also means that major Party organs, especially newspapers, are monotonous and detached from the people. Indeed, a growing number of people do not bother to open major Party organs. "Editors of major newspapers, why are your headlines so dull? . . . You spend your time in meetings or rehashing official documents and languishing in the corridors of power. How can you produce papers that please the masses?" Even the official *Outlook* (Liaowang) news magazine has began to ask such questions.[8]

Circulation of major Party organs has dropped significantly despite mandatory subscriptions. *Guangming Daily* dropped from 1.5 million in 1987 to 800,000 in 1993. To survive, like many other Party organs, the paper has decided to "use fewer political articles and more culture and science news."[9] The result, of course, is less straightforward political propaganda.

The differentiation policy has another repercussion. The personal is political, as Chinese authorities are newly discovering, so even nonpolitical topics are not necessarily politically safe. In Beijing, a popular late night phone-in talk show on Beijing People's Radio was ordered by the Party's Propaganda Department to shut down less than forty days after its inauguration. The show upset the Party, among other things, because it "revealed the ugly side of life in Beijing and exposed the city's social and psychological problems."[10]

As there is a difference in control over hard and soft news, there is also a significant difference between central and local levels. With the proliferation of outlets, monitoring becomes increasingly difficult. Central authorities keep key Party organs—major newspapers and national broadcast networks—in check. Provincial authorities maintain control of news organs under their direct supervision (although perhaps not as tight as at the central level). But at municipal and county levels, as well as media outlets not directly under national or provincial Party committees, control is much looser. Thus, audiences have compared CCTV programming with "distilled water," television programming by provincial stations with "boiled water," and municipal and county level stations—filled with Hong Kong and Taiwan productions packed with action, violence, and sentimental love stories—with "Coca-Cola."

Indeed, the rapid development of local television stations and cable networks has greatly reduced audiences for centralized propaganda, particularly for CCTV. Previously, county-level stations were merely relays, but since 1983 they have been allowed to broadcast their own programs. With the introduction of cable in the mid-1980s, many municipalities and counties, as well as large government units and businesses with their own residential areas for employees, established local cable networks. Because cable stations charge monthly fees, they do not need government investment. As a result, they have developed at an explosive rate and have become highly decentralized. As of the first half of 1993, there were more than two thousand cable networks in the country—with varying levels of technological sophistication—reaching into 20 million households. Approximately eight hundred were full-scale cable stations, broadcasting videos or self-produced programming. Two hundred of these were run by large-scale state-owned business enterprises.[11] At the end of 1995, the number of full-scale cable stations had reached twelve hundred, with an estimated audience of 200 million. Cable viewership is expected to increase by 50 percent between 1996 and 2000, eventually reaching 300 million people in 60 million households. This will make China the biggest cable television market in the world.[12]

The rapid growth of cable television and the decentralization of the television industry have threatened the domination of CCTV. Its president, Yang Weiguang, reported in 1991 that despite the rapid development of television in the previous decade, the audience for CCTV had actually declined, while the reach of local stations had increased.[13] Previously, when provincial stations could not fill their broadcast time, they transmitted CCTV programs. But with more provincial programming available, these stations use their powerful transmitters for their own programming while carrying CCTV programming on less powerful transmitters.

The transmission of CCTV's complete programming is often limited to provincial capitals. Although CCTV shows are now carried by satellite, in areas where there are no satellite receiving stations most CCTV programming cannot reach local audiences.

Municipal and county-level stations further cut the reach of CCTV. Because the channels assigned to county-level television stations are usually at a higher spectrum and thus are difficult to tune in, county-level stations often use the CCTV channel to broadcast local programs. A resident in one county complained: "For a long time, our county's television relay station has disregarded repeated orders from authorities and . . . replaced most CCTV programs with Hong Kong and Taiwan video tapes for private gain."[14] Another viewer complained in a letter to CCTV that the county station replaced CCTV programs with its own advertising and video show and even asked each household to send it a 100–500 yuan "video fee."[15]

Even in places with both satellite relay and cable distribution, a technological combination that is capable of distributing the entire CCTV package, the Party can no longer control what the people are exposed to. Indeed, given the choice, the majority of the audience prefers the "Coca-Cola" offered by local cable stations to the "distilled water" of CCTV. The more localized the station, the higher the audience rating. Thus, as Yang Weiguang complained, "because of the lack of management, the rich resources of cable have not been used to promote positive propaganda, instead, it has provided convenience for those who choose to watch low quality programming. . . . As a result, the influence of CCTV on the national audience is undermined. Consequently, the role of CCTV in using the Party's thoughts to unify the thinking of the people in the whole nation is weakened."[16]

The lack of production capacity at the local level means that "local programming" really means "imported programming," particularly Taiwan and Hong Kong entertainment shows. A 1994 survey of more than ten municipal cable stations revealed that over 90 percent of the programs were Hong Kong, Taiwan, and foreign imports, which are considered by the Party as ideological instruments of "peaceful evolution" to capitalism.[17] Except for local news, which is usually a propaganda outlet of local Party and government authorities, the primary form of local expression on local cable stations has been the lucrative business of song requests. For a fee, a station dedicates requests, usually to celebrate birthdays or weddings. The names of both sender and receiver are often displayed on the screen. Because profit is the only consideration, cable stations usually do not exercise much control over requests. The few songs broadcast repeatedly are mostly Hong Kong and Taiwan pop songs. The Party has intended to use the mass media to resist "peaceful evolution" and promote "socialist spiritual civilization." In 1993, a top leader at the Ministry of Radio, Film, and Television warned: "We can't spend money to buy peaceful evolution!"[18]

CCTV president Yang Weiguang has argued that for control to be effective, the Party cannot let local stations do as they please. The country is so large that central policies have to pass through several administrative levels. Technological developments are too fast for the Party and the government to respond to. And, most importantly, local—especially county-level—officials are less interested in ideology. Regulations are simply ignored or at best loosely enforced. For example, according to government policies, the foremost duty of county-level stations is to transmit CCTV-1 in its entirety; they are not to carry advertising and their own entertainment programs. Although they are supposed to provide only local news and features on local topics, few stations obey. Moreover, there are many loopholes as well as problems for which there are no policies.

While both CCTV and provincial television stations are facing challenges from municipal and county-level stations, CCTV also faces competition from provincial stations. In addition to CCTV's four primary channels, the stations of Sichuan, Yunnan/Guizhou, Xinjiang, and Tibet also relay their signals to satellites and thus reach a national audience. More influential provincial stations in coastal provinces also want to reach a national audience through satellites. As of late 1994, Shandong Television and Zhejiang Television had each sent one channel to national audiences through satellites. With the help of local cable networks, many cities and even some rural areas can receive more than a dozen channels.

External Political and Commercial Pressures

External challenges to the Chinese media system have never been so strong. The news media of Hong Kong and Taiwan are increasingly influential, with better economic integration and a common cultural background. Although the Party has tried hard to contain the influence of the Hong Kong press on the mainland, sources of external influence go far beyond the East. Western media influences come in many technological forms—shortwave radio to satellite television to the Internet—and are driven by both political and commercial imperatives.

Since China opened up to the outside world, foreign shortwave radio has become an important alternative source of news, particularly for intellectuals and university students. A 1990 survey found that 10.6 percent of the Beijing population frequently listened to foreign radio.[19] As of 1993, twenty-seven outside broadcasters (including five in Taiwan) provided Chinese-language broadcasts, using a total of 185 channels.[20] Influential foreign shortwave stations like the Voice of America and the BBC have played a critical role in challenging the Party's monopoly on information, especially with their reports about events in China during political upheavals. Indeed, the Party blamed the Voice of America for stirring up students during the 1989 democracy movement. In Beijing, audiences listened to nearly twenty foreign stations. Fifteen had an audience rating of above 1 percent. The Voice of America has the highest rating, with approximately 1.3 million listeners.[21]

International broadcasting has always been an instrument of foreign policy, and the Chinese authorities are certainly right to argue that the main purpose of Western stations' broadcasting in the East is ideological penetration and the promotion of Western values. For a long time, Western stations focused on the former Soviet Union and eastern Europe. With the collapse of communist regimes there, Western attention has turned to communist regimes in Asia. Territories of the former Soviet Union, previously targets of Western broadcasts, have become bases for directing programs to China, currently the most important propaganda target. If previously China was partially under siege from Western shortwave signals coming mainly from Southeast Asia, now China has been encircled by them.

Since the early 1990s, the United States has closed the offices of Radio Liberty and Radio Free Europe in many western European capitals and drastically cut their budgets.[22] Concurrently, the broadcast time of the Voice of America has been increased from 8 hours a day in 1989 to 12 hours, and more than $300 million has been spent on expanding and upgrading facilities in Asia.[23] The Voice of America uses twenty-four channels for more than 10 hours daily to aim programs at China.[24] The BBC increased its daily broadcasting to China from 2.75 hours to 3.5 hours in 1990; in 1992, it began to rent three Russian broadcasting facilities in central and far east Asia and provided 9.5 hours of daily programming into China and India in five languages; since 1993, its broadcasting has increased to 15 hours. Germany also began leasing three radio transmission stations in central Asia to provide a daily broadcast of 19.5 hours to Asia, mainly to China.

On September 29, 1996, the United States launched Radio Free Asia. Created by the U.S. Congress and designed to copy the success of Radio Free Europe in combating communism during the cold war, Radio Free Asia has a clear anti-Communist mandate and is aimed specifically at China, North Korea, Vietnam, Cambodia, and Laos. Given that China is its primary target, it is not surprising that the station, with a $10 million annual budget from the U.S. Treasury, began its operation with a half-hour newscast to China in Mandarin. Unlike the Voice of America, which provides worldwide news and sometimes editorials that reflect the viewpoints of the U.S. government, Radio Free Asia has no editorials representing official U.S. policy. It concentrates heavily on domestic news in China and provides an outlet for the views of critics of the Chinese regime, especially exiles and dissidents. According to one initial report, one of Radio Free Asia's regular commentators would be Liu Binyan, the journalist and writer who has made a career of exposing official corruption within the Chinese Communist party.

Currently broadcasting a half-hour news show repeated three times a day with news updates, this semiclandestine station (both its frequencies and the location of its transmitters are kept secret, to prevent jamming and avoid embarrassment to the hosts of its transmitters in Asia) is planning to increase its Chinese programming to five and half hour a day in the first quarter of 1997 and to reach 90 percent of China's population.[25] With one of its newscasts broadcast at 7:00 A.M. local time, Radio Free Asia is potentially in direct competition with domestic Chinese radio stations, including Central People's Radio, for morning radio listeners. The fact that Radio Free Asia's frequencies are not announced is not likely to significantly reduce the number of potential listeners in China. Indeed, shortwave dials on most Chinese radio receivers are so inexact that most listeners are constantly turning the dial in search of a clear and interesting foreign signal anyway. Publications in Chinese trade and internal policy journals show that Chinese broadcast authorities had felt the pressure of this new station long before it went into operation.[26] One report, for example, describes the station as a powerful U.S.-sponsored propaganda machine that will be on the air twenty-four hours a day, with personnel recruited from Chinese-speaking broadcasters and journalists in the United States and with broadcasting facilities in Taiwan to the east, the Philippines to the southeast, Thailand to the south, and Russia to the northwest.[27] If the Party feels threatened by the Voice of America, it now faces a more direct threat from Radio Free Asia, given this new station's more flexible policy, greater coverage of Chinese domestic affairs, and more straightforward political objectives. The official media's attacks on the new station may have the unexpected impact of publicizing the station among the Chinese population.

Direct satellite television broadcasting is another threat to the Party's monopolistic control of news and ideology. In addition to CNN and the BBC, more than twenty outside television channels broadcast by satellite into China, including both commercial and government-sponsored stations in such places as Hong Kong, Australia, Japan, France, Germany, and Russia.[28]

Although the Party and the government, out of fear of ideological influence from the West, generally forbids the reception of all external television, foreign satellite television has gained considerable influence because of a number of factors—among them, an initial relaxed broadcast policy, pursuit of commercial interests by local stations, and ineffectual enforcement of government regulations. As a reflection of relaxation of control, a 1990 government regulation stated that—with government approval and a license—education, science, news media, financial and trade institutions, and hotels and apartments for foreign guests could install satellite dishes to meet their business needs. The regulation, however, left a loophole by not specifically excluding individual households. Costing about the same as a television set, satellite dishes soon entered many homes in the early 1990s, especially once businesses realized a lot of money could be made by making, selling, and installing them. The media themselves publicized satellite reception both in their advertising and news reporting.[29] By late 1993, more than 11 million Chinese households had satellite dishes.[30]

In 1985, China began to lease international satellites to transmit domestic radio and television programs. By 1993, the country had opened eleven satellite television transmission channels, carrying twelve television programs and thirty sets of radio programs. It had also built 54,084 satellite ground reception stations.[31] As with shortwave radio, China originally moved into satellite broadcasting to improve signal reception and to expand the reach of domestic stations, particularly CCTV and the stations in Sichuan, Yunnan, Guizhou, and Xinjiang, where geography makes microwave transmission difficult. Once dishes are installed, however, they can receive all programs carried by the same satellite.

The most wide-reaching outside threat comes from Hong Kong–based StarTV. In 1992, three domestic television channels, CCTV-4, Guizhou TV, and Yunnan TV, began to transmit from the satellite AsiaSat I, the same one that carries StarTV's programming. Among the 11 million Chinese households that owned satellite dishes, 45 percent, i.e., 4.8 million, are capable of receiving StarTV. The Hong Kong station was established in 1990 as the first commercial pan-Asia television service. By leasing twelve transponders from AsiaSat 1, its programs reach thirty-eight countries with a potential audience of 2.7 billion. StarTV offers a total of five channels, including MTV, sports, news from BBC World Service Television (partially translated into Mandarin), family entertainment, and a channel of broadcasts in Mandarin, all on the air twenty-four hours a day. With the exception of the Chinese channel, which carries programs made in Hong Kong, Japan, Taiwan, and China, the other four channels are devoted mainly to Western programs obtained through contract suppliers or the international market.[32]

StarTV's Chinese language news program provided by BBC World Services Television is a major threat to the Party's control over information. In the words of Liu Xiliang, deputy minister of Radio, Film, and Television, the news program "contains a lot of distorted reports about China, and it frequently attacks China's domestic and foreign policies."[33]

The potential threat of outside television is much larger than that of foreign radio. Unlike radio, whose reception is individually decided and often poor, satellite television is often amplified and transmitted collectively by local cable networks and common antenna systems. In late 1993, StarTV programs were being seen in more than 30 million Chinese households.[34]

StarTV was originally controlled by the Hong Kong tycoon Li Ka-shing, who has many business interests in China and close ties with China's top leadership. Initially, China took its protest to StarTV and while the two sides were in dispute in July 1993, Li suddenly sold 64 percent of StarTV to Rupert Murdoch's News Corporation. This change of ownership from a friendly Hong Kong businessman to an international media baron, of course, further diminished the Chinese government's possibility of cutting off unwanted news.

Seeing the increasing popularity of Hong Kong and foreign television broadcasts and realizing the difficulty of exerting direct pressure on foreign broadcasters, the State Council in October 1993 banned unauthorized production, sale, and installation of satellite dishes.[35] StarTV programs, particularly its Chinese news program, were prohibited from being received and transmitted. Owners of all satellite dishes were required to report their existence and get proper licenses for them. Although this order put a temporary halt to the rapid expansion of StarTV audiences, it still proved to be partially ineffective. In addition to the massive work required to process licence applications for the millions of dishes already installed and the police strength required to remove illegal ones, local interests have further hindered the effectiveness of the ban.

For example, a Ministry of Radio, Film, and Television internal publication disclosed in July 1994 that despite the State Council ban in 1993, "a number of local cable networks and common antenna systems continue to receive and transmit foreign television programs, including StarTV."[36] In fact, under the very nose of the central authorities, Beijing Cable Television continued to relay sports programs of ESPN for fifteen hours daily until well into February 1994. It was forced to stop only because CCTV, which viewed it as a competitor for its own sports programs, put pressure on the Ministry of Radio, Film, and Television.[37]

In addition to illegal transmissions, many local television authorities are setting up subscription television, which could potentially provide a long-term redistribution network for StarTV.[38] Joseph M. Chan, for example, cited a cable network in Wuhan that already offers all but the news channels of StarTV. Chan also noted that there are policy differences over satellite television regulations. While ideological departments prefer tight control, technical departments that manufacture the dishes advocate a more liberal policy.[39]

Moreover, the simple technological factor that some of the domestic television programs are also carried by the same satellites that carry foreign programs makes control very difficult. Central ideological authorities are facing a formidable challenge from an increasingly influential technological configuration: the foreign satellite television broadcasting/local cable network transmission combination, linking international and local interests.

In addition to satellite television, telephone and fax lines also threaten the Party's information control. Such a threat was clearly demonstrated during the 1989 student movement when democracy activists outside the country faxed relevant news to those in China. Moreover, access to the Internet is expanding rapidly and the Party's Propaganda Department is again falling behind government departments that have technological and commercial interests in promoting it. China's first electronic mail message was sent through an international connection to a German mail gateway in September 1987. Among the more than 190 national and regional computer networks registered in China in 1996 are two major academic networks, the China Education and Research Network (CERNET), and the China Academic Science Network (CASNET). These two networks link hundreds of Chinese universities and research institutions to the outside world. In addition, the Ministry of Posts and Telecommunications operates the Chinanet, which began to provide commercial access to the Internet in May 1995. The Ministry of Electronic Industry is also installing an Internet service. By early 1996 about 100,000 people in China had logged onto the Internet. Government statistics estimate that market demand for personal computers will increase by 50 percent by the end of 1996 to 1.7 million units.[40] With the growing popularity of telephones and home computers, many more institutions and urban households will soon access the Internet. Unlike satellite television, where a receiving dish is easy to see, the Propaganda Department cannot simply ban computer and telephone use without crippling the economy.

Party Policies: A New Leap Backward?

Does the Party have a coherent policy regarding the news media and information or does it simply respond to challenges as much as possible? To be sure, there are officially sponsored research projects on media policies, such as the News Media and Modernization research project in the social sciences during the Seventh Five-Year Plan (1986–90). Its report, entitled *News Media and Modernization in China* (Xinwen shiye yu Zhongguo xiandaihua) and published in 1992, contains many proposals in specific areas, but it simply reiterates the Party line for media policy.[41] The official research project for the Eighth Five-Year Plan (1991–95), News Media Reform in China, was supposed to provide an overall scheme for media reform and strategies for its implementation.[42] Viewed from its outline, the report of this project, like the first, is not likely to suggest any major breakthroughs.

Despite attempts at the bureaucratization of decision-making in many areas, there is still a lack of institutionalization at the top of the political system with regard to basic political decisions in China. Moreover, there is also a "fundamental lack of agreement among the top political leadership over the *procedures* for sorting out policy alternatives."[43] This is certainly the case for media policy, a politically highly sensitive area. Indeed, the Party's policies toward the media have been rather chaotic in the 1990s. Uncertainty about leadership after the death of Deng Xiaoping has led to a regime of media policy-making that is characterized by short-term responses rather than long-term planning. Suppression of not only press freedom but also theoretical debate and academic freedom certainly has not contributed to the formation of a viable and coherent media policy.[44] Notwithstanding initial discussions of plans for the commercialization of the press by the State Press and Publications Administration following Deng's southern visit and the Party's Fourteenth National Congress in 1992, the Party still refuses to recognize commercialization as an explicit policy objective.

In late 1994, the Propaganda Department's six no's were circulated in top journalism and news media research circles:[45] no private media ownership, no shareholding of media organizations, no joint ventures with foreign companies, no discussion of the commodity nature of news, no discussion of a press law, and no openness for foreign satellite television. This is by far the most important media policy statement made by the Party in the 1990s. Its negative and colloquial formulation are illustrative of the ad hoc, informal, and reactive nature of media policy-making by the Party. As discussed previously, the commodification of news has been openly debated in theoretical literature and commercialism has been carried to the extreme in practice. Although preparation work for the drafting of a press law was halted in 1989, some people still pursue the idea. The first shareholding newspaper enterprise was established in Sichuan and received wide publicity in the media. And there are many proposals from domestic and foreign businesses for privately owned operations and joint ventures, especially from media interests in Hong Kong and Taiwan—indeed, there are already some small-scale joint ventures in business information and entertainment.[46]

Policy actions and statements in 1996, however, indicate that the Party is not only adhering to the six no's but also taking a more active and interventionist approach toward news media and ideology. Control of the business information sector has been strengthened. In January 1996, authorities centralized the distribution in China of business, economic, and financial news and data by ordering foreign news providers and their subscribers to register with the state monopoly, Xinhua News Agency. Although the Party had always limited foreign political news, as part of its differentiated approach to information control, it had allowed foreign business information. The opening of stock markets since the early 1990s and the increased volumes of foreign trade have created the need for timely access to business information by Chinese government departments and business organizations. Because business news has become a hot commodity, foreign news services such as Reuters and Dow Jones have developed a business worth tens of millions of dollars by selling up-to-the-minute stock market prices and news to more than one thousand private and company clients in China.[47] But the January 1996 regulations put strict curbs on foreign news services in reaping profits from this lucrative business. The new regulations allowed Xinhua to filter news that is "forbidden" or that "slanders or jeopardizes the national interest of China." Xinhua would also decide how and at what price foreign-produced business news would be distributed. The regulations banned foreign news services from setting up joint ventures with Chinese partners to distribute news in China. Nor were Chinese news media organizations allowed to subscribe to any foreign news services directly. While Western observers denounced the new regulations, arguing that they went against the idea of economic reform and will harm business in China, the Party had its own rationale. It contended that "the purpose of taking the move is to safeguard the state sovereignty, protect the legal rights and interests of the Chinese economic information users and promote the healthy development of the country's undertaking of economic information."[48] Political considerations and the intention to protect a domestic monopoly in the information market are thus the apparent reasons.

The same concerns have also underscored attempts at controlling the flow of foreign information and media content through other channels, notably the Internet and satellite and cable television. The Party paved the way for centralized control of the Internet in early 1996 by ordering that all Internet servers in China go through the Ministry of Post and Telecommunications. In September 1996, government authorities imposed broad censorship by blocking as many as one hundred English and Chinese Web sites, including those sponsored by U.S. news media such as the *Los Angeles Times,* the *Wall Street Journal,* the *Washington Post,* and CNN, as well as those sponsored by the Taiwan government and overseas human rights and dissidents groups. In addition, Internet users have been ordered to register with the police. Shortly before that, in mid-August, after trying in vain for five years to stop people from tuning into StarTV, the Ministry of Radio, Film, and Television finally ordered three domestic satellite television broadcasters to switch from AsiaSat 1 to AsiaSat 2, from which StarTV can transmit only encrypted channels.[49] Rather than peep into living rooms to see what channels are being watched, government inspectors now need only check how dishes are adjusted. This move was certainly another major setback to Rupert Murdoch's plan to enter the Chinese media market. Although the switch of satellites means more expensive fees for Chinese domestic broadcasters, the government has demonstrated its willingness to go to great lengths to beat Murdoch, who claims that the successful penetration of satellite television would spell the end of totalitarian regimes.

Similarly, despite initial reports of joint ventures in cable television, foreign attempts at getting a slice of the rapidly expanding Chinese cable market have not yielded results. To be sure, there have been many rumors about various joint ventures. In April 1996, Murdoch's StarTV reportedly was close to striking a deal with CCTV to set up a cable television network using rebroadcasted programming from its satellite operation. Later on, rumors about the establishment of a Chinese-language cable service known as Phoenix, involving Hong Kong–based partners with "good mainland connections," were also circulated in certain quarters. Both deals came to nothing.[50] Indeed, commenting on Murdoch's claim that he was on the verge of securing access to China through cable, an official at the Ministry of Radio, Film, and Television was quoted as saying: "Mr. Murdoch has a lot of beautiful dreams, but at this stage I don't think it will be possible in China for him to realize them."[51] Thus, while foreign media companies and Chinese news organizations are eager to do business together and are engaging in all kinds of deal-making, the central authorities, which have the final say, are not ready to break the six no's.

At the same time, the Party has tightened up control of domestic media content, including the popular commercial news media sector and small news media outlets on the margins of the system. It seems that it is taking back the limited space of relative autonomy that popular commercialized media outlets have carved out for themselves in the past few years. *Beijing Youth News* was disciplined in September 1996 after it ran a story about a poisoning case involving a state-run beverage producer and its publisher, Cui Enqing, was replaced by a more reliable figure.[52] *Economic Work Monthly,* a journal published in the remote Guizhou Province, was suspended in August 1996 after it carried an article criticizing claims that economic reforms were undermining Communist Party rule. *Focus* magazine in Shenzhen had suspended publication for two issues by November 1996 after a Hong Kong newspaper reported that the magazine defied propaganda authorities and ran a cover story on the anniversary of the 1966–76 Cultural Revolution. Propaganda authorities were also reportedly debating the fate of the Beijing-based magazine *Orient* in November 1996 after it defied a Propaganda Department gag on debates on the thoughts of writer Gu Zhun by running a series of book reviews of the *Collected Works of Gu Zhun.* Gu's writing had angered the Party before his death during the Cultural Revolution because he openly opposed authoritarianism and supported the rule of law and civil rights.[53]

There are also signs of renewed emphasis on orthodoxy and discipline by the central Party leadership on the wider political stage. On September 26, 1996, Party General Secretary Jiang Zemin paid a visit to the headquarters of the *People's Daily* to reinforce his grip. Jiang reiterated the Party principle and the primacy of positive propaganda in a hardline speech. Implicitly addressing popular sayings in the news media that an editor-in-chief who does not know how to make money is not a good one, Jiang emphasized that the news media must be run by people of the political type and that "the leadership of the news media must be tightly held in the hands of those who are loyal to Marxism, the Party, and the people." He also insisted that the news media must put the objective of maintaining a "correct political direction" ahead of any other considerations.[54]

Jiang's renewed emphasis on ideological orthodoxy and strict adherence to the Party line was further articulated and formalized in the Party's resolution on the construction of "socialist spiritual civilization," passed at the Sixth Plenary Session of the Fourteenth Communist Party Central Committee Congress on October 10, 1996. The resolution not only reiterated the main ideas of Jiang's speech at the *People's Daily* but also went further in a number of specific areas.[55] It stressed that the Party must strengthen the macro-management of news media by making the transition from an emphasis on quantitative growth in the number of media outlets to the quality and effectiveness of propaganda. It continued that media outlets that "have repeatedly violated regulations and created problems" or have failed to meet the basic operational requirements must be closed down. While noting that the news media should continue to explore multiple channels of financing, the resolution called on central and local governments to provide more funding to media and cultural institutions, specifying that the rate of increase in government funding should not drop below the rate of increase in government revenues.

Neither Jiang's speech nor the Party's resolution mentioned the term "journalism reform." Nor did they have much to say about the commercialization of news media—except for pressing journalists to devote themselves to Party journalism; resist money worship, denounce paid journalism, and maintain high ethical standards. In contrast to the intense hard-line actions and harsh rhetoric of 1996, Jiang's report to the Party's Fifteenth National Congress in September 1997 took a low-key approach. It required the news media to adhere to the Party principle and to maintain correct guidance over public opinion but it did not explicitly invoke the term "mouthpiece." In fact, the report downplayed the political role of the news media and said nothing specific about journalism at all. It referred to the news media only as part of the Party's "cultural undertakings" and spoke in very general terms about the need to strengthen their supervision in order to optimize "their structures" and improve "their quality."[56] It is not clear whether the report signaled any change in the Party's policy toward the news media. A more likely interpretation is that since the Party had already consolidated its control in 1996, it simply did not want to bring the issue up again.

One thing is clear, however. The contradictions and tensions in the news media system will be further intensified under the current regime. The Party cannot simply pretend that nothing has happened and that it can resort to old forms of control by simply reiterating the Party line. The enormous energy for commercialization and democratization will find outlets one way or another. Extreme control of domestic news, for example, will inevitably create a willing audience for foreign news outlets like the Voice of America and Radio Free Asia. While the

Party can jail individuals, the lack of formal public channels for the expression of different views within the Party means that "rumors" about Chinese politics, especially about power struggles at the top and differences of opinion among central leaders, will continue to proliferate and feed the Hong Kong and Taiwan news media, which will send them back to China. Indeed, even the Party leadership has acknowledged that those engaged in "rumor-mongering" include Party members.[57] Similarly, although the Party prohibits Chinese businesses from owning and operating general interest media, they have entered and will continue to enter the media sector through the back door, engendering Chinese forms of business control of the media that are more blunt than in the West. Finally, despite official bans, many organizations and individuals will continue to turn their satellite dishes toward StarTV and find ways to receive news from foreign news services and bypass Party censors on the Internet, while the Murdochs and their representatives will continue to knock at the doors of the Party's Propaganda Department.

9

Media Reform beyond Commercialization

In the West, liberal and critical media scholars and persons involved in the alternative media alike criticize the limitations imposed by advertising and the inadequacy of the commercial media system as a democratic forum. In addition to defending public broadcasters such as the BBC and the Canadian Broadcasting Corporation, democratic media reformers argue for a "maximum feasible decommodification and 're-embedding' of communications media in the social life of civil society as vital for freedom from state and market censorship."[1] In China, while traditional Party ideologues continue to denounce the negative impacts of commercialization and may even attempt to curb its wave, some newly commercialized media outlets are considered by reformers as the most promising in the media system. When the media are under strict Party supervision and are plagued with more blunt and problematic forms of commercialism, it is not surprising that media reformers see the establishment of "genuine" market logic—the selling of media audiences to advertisers—as the objective of reform. Many media reformers, particularly those in the academy and in various levels of media management, are currently pushing for the further commercialization of the news media.

Although some have argued that the Party principle and the market are not incompatible, arguments for further commercialization contain a potential challenge to Party logic. While few have held that editorial freedom is necessary for market success, many have begun to maintain that if the media are to be run as businesses, they should have relative autonomy in editorial policy. When commercial logic is carried to its conclusion, as some have done, it means that just as factory managers have autonomy in determining what to produce, editors should have the right to determine what to report; and just as factory products are manufactured to meet the needs of consumers, news should be produced to meet the needs of readers and audiences, not just the propaganda imperatives of the Party. Moreover, if the market is to play a major role in the allocation of resources, then communicative resources such as the broadcast spectrum should be commercialized and distributed through the market, not monopolized by the state. But there is evidence of reification of the market in much of the literature advocating commercialization of the Chinese news media.

Full-Scale Commercialization?

To be sure, as John Keane has put it, market mechanisms are useful accessories of a complex and pluralistic civil society. Market transactions enhance a society's productiveness, flexibility, and efficiency. Similarly, "market-influenced media can also function as important countervailing forces in the process of producing and circulating opinions" because they are "sites of signification that often run counter to opinion-making monopolies operated by churches and states."[2]

It is precisely for this reason that the introduction of market mechanisms into the Chinese economy, including the current spin-off to the news media sector, has its progressive aspects. Commercialization has led to the development of an elaborate media infrastructure and has made some parts of the system more responsive to readers and audiences. It has also modified the elitism of media professionals and given rise to populist sensibilities. But because of its inherent limitations and structural biases, the market is not a value-neutral mechanism. It is important not to equate reform with commercialization or reduce reform to commercialization.

In the West, a growing critical literature has raised serious questions about the adequacy of the market model as a democratic form of communication. Profound contradictions between the democratic ideals and the institutional arrangements of market-driven media have been identified. The mass media have been linked to a "decline of democracy" or "the crisis of democracy."[3] Strong arguments have been made that, despite formal institutional independence, the media act more like lap dogs than watchdogs because of institutional pressures. Indeed, the operation of advertising logic in the free market has acted historically as a powerful and effective form of political censorship.[4] The media's effort to satisfy the audience is not democracy of the one-person-one-vote variety. It has been argued that "market relations can inhibit popular democratic communication just as easily as the state."[5] While acknowledging the progressive functions of the market, John Keane, for example, has also criticized the structural limitations of the market in the following terms: "Market competition produces market censorship. Private ownership of the media produces private caprice. Those who control the market sphere of producing and distributing information determine . . . which opinions officially gain entry into the 'marketplace of opinions.'"[6]

Moreover, "individuals are treated as market-led consumers, not as active citizens with rights and obligations."[7] The peculiar nature of news as a commodity means that "the logic of maximizing return often conflicts with the logic of maximizing public understanding."[8] Thus, "serving the market was not the same as serving the public."[9] In contrast to the notion of consumer sovereignty, critics have argued that commercial media do not actually "give people what they want" but rather part of what some of the people think they want. Commercial media "satisfy precisely those needs that are compatible with the marketing of commodities. Needs that no one can make money from or that threaten our consumer culture are left unattended. These include the need for democratic communication."[10]

It is clear that press freedom resting on the market is not sufficient for a fully democratic system of communication. Albert Camus's 1944 statement that "the press is free when it does not depend on either the power of government or the power of money" has been strongly felt in democratic circles in the West.[11] Normative theories of the press, for example, have long gone beyond the four proposed by Fredrick S. Siebert, Theodore Peterson, and Wilbur Schramm.[12] Already in the early 1960s, instead of adopting the us-versus-them cold war mentality and liberal framework, Raymond Williams proposed four models of the press (authoritarian, paternal, commercial, and democratic) that refuse to equate the market model with a democratic model.[13] More recently, a "democratic participant" model has been elaborated in the West to take into account emerging democratic media theories and practices.[14] Drawing from the experiences of the Nordic press, Robert Picard has distinguished a "social democratic" version, which, in contrast to "libertarian" and "social responsibility" theories, provides legitimation for public intervention and collective ownership to ensure media independence not only from the state but also from other vested interests.[15] James Curran, meanwhile, has put forth a "radical democratic tradition" of the media that can be differentiated from the traditional liberal model on the one hand and from Stalinist practices and Marxist critiques of the liberal model on the other hand.[16] This long-standing critique of the limitations of the liberal model and traditional binary thinking about press systems has also been eloquently articulated by eight communication scholars at the University of Illinois, where the four theories of the press originated several decades ago.[17] With penetrating critiques of both its external articulation with the cold war logic and its internal theoretical and empirical inconsistencies and inadequacies, these scholars have given the four theories of the press a decent funeral. While these scholars do not offer a clearly defined alternative model, they unequivocally call for alternatives that are neither profit-motivated nor totalitarian. They have also demonstrated that any thoughts about alternatives should go beyond the liberal equation between a "free" press and "the U.S. system of privately capitalized, profit-driven newspaper publishing."[18]

Currently, the Chinese media are celebrating the liberating effects of the commercial logic of dependence on advertising—no dependence on government subsidies or paid journalism. To be sure, pursuing market success through attractive media content is more desirable than simply producing single-minded Party propaganda. For journalists, earning a decent salary from a commercially successful news media operation is much more dignified than taking a bribe or blurring advertising and news functions. However, even if the market logic is fully established and functions "normally" without all the illegal and unethical practices, as critics of commercial media systems in the West have demonstrated, serving the market is not the same as serving the public.

Indeed, full-scale commercialization may lead to destruction of some of the gains of past reform. In the 1980s special interest newspapers run by China's version of civil organizations grew markedly. Although their parent organizations lack the autonomy to fully express the interests of their readers because readers are considered political, social, and cultural constituents instead of consumers, once political control is loosened these papers could become potential forums for different economic and social groups.

As discussed in chapter 3, commercialization has already led to the decline of newspapers oriented toward the peasantry. It remains to be seen whether specialized organs such as workers' and women's newspapers can attract enough advertising to become commercially viable. Certainly full-scale commercialization would force some of these papers to close while others would have to turn themselves into general interest papers, thus destroying the current structure. Such a tendency is already apparent both in the expanded pages of specialized papers and their weekend supplements. For those that continued to survive as special interest papers, heavy dependence on advertising would certainly change their editorial orientation. For example, instead of resisting commodification and objectification of women, a women's paper might end up contributing to them.

In addition to commercialized financing, reforms in media micro-management have so far focused on introducing market mechanisms in the newsroom, including connecting journalists' news output with material incentives, increasing income differentials among journalists, and replacing job tenure with short-term (usually one-year) contracts. Such measures are meant to increase productivity but frequently introduce new forms of control as well. The lack of job security, for example, may encourage self-censorship.

Currently, many media organizations are confronting poor news quality and low morale among journalists. Although media management and trade journal articles tend to blame equality of pay, job tenure, and lack of competition for these problems, they result more from political constraints than from the absence of market mechanisms. If solutions to political problems are mistakenly sought through commercial means, the result could be dual repression.

Indeed, the lack of productivity and creativity have less to do with job security and material incentives than with the lack of autonomy and the sense of responsibility that comes with it. If topics are assigned from above anyway, why bother to be diligent or to pursue investigative journalism, which might cause political trouble? Already, management and personnel reforms in Shanghai People's Radio have led to the conclusion that increased journalistic autonomy, reduced levels of bureaucratic control in news production, and, most importantly, a sense of job satisfaction derived from the relevance of their work to the daily life of their audiences are journalists' principle "motivating forces."[19]

My impressions of journalists working under different institutional settings support this conclusion. Those with relatively more autonomy in news reporting have a better sense of achievement and job satisfaction. They are more dedicated and derive more social meaning from their work. On the other hand, although some journalists actually have a higher income thanks to paid journalism, their lack of opportunities to practice enterprising journalism make them feel that journalism is just a means of earning an income.

Another case in point is competition. One argument put forward by those in favor of commercialization is that the current system lacks a mechanism for competition, which a market mechanism can bring about. But what type of competition and at what level? Without press freedom, competition often means merely rivalry in the format and presentation style of safe subjects. Only with different media sectors and different opinions will competition be more meaningful. In the broadcast sector, for example, specialized radio and television channels compete by offering the same fare of light entertainment. Thus, while Party control has created a monotonous media system, market competition also has a homogenizing impact on media content. It may well create "rivalry in conformity."[20]

The most crucial issue, though, is the relationship between private ownership of news media and press freedom. In eastern Europe, as Slavko Splichal has observed, after decades of a state-controlled economy, "it is largely believed that freedom of ownership and particularly private ownership are the guarantors of democracy and a free press. Privatization is seen as the only instrument that can reduce and possibly abolish state intervention in the media."[21] In China, the issue of private ownership of media of communication is still being suppressed, despite its brief appearance during the 1989 democracy movement when an argument was made that the right of individual citizens to publish newspapers is inherent in the constitutional guarantee of press freedom.[22] While some reformers have explicitly argued for private ownership, others use the more broad and vague term of nonofficial newspapers (*minban*). Since the 1990s, many entrepreneurs have wanted to establish private and profit-oriented news operations.

Certainly, the establishment of independent media outlets would be the most important step toward the democratization of the media system. But there is the inevitable question of exactly what kind of ownership and financing structures independent outlets should take. It is important to note that although privately owned, advertising-supported, and profit-oriented media have traditionally been associated with press freedom in the West, and that there is a common assumption that property rights are the foundation of press freedom, there is also a growing literature that challenges these views. Thus, "the case for equating press freedom with property rights is far from conclusive."[23] Even in the United States, "authoritative accounts of the theory of the American First Amendment do not always support the equation of economic freedom with press freedom nor the argument for private ownership as a necessary condition."[24] It is important, therefore, not to equate independent news media with privately owned and profit-seeking media.

Toward a Framework for a Democratic News Media System in China

The current intertwining of Party control and market forces is highly problematic, but complete commercialization and the replacement of Party control by market control alone will not lead to a democratized system of media communication either. Media developments in the former Soviet Union and Eastern Europe are illustrative. While governments still control the broadcast media in one form or another in these postsocialist societies, the print media, newly freed through progressive legislation that abolishes formal censorship, are facing strong economic pressures and are in danger of falling under the control of domestic and international capital.[25] The print media in Russia, for example, after press freedom during the perestroika years of the late 1980s, have faced severe economic pressures and become increasingly dependent on government subsidies. Lacking a material foundation for freedom, the press "is becoming a kind of product that not many people care to produce, sell, or buy," while the government has quickly learned "that economic pressure provides as effective a tool for control over editorial policies as did the ideological and political dictate exercised by the Communists."[26]

Although market forces have partially taken over the Chinese news media and the contractual system has served as a surrogate for private media ownership in some cases, the Party still rejects private ownership of and direct domestic and foreign business involvement in the news media. The Party still rejects complete commercialization of the news media as a matter of principle, and if the policy directives of September and October 1996 are any indication, there may be a conservative backlash against further commercialization in communication and culture. It is important, and perhaps still possible, for those who pursue media democratization not to reduce reform to commercialization. This would require critically examining the implications of the current wave of commercialization, insisting on the specificity of the media industry, and not allowing commercial logic to take over completely. Since the Party is still rhetorically committed to the socialist values of justice and equality, it is vital for democratic forces to appropriate the Party's language and struggle for a different articulation of this language (including key terms like "socialism with Chinese characteristics," "reform," and a "socialist market economy"), rather than jump from anticommercialization to market fetishism. Neither Party journalism as usual nor market-driven journalism speaks to the democratizing impetus that China sorely needs.[27]

In her study of rural economic reform in the early 1980s, Pat Howard warned: "There is a very real danger that overcoming utopianism will mean reversion to a pragmatism more or less devoid of social ideals. There is a danger that the rejection of the moralizing of the Cultural Revolution will involve a rejection of ethics altogether. There is also the danger that rejection of large-scale class struggle will involve elimination of struggle over questions of equity and justice. All of this would add up to a triumph of pragmatism over practical reason."[28]

This is precisely what is happening in China in the 1990s. Although there is plenty of room to get rich and get corrupt, there is little space for political imagination. The Party has sunk into ideological and moral bankruptcy. Its objective of "socialism with Chinese characteristics" has little credibility, and although there is nothing wrong in defining a cultural dimension of modernization, the Party's social engineering project of building "socialist spiritual civilization" in ideology, culture, and morality is highly problematic. Binary thinking and extreme politicization of criticism has made any analytical thinking difficult, if not impossible. In the late 1980s and early 1990s, if you mentioned concepts like "cultural imperialism" in some academic and cultural circles, you were likely to be "accused of harbouring leftist sentiments" that "should be buried along with the Cultural Revolution."[29] You were necessarily identified with conservative Party ideologues. Indeed, to some Chinese scholars, the flow of Western, especially American, commercial culture and values to China should be seen as natural as the flow of water from a higher vintage point to a lower one.[30] In the mid-1990s, however, the pendulum seemed to have swung to the opposite extreme, with raising nationalistic and anti-foreign, especially anti-American, sentiments. In 1988 and early 1989, "River Elegy," the popular television program that served as a political manifesto for liberal reformers, celebrated "Blue Civilization" (Western civilization) and condemned "Yellow Civilization" (Chinese civilization). In the summer of 1996, however, the best-seller *China Can Say No: Political and Emotional Choices in the Post-Cold War Era* (Zhongguo keyi shuobu: Lengzhan huoshidai de zhengzhi yu qinggan xuanze) has gone to the other extreme by espousing ultranationalist sentiments mixed with harsh criticisms of post–cold war American government and media treatments of China. Written by five young journalists and lecturers who recounted their personal experiences and opinions that evolved from admiring to reviling the United States, this book has captivated its readers with chapter titles such as "Burn Down Hollywood" and "The Blue Sky Must Die, the Yellow Sky Must Rule." Although Party authorities have disassociated themselves with the book and the official press has even criticized it, it must have added confidence to the current leadership's own attempt to fill the ideological vacuum left by the reforms with appeals to nationalism and traditional Chinese values.

Outside China, some dissidents are still fighting over whether the 1989 democracy movement should be critically assessed.[31] Reflection on it can be viewed with suspicion and runs the danger of being perceived as "standing in line" with the Party.[32] It is very difficult to articulate anything outside the dominant ideological framework that defines democracy in liberal terms, anything beyond the "Capitalism Triumphant: No Third Way" mode of thinking.[33] The result is a volatile scene of extreme political and ideological polarization.

But the goal of democratic socialism has not been totally abandoned. Inside China, media scholars such as Gan Xifen and Sun Xupei are trying to define some form of socialist press freedom and ideological pluralism that differs from either Party journalism or market-driven journalism. Outside China, Ruan Ming, for example, has spoken out about the "ideological bankruptcy" of the 1989 democracy movement and argued that movement leaders, Party reformers, and journalists "should keep in mind that the goal of socialism is not modernization through authoritarianism, but human emancipation."[34]

The Chinese people suffered when the political imagination of one man, Mao Zedong, was imposed as articles of faith on the whole population. The lack of fundamental change in political communication means that again there is the danger that the whole nation may suffer from the domination of the pragmatism of another old man, Deng Xiaoping. While the Cultural Revolution is remembered for its "Great Criticisms," Deng's closure of any substantial public debate on the future direction of the country and the ethical and political implications of reforms is no less problematic. Both are undemocratic. Nor is the post-Deng leadership's reaffirmation of ideological orthodoxy and formal codification of Deng Xiaoping Theory a viable and attractive alternative.

While some people still believe that China's capitalist revolution will eventually lead to a democratic political system, there is no necessary relationship between capitalism and political democracy even though capitalism and liberal democracy have been ideologically and historically fused together in the West. Indeed, there is a real possibility that global capitalism will become increasingly authoritarian. Although the current hegemony of neo-liberalism makes it difficult to imagine and discuss alternatives, capitalism is not the only possible future for humanity. Nor does liberal democracy have an exclusive claim on democracy.[35] To be sure, just as the market has an vital role in the organization of human society, liberal democracy contains important principles that constitute significant achievements of human civilization. Such principles include the rule of law, equality before the law, respect for individual human dignity and rights, accountability of the government to the governed, and the right to participate in choosing those who rule. On the other hand, the brutality and bankruptcy of Stalinism and Maoism do not invalidate critiques of the fundamental flaws and blind spots of liberalism, capitalism, and liberal democracy. Here are just a few of the criticisms.[36]

First, liberalism virtually equates freedom with ownership of property. Based on the notion of acquisitive, possessive individualism, capitalism has produced massive poverty as the counterpart to the extreme concentration of wealth.

Second, liberalism assumes the nation-state as the repository of political virtue and the guarantor of political rights. But the nation-state faces dissolution from above by the process of globalization and the associated growth and power of unaccountable, hierarchical supranational organizations and arrangements that represent elite interests, such as the World Trade Organization and the International Monetary Fund, and disintegration from below by the growing anarchy in many developing nations, by the growing millions of effectively stateless refugees and "guest" workers, and by the upsurge of racism, ethnic violence, and micro-nationalism in many countries, including Europe and North America. Citizenship based on nation-states is not enough.

Third, from an ecological perspective, liberalism has no notion of the limits of growth. Its assumption of the limitless expansion of human wants leads to a continuing crisis of overconsumption and destruction of resources and local ecologies.

Fourth, the homogenizing impact of market relations has undermined more traditional values of kinship, community, place, ethics, and mutual obligation and has contributed to the backlashes of racism, fundamentalist religions, and micro-nationalism in many parts of the world.

Fifth, from a feminist perspective, neither liberalism's notion of elected, representative institutions as the embodiment of the public sphere nor its definitions of individual rights in the private sphere addresses the political economy of the domestic household and the exploitation of women's labor.

Finally, despite its achievements, liberal democracy is insufficiently democratic—partly because of the discrepancy, oft noted by socialists, between formal legal and political equality on the one hand and substantive inequalities of social class, which lead to inequalities in communicative and political power, on the other. A related critique is that the political institutions of contemporary liberal democracies (parties, elections, parliaments) sharply curtail the opportunities for genuine political participation. They have become simply mechanisms by which citizens can at best select candidates and parties from a narrow range of alternatives. Once in power, those parties are in turn so strongly influenced by the society's most powerful unelected elites and systemic problems (e.g. the debt crisis of the capitalist state) that they can no longer function as popular representatives. North America's populist revolts, symbolized by Ross Perot in the United States and the

Reform party in Canada, are partly products of a political malaise, of a perceived gap between the system's democratic legitimation and its actual performance.

While democracy has often been defined in a narrow sense as "meaning simply a system of choosing and authorizing governments," as C. B. Macpherson has effectively argued, broadly democracy "has always contained an idea of human equality, not just equality of opportunity to climb a class ladder, but such an equality as could only be fully realized in a society where no class was able to dominate or live at the expense of others."[37] Thus, democracy not only has a political dimension, as a system of government that provides "to the people (all members of a collectivity) a certain degree of political equality and the fullest possible involvement in procedures for arriving at collective decisions about public affairs,"[38] but also a social dimension. It also means a kind of society.

Much has been written on prospects for political democratization in China.[39] The question is not whether China should or can be democratized but which definition of democracy will prevail in the process. Indeed, even the Communist party proclaims that its objective is to build a "civilized, democratic and prosperous China." In the West, where democracy in the narrow sense has been achieved, democratic forces are struggling for a broadened definition of sustainable democracy with a focus on equality while fighting against the deterioration of existing democratic institutions and various anti-liberal democratic backlashes. In China, democratic forces should struggle to achieve democracy in the narrow sense while at the same time guarding against losing the progressive gains of the socialist revolution and whatever has been achieved in the name of a broad definition of democracy. These forces should aim at the democratization of all aspects of the Chinese society, including political, economic, social, and communication and cultural spheres, as all these are interrelated and interdependent. Indeed, one does not have to choose between economic and social rights on the one hand and civil and political rights on the other: "One can have both food and freedom."[40] Neoauthoritarian theory and the success of a handful of authoritarian market societies in Asia notwithstanding, there are many instances of such regimes that have failed in providing the basic needs for the poor. On the other hand, there are examples of states that have succeeded in achieving economic prosperity while protecting essential political freedoms. The social democracies in northern Europe are good examples. Some Asian and African countries have also opted to secure basic political freedom and democratic governance, achieve economic prosperity, and strive for more equitable distribution of wealth among different social groups at the same time.[41]

Such an option would necessarily involve the reconceptualization and restructuring of the complex relations among the state, the media, and civil society. The party-state system must be democratized through measures such as the strengthening of existing democratic institutions, including the National People's Congress, the introduction of a multiparty system, and the democratization of the Communist party itself. The Party's pseudo-version of civil organizations would need to become truly independent, and new ones would need to be encouraged. The dominant ideology of Marxism, Leninism, Mao Zedong Thought, and its latest addition, Deng Xiaoping Theory, should be critically reexamined, adapted, and amended to allow ideological diversity within the broad framework of socialist pluralism. A reinvigorated democratic state that has popular support and a strong commitment to economic and social justice, a vigorous civil society guaranteed by democratic state institutions, and a reconstructed news media functioning as an independent public sphere are all urgently needed to check both unaccountable political power and the structural biases of market forces.

In the area of communication, a broad definition of democratization means that it is necessary to struggle not only for freedom but also for equality and for a sense of community. While freedom and rights of communication defined in the traditional liberal sense of negative liberty is a necessary base, as Slavko Splichal has contended, "the question of democratization ultimately rests with a *material base* that does (or does not) provide for the realization of the political and social rights declared in a society."[42] Democratization should dismantle such barriers to communication as class privilege, gender preference, racial discrimination, exclusion on the basis of age, regional disparities, and a division of labor that awards authority to a relative few and mandates compliance to a large majority. Writing in the context of post-socialist societies in eastern Europe, Splichal argues that a process of societal democratization implies a transition from "political democracy" in the strict sense to "social democracy" infiltrating various spheres of civil society. Democratization implies and should mean more than the overthrow of a government that was not elected democratically and the turn to a market economy. It should also involve a concern over the "the management and control of information *within and between groups.*"[43] This observation is highly relevant to the Chinese struggle for democratization. The democratization of media communication should mean much more than a press law that protects journalists from the heavy hand of the Party and allows the publication of private newspapers.

As Raymond Williams puts it, the "basic choice is between control and freedom, but in actual terms it is more often a choice between a measure of control and a measure of freedom, and the substantial argument is about how these can be combined."[44] Denis McQuail has grouped the basic values of public communication in terms of three fundamental principles, freedom, equality, and order/cohesion.[45] Each value is further divided into a number of subsets, including independent status, access, diversity of supply and content, objectivity of content, control and solidarity in the social domain, and quality and authenticity/identity in the cultural domain. These values, of course, are both complementary and contradictory, and none is absolute. The struggle for a democratic communication system requires finding the best ways of achieving a maximum balance in their realization. In China, for example, freedom has been compromised to its extreme in the name of achieving equality and cohesion, but the result has been neither equality nor cohesion. Similarly, the Party has persistently invoked the relativity of freedom to suppress freedom. While there is no absolute freedom and autonomy, there is a substantial difference between legally sanctioned freedom, relative autonomy, and none at all. At the same time, while expanding media freedom, it is also important to safeguard and expand equality, including media services and access for such groups as children, women, peasants, seniors, and ethnic minorities, particularly in light of mass commercialization. Basic access to the news media has been very unequal in China. For example, while most of the urban population enjoys multiple radio and television channels and, increasingly, Internet connections, close to 20 percent of the population in the countryside receives no radio or television signals at all.[46]

If anything, experience makes clear that the domination of one mechanism of control—either the market or the state—is unsatisfactory for a democratic system of communication. At present, the idea of a multisector, multitiered, pluralistic media system organized around different principles and logics within a democratically constructed legal framework is perhaps the best alternative. The struggle for such a system should be part of the struggle for the democratization of Chinese society.

Strikingly, but perhaps not surprisingly, there are elements of similarity between media democratization proposals developed by democratic forces in China and in the West. In the conclusion to the November 1988 survey report on press reform, perhaps the most eloquent and best-formulated statement produced by the Chinese journalism reform movement so far, two high-profile institutional coauthors, the Journalism Research Institute of the Chinese Academy of Social Sciences and the Capital Journalism Society, wrote: "Ideological pluralism means ending the monopoly structure of the Party press. It means that government press, partisan press, public service press [*gonggong xinwen shiye*] and civic press [*minying xinwen shiye*] develop and compete on an equal basis within a constitutional and legal framework. It means a multi-dimensional structure with different tiers, different levels and different forms of ownership."[47]

Elsewhere, ideas such as "many voices, one direction [socialism]," originally proposed by People's University professor Gan Xifen, and "a multi-tiered, multi-structured socialist press system with the Party press at the center," originally proposed by Sun Xupei, have also been expressed.

There are similarities between these ideas and James Curran's "model of a democratic media system," which "draws upon and composes features derived from the practice of different European countries." In this model, a core sector is surrounded by media organizations that are organized on different principles. The core is composed of general interest TV channels that "reach a mass audience and provide a common forum of societal debate . . . and a common symbolic environment that reinforces ties of mutuality." The peripheral sectors are composed of "media reaching more differentiated audiences, and are organized in a way that is designed to produce a vigorous plurality of competing voices," including a private enterprise sector, a social market sector, a professional sector, and a civil sector.[48]

While Curran's model reflects the centrality of television, the proposals of Chinese scholars have been heavily biased toward print journalism, primarily because many leading scholars were press scholars to begin with and because the press has been at the center of both Party journalism and journalism theory in China. But such a bias is no longer justified. Given that television has become the most important medium, especially for rural residents who have skipped the era of the popular press and jumped directly into the age of satellites and cable, television should be at the center of reconstruction of the media system. On the other hand, while Curran's model assigns a significant role to a private enterprise sector, which is the dominant sector in current Western media systems, Chinese scholars have maintained the centrality of the Party/state sector and few have so far explicitly advocated the establishment of privately owned and profit-driven news media. If, as Sun Xupei writes, the ultimate goal of media democratization is the liberation of the communications media from subordination either to private capital or to the state,[49] then there is no reason why a media sector that is controlled by private capital and driven by the profit motive should be introduced in China in the first place.

Although discussions about democratic alternatives sound extremely idealistic at the present, it is important to note that a democratized media system does not have to start from scratch in China. A publicly owned commercialized sector has already gained ground within the current Party-controlled media system. An independent and regulated commercial news media sector can be established on the basis of existing advertising-supported "economic" broadcasting channels and evening papers. A civil sector in the print media can be (re)established through transformation of existing newspapers run by women's federations, trade unions, and other social groups as part of the process of reconstituting an independent civil society. These newspapers will serve both as channels of communication among members of a group and as the collective voice of special groups in discussion of public issues. Similarly, the idea of newspapers run by professionals without external political and commercial control (*tongren banbao*) has always been an important dream of Chinese journalists under different political regimes. This sector can take the form of subscription-based, nonprofit journalist cooperatives democratically managed and operated in a nonhierarchical structure so as to ensure a maximum of freedom and a minimum of organizational constraint. The first step toward establishing such papers could be the transformation of *Guangming Daily* in Beijing and *Wenhui Bao* in Shanghai by cutting their institutional ties to the Party and reorganizing them into worker-owned cooperatives. Both have some tradition of professionalism and nonpartisanship, especially before 1957.

In broadcasting too, a professional sector has already emerged in embryonic form through the contracting-out arrangement of CCTV's News Commentary Department. A civic sector can be established by the assignment of special channels to civil organizations such as trade unions and women's federations. Taxes and revenues from the commercial sector, as well as an advertising surtax administered by an independent body, can be used to provide financial support to nonstate, noncommercial sectors.

Community space is also important. Here again, the infrastructure is already in place. The key issue is democratization. In broadcasting, for example, there is already an elaborate infrastructure for community programming in various independent local cable networks. The current drive for technological standardization and convergence of unconnected cable networks into one big network in metropolitan areas should not lead to the elimination of the relative independence of the constituent local networks. Local cable as a communication resource should not simply be used as a propaganda organ of local Party authorities and a profitable outlet for Hong Kong, Taiwan, and foreign videos. Local expression needs to go beyond "on call" popular songs to include the discussion of community issues and the promotion of local and folk cultures.

There can be no single agent of change. Reformers within the Party, journalists, and democratic forces throughout society must act together to bring it about. The spring of 1989 was a moment of hope, but Party reformers and democratic forces failed to forge a successful alliance and win the battle for democracy. However, the objectives articulated by these forces in 1989 are still highly relevant, especially in light of the current intermingling of Party logic and market logic and the Party's possible abandonment of the project of media reform altogether:

> The overall objective of journalism reform is the democratization of every aspect of news communication and the establishment of a Chinese socialist news media system that has a high level of democracy, a comprehensive legal framework, unimpeded communication channels, a fair structure, and maximum vitality.[50]

> In short, the key issue in reforming both the economic system and the political system is democracy. The crucial point to economic reform is the democratization of the economic sphere so that producers obtain economic rights and financial benefits and assume responsibilities as masters of society. Vitality and efficiency are the results of voluntary participation on the basis of democracy. Herein lies the true meaning of journalism reform as well.[51]

Notes

Introduction

1. Joseph M. Chan, "Commercialization without Independence: Trends and Tensions of Media Development in China," in *China Review 1993*, ed. Joseph Cheng Yu-skek and Maurice Brosseau (Hong Kong: Chinese University Press, 1993), 25.2.

2. Joseph Fewsmith, "Institutions, Informal Politics, and Political Transition in China," *Asian Survey* 36.3 (Mar. 1996): 243.

3. Chin-Chuan Lee, "Ambiguities and Contradictions: Issues in China's Changing Political Communication," in *China's Media, Media's China*, ed. Chin-Chuan Lee (Boulder: Westview Press, 1994), 16.

4. Tsan-Kuo Chang, Chin-Hsien Chen, and Guo-Qiang Zhang, "Rethinking the Mass Propaganda Model: Evidence from the Chinese Regional Press," *Gazette* 51.3 (1993): 175.

5. See, for example, Franklin Houn, *To Change a Nation* (New York: Free Press, 1961); Alan P. L. Liu, *Communication and National Integration in Communist China* (Berkeley: University of California Press, 1971); and Frederick T. C. Yu, *Mass Persuasion in Communist China* (New York: Frederick A. Praeger, 1964).

6. See, for example, Judy Polumbaum, "The Chinese Press and Its Discontents," *China Exchange News* 16.4 (Dec. 1988): 2–5; Judy Polumbaum, "Outpaced by Events: Learning, Unlearning, and Relearning to Be a Journalist in Post–Cultural Revolution China," *Gazette* 48.2 (1991): 129–46; Judy Polumbaum, "The Tribulations of China's Journalists after a Decade of Reform," in *Voices of China: The Interplay of Politics and Journalism in China*, ed. Chin-Chuan Lee (New York: Guilford Press, 1990), 33–68; Lynn T. White III, "All the News: Structure and Politics in Shanghai's Reform Media," in *Voices of China*, 88–110; Yu Jinglu, "The Structure and Function of Chinese Television, 1979–1989," in *Voices of China*, 69–87; James Lull, *China Turned On: Television, Reform, and Resistance* (London: Routledge, 1991); Glen Lewis and Sun Wanning, "Discourses about 'Learning from Japan' in Post-1979 Mainland Chinese Management Journals," *Issues and Studies* 30.5 (May 1994): 63–76; and Chang, Chen, and Zhang, "Rethinking the Mass Propaganda Model."

7. Chin-Chuan Lee, "Mass Media: Of China, about China," in *Voices of China*, 3–32.

8. Lee, "Ambiguities and Contradictions," 12.

9. See, for example, Yu Huang, "Peaceful Evolution: The Case of Television Reform in Post-Mao China," *Media, Culture, and Society* 16.2 (1994): 217–41; Leonard L. Chu, "Continuity and Change in China's Media Reform," *Journal of Communication* 44.3 (Summer 1994): 4–21.

10. The "end of ideology" thesis was originally put forward by Daniel Bell in his classic book of the same title (New York: Free Press, 1960). It is part of a broad "theory of indus-

trial society" that dominated American social sciences in the 1950s. According to this theory, a "normative consensus" had been achieved in Western industrial societies and the major ideological struggles characteristic of the transition from "traditional" agrarian to "modern" industrial societies had essentially disappeared. For critiques of this argument, see John B. Thompson, *Ideology and Modern Culture: Critical Social Theory in the Era of Mass Communication* (Stanford: Stanford University Press, 1990); see also Larry Portis, "On the Rise and Decline of Totalitarian Liberalism: Schlesinger, Bell, Larouche," *Canadian Journal of Political and Social Theory* 12.3 (1988): 20–36.

11. For overviews of the broader concept of ideology in the critical media literature, see Stuart Hall, "The Rediscovery of 'Ideology': Return of the Repressed in Media Studies," in *Culture, Society, and the Media,* ed. Michael Gurevitch, Tony Bennett, James Curran, and Janet Woollacott (New York: Routledge, 1982), 56–90; see also Stuart Hall, "Culture, the Media, and the 'Ideological Effect,'" in *Mass Communication and Society,* ed. James Curran, Michael Gurevitch, and Janet Woollacott (London: Arnold, 1977), 315–48.

12. See, for example, John Hartley, *Understanding News* (New York: Routledge, 1982).

13. John Hartley, "Ideology," in *Key Concepts in Communication and Cultural Studies,* ed. Tim O'Sullivan, John Hartley, Danny Saunders, Martin Montgomery, and John Fiske, 2d ed. (New York: Routledge, 1994), 143. For a more elaborate critique of the ideological implications of the conventions of journalistic objectivity, see Robert A. Hackett and Yuezhi Zhao, *Sustaining Democracy? Journalism and the Politics of Objectivity* (Toronto: Garamond Press, 1997).

14. Post-structuralism has further extended the analysis of power and relations of domination from the level of consciousness and ideology to the level of the unconscious and the physical body. At the same time, it emphasizes the subversion of ideological constructs by active social agents. For a concise overview of the concept of ideology in the post-structuralist, post-modernist, and post-marxist literature, see Yuezhi Zhao, "The 'End of Ideology' Again? The Concept of Ideology in the Era of Post-Modern Theory," *Canadian Journal of Sociology* 18.1 (Winter 1993): 70–85.

15. Thompson, *Ideology and Modern Culture,* 58, emphasis in the original.

16. Anne Thurston, "Frenzy for Money Masks a Dynasty in Decline," in Alison L. Jernow, *Don't Force Us to Lie: The Struggle of Chinese Journalists in the Reform Era* (New York: Committee to Protect Journalists, 1993), 14.

17. I am indebted to Pat Howard for the formulation of this idea.

18. "Peaceful evolution" is cold war political terminology that is often invoked by the Chinese Communist party. According to Party propaganda, it describes a Western strategy, initiated and championed by the U.S. government since the late 1940s, to transform existing socialist regimes into capitalist formations through systematic, gradual, and peaceful political, economic, cultural, and ideological penetration.

19. Jernow, *Don't Force Us to Lie,* 79.

20. Actually, these editorials expressed ideas formulated by Deng Xiaoping. During the Spring Festival in 1991, Deng visited Shanghai and stated that to develop Shanghai's Pudong District, the city should take bold measures and leave behind the debate on whether certain reforms are capitalist or socialist. *Liberation Daily* used three editorials (March 2,

March 22, and April 12, 1991) to carry the main ideas of Deng's talks. See Wu Jianguo, Chen Xiankui, Liu Xiao, and Yang Fengcheng, *Ideological Winds in Contemporary China* (Beijing: Police Education Press, 1993), 574.

21. Hsiao Ching-Chang and Yang Mei-Rong, "Don't Force Us to Lie: The Case of the *World Economic Herald*," in *Voices of China*, 111–21. See also Kate Wright, "The Political Fortunes of Shanghai's *World Economic Herald*," *Australian Journal of Chinese Affairs* 23 (Jan. 1990): 121–32; and Jernow, *Don't Force Us to Lie*, 31–49.

22. Hsiao and Yang reported that even "Zhao Ziyang had to say that Qin Benli had 'made a serious mistake and must be dealt with sternly.'" See Hsiao and Yang, "Don't Force Us to Lie," 120.

23. Hsiao and Yang's article on the *Herald* appears in Chin-Chuan Lee's 1990 volume on the news media in China and American media reporting of China. It is worthwhile to note that articles in Lee's second volume on the same theme (*China's Media, Media's China*, Boulder: Westview Press, 1994) have substantially contextualized the kind of press freedom described by Hsiao and Yang. Marlowe Hood points out that the Chinese press during the extraordinary moment of April and May 1989 "was operating roughly within the perceived guidelines of a particular faction, albeit a losing one, within the central leadership." "The Use and Abuse of Mass Media by Chinese Leaders during the 1980s," in *China's Media, Media's China*, 38. Hood even goes so far as to suggest that "we must recognize the extent to which the explosion of 'press freedom' was politically guided and manipulated by Zhao Ziyang and his allies" (52). Using the more structurally oriented concept of the public sphere, Lowell Dittmer notes in the same volume ("The Politics of Publicity in Reform China," 89–112) China's emerging public sphere's continuing dependence on leadership patronage and the "formal and informal ties" between relatively autonomous enterprises such as the *Herald* and the regime. See also Lowell Dittmer, *China under Reform* (Boulder: Westview Press, 1994), 109–58.

24. See Cheng and White, "China's Technocratic Movement," 345. Hsiao and Yang mentioned that "General Secretary Zhao Ziyang spoke out in support of the *Herald* for being on the front lines of reform, and helped it weather the storm [of those inside the Party who want to close the newspaper]." "Don't Force Use to Lie," 118. Jernow also suggests that the direction and fate of the newspaper was closely related to Zhao Ziyang. For example, the *Herald*'s adoption of a more radical stance was the result of an affirmation Qin received "from above, most likely from someone affiliated with Zhao Ziyang, that it was okay to promote political reform." Moreover, when the newspaper was under pressure from hardliners, Zhao twice came to its rescue. See Jernow, *Don't Force Us to Lie*, 34–35. Merle Goldman concludes more definitively that "The *Herald* was only able to survive because of Zhao's protection." "The Role of the Press in Post-Mao Political Struggles," in *China's Media, Media's China*, 30.

25. Fred S. Siebert, Theodore Peterson, and Wilbur Schramm, *Four Theories of the Press* (Urbana: University of Illinois Press, 1956).

26. Developed at the end of the cold war and the collapse of Soviet Union and communist regimes in eastern Europe, the "end of history" argument celebrates the alleged global triumph of a liberal democratic consensus and sees liberalism and capitalism as the only

possible human future. See Francis Fukuyama, *The End of History and the Last Man* (New York: Free Press, 1992). For a critique of this argument, see Alan Ryan, "Professor Hegel Goes to Washington," *New York Review of Books,* Mar. 26, 1992, 7–13.

27. Mark R. Levy, "Editor's Note," *Journal of Communication* 44.3 (Summer 1994): 3.

28. One notable exception to this liberal framework is Seung-Soo Kim's Ph.D. thesis, "The Communication Industries in Modern China: Between Maoism and the Market" (University of Leicester, 1987). Kim analyzes the structure of the Chinese mass media and its transformation in response to market mechanisms in the first half of the 1980s from the perspective of Marxist political economy. His occasional romanticization of the Cultural Revolution is rather problematic, and much of the material is dated.

29. C. B. Macpherson, *The Real World of Democracy* (Toronto: Canadian Broadcasting Corporation, 1965), 4.

30. Denis McQuail, *Media Performance* (London: Sage, 1992), 103.

31. Norberto Bobbio, *The Future of Democracy: A Defense of the Rules of the Game* (Cambridge: Polity Press, 1987), 25, cited in Slavko Splichal, *Media beyond Socialism: Theory and Practice in East-Central Europe* (Boulder: Westview Press, 1994), 1.

32. A list of the major Chinese academic and trade journals used in this study is included in the bibliography. I have also included the names of their publishers, as such information is important for evaluating the significance of the publication.

33. Unless specified, all translations of Chinese documents, including phrases and titles, are mine. Pinyin for the titles of Chinese books and periodicals is included in the bibliography.

Chapter 1: Party Journalism in China

1. James Curran, "Rethinking the Media as a Public Sphere," in *Communication and Citizenship: Journalism and the Public Sphere,* ed. Peter Dahlgren and Colin Sparks (New York: Routledge, 1991), 35.

2. Based on her field research in the relatively open period of the mid-1980s, Judy Polumbaum observes that the media control system "leaked like a sieve." See "Outpaced by Events: Learning, Unlearning, and Relearning to Be a Journalist in Post–Cultural Revolution China," *Gazette* 48 (1991): 140. Edward Friedman provides numerous examples of oppositional reading of the official media by readers in post-1989 China. See "The Oppositional Decoding of China's Leninist Media," in *China's Media, Media's China,* ed. Chin-Chuan Lee (Boulder: Westview Press, 1994), 129–46.

3. For an overview of the development of the radical students' press and the communist press in the 1920s, see S. S. Kim, "The Communication Industries in Modern China: Between Maoism and the Market" (Ph.D. diss., University of Leicester, 1987), 36–41.

4. Fang Hanqi, Chen Yeshao, and Zhang Zihua, *A Brief History of Chinese Journalism* (Beijing: Chinese People's University Press, 1982), 152–53.

5. Timothy Cheek provides an excellent discussion of the Yan'an legacy for propaganda and newspapers under the Party. He argues that the Party's current model for propaganda and newspapers was set during the recitification movement and the reorganization of the

Party press in April 1942. See "Redefining Propaganda: Debates on the Role of Journalism in Post-Mao Mainland China," *Issues and Studies* 25.2 (1989): 56–58. See also Patricia Stranahan, *Modeling the Medium: The Chinese Communist Party and the Liberation Daily* (Armonk, N.Y.: M. E. Sharpe, 1990), for an insightful and detailed analysis of the legacy of the *Liberation Daily* in Party journalism.

6. Fang, Chen, and Zhang, *A Brief History,* 205–6.

7. Zhang Tao, *A History of Journalism in the People's Republic of China* (Beijing: Economic Daily Press, 1992), 59.

8. Sun Xupei, "The Take-over and Transformation of the Old Press in the Years after Liberation," *Journalism Research Material* 43 (Sept. 1988): 61.

9. In 1953, the newspaper became the joint organ of China's eight democratic parties (Revolutionary Committee of the Kuomintang, China Democratic League, China Democratic National Construction Association, China Association for Promoting Democracy, Chinese Peasants' and Workers' Democratic Party, China Zhi Gong Dang, Jiu San Society, Taiwan Democratic Self-Government), the All China Industrial and Commercial Association, and a number of nonpartisan political personalities who were delegates to the Chinese People's Political Consultative Conference.

10. Zhang, *A History of Journalism,* 33.

11. Sun Xupei, *New Theories of Journalism* (Beijing: Contemporary China Press, 1994), 318–19.

12. China Statistics Bureau, *China Statistical Yearbook, 1993* (Beijing: China Statistics Press, 1993), 785.

13. Readership Survey Team of the Capital Journalism Society, "A General Survey of Newspapers," in *China Journalism Yearbook 1986,* Journalism Research Institute of the Chinese Academy of Social Sciences (Beijing: Chinese Social Sciences Press, 1987), 122.

14. Journalism Research Institute of the Chinese Academy of Social Sciences, *China Journalism Yearbook 1993* (Beijing: Chinese Social Sciences Press, 1994), 373.

15. Tong Bing and Cheng Mei, *A Teaching Program for Journalism Theory* (Beijing: Chinese People's University Press, 1993), 148.

16. Quoted in ibid., 147.

17. Mao Zedong, "Strengthening the Party Principle in Newspaper Propaganda," in *Selections from Documents on Journalism,* ed. Journalism Research Institute of Xinhua News Agency (Beijing: Xinhua Press, 1990), 68–69, 76–77.

18. Hu Yaobang, "On the Party's Journalism Work," *People's Daily,* Aug. 14, 1985, 1.

19. Ibid.

20. Jiang Zemin, "Issues on the Party's Journalistic Work," in *Selections,* 199.

21. Su Shaozhi provides a penetrating account of the Party's ideological control in broader terms. See "Chinese Communist Ideology and Media Control," in *China's Media, Media's China,* 75–88.

22. "Central Party Committee Circular on the Writing of Reference Material by Xinhua News Agency Correspondents," July 1953, in *Selections,* 262.

23. The relevant passage from this document is in *Selections,* 276.

24. Central Party Propaganda Department, Central Party External Propaganda Group, Xinhua News Agency, "Several Suggestions on Improving News Reporting," issued on July 18, 1987, in *Selections,* 303–12.

25. Xinhua News Agency, "The True Face of the *World Economic Herald* Incident," *People's Daily,* overseas ed., Aug. 19, 1989, 4.

26. Zhang, *A History of Journalism,* 125, 141.

27. See Fang Hanqi and Chen Yeshao, *A History of Contemporary Chinese Journalism, 1949–1988* (Beijing: Xinhua Press, 1992), 99–113.

28. *China Women's News,* for example, has been concerned with women's equality in the workplace, women's health, and family issues. It has also taken a critical stance against the commodification of women.

29. Film was originally under the jurisdiction of the Ministry of Culture. It was shifted to the Ministry of Radio and Television in 1986.

30. The agency was established January 27, 1987, at the height of the Party's Campaign against Bourgeois Liberalization. For this reason, Timothy Cheek argues that the agency is "a child of Party conservatives and the struggle against bourgeois liberalism." "Redefining Propaganda," 60. Although there is perhaps some truth in this observation, it must be noted that it is also a child of political reform, especially the move to separate government and the Party. It was also created out of the perceived necessity of regulating the proliferation of non-Party newspapers. The agency is, as Judy Polumbaum observes, an important administrative innovation that contributes to the institutionalization of media management through bureaucratic organizations. See "Striving for Predictability: The Bureaucratization of Media Management in China," in *China's Media, Media's China,* 113–28.

31. Pat Howard, *Breaking the Iron Rice Bowl: Prospects for Socialism in China's Countryside* (Armonk, N.Y.: M. E. Sharpe, 1988), 21.

32. Mao Zedong, "Some Questions concerning Methods of Leadership," *Selected Works,* vol. 3 (Beijing: Foreign Languages Press, 1967), 120, cited in Howard, *Breaking the Iron Rice Bowl,* 20.

33. Cheek, "Redefining Propaganda," 57.

34. Deng Tuo, "Review and Prospects of *Resistance News* upon Its Fiftieth Issue," *Resistance News,* June 27, 1938, cited in Cheek, "Redefining Propaganda," 58.

35. Cheek, "Redefining Propaganda," 58.

36. Liu Shaoqi, "A Talk to the Northern China Press Crops," in *Selections,* 94.

37. Andrew J. Nathan, *Chinese Democracy* (Berkeley: University of California Press, 1985), 154.

38. Mao Zedong, *Selected Works* (Beijing: Foreign Languages Press, 1961–77), 4:241.

39. Mao Zedong, "A Talk to the Editorial Staff of *Jinshui Daily,*" in *Selections,* 72, my emphasis.

40. Peter Kenez, *The Birth of the Propaganda State: Soviet Methods of Mass Mobilization, 1917–1929* (Cambridge, Mass.: Cambridge University Press, 1985), 4, cited in Cheek, "Redefining Propaganda," 52.

41. Mao Zedong, "A Letter to Liu Jianxun and Wei Guoqing," Jan. 12, 1958, in *Selections,* 88.

42. Quoted in Zhu Yan, "The Guiding Role of the Theory of Socialist Market Economy in Broadcasting Reform," *Chinese Journal of Broadcasting* (Apr. 1994): 5.

43. Cheek, "Redefining Propaganda," 53.

44. Ibid., 54.

45. Gan Xifen, "Debates Contribute to the Development of the Journalistic Science," *Journal of Communication* 44.3 (Summer 1994): 45.

46. Quoted in Cheek, "Redefining Propaganda," 58.

47. Tong and Cheng, *A Teaching Program*, 98.

48. Cited in ibid., 94.

49. Pei Zheng, "*People's Daily* Emphasized the Reporting of Role Models That Reflect the Spirit of the Time," *China Journalism Yearbook 1993*, 175–77.

50. Both Lei Feng and Jiao Yulu are famous role models set up by the Party in the 1960s.

51. Howard, *Breaking the Iron Rice Bowl*, 20.

52. Ibid., 181.

53. Nathan, *Chinese Democracy*, 8.

54. For an extended account of this type of criticism and self-criticism, see Nathan, *Chinese Democracy*, 155–56.

55. Fang and Chen, *A History of Contemporary Chinese Journalism*, 226.

56. Howard, *Breaking the Iron Rice Bowl*, 15.

57. For example, during the famine in the early 1960s, the peasants who grew the grain suffered massive starvation, while the urban population suffered less because they were protected by the state's ration and grain coupon systems.

58. Fang and Chen, *A History of Contemporary Chinese Journalism*, 71–75.

59. Quoted in Fang, Chen, and Zhang, *A Brief History*, 209.

60. Ibid.

61. When I worked as a news editor intern at Jiangsu People's Radio in 1984, I personally processed many news reports supplied by local amateur correspondents. Andrew Nathan noted that such correspondents "submit their own work to their own party secretaries" before sending it to the news media. *Chinese Democracy*, 153. The more common practice is to simply get a seal from the unit's propaganda department, which usually previews such items.

62. See Leonard L. Chu, "Continuity and Change in China's Media Reform," *Journal of Communication* 44.3 (Summer 1994): 12–14, for a brief account of the Party's past and present media reforms. While Chu emphasizes that past reforms were aimed at reinforcing Party control, it is also important to note that all these reforms simultaneously aimed at bringing the media closer to the people.

63. Contrary to Chu's argument that this reform movement was "modeled after the former Soviet Union's media concepts, structure and operation," this reform was actually an attempt to rethink the Soviet model. See Chu, "Continuity and Change in China's Media Reform," 14.

64. Fang and Chen, *A History of Contemporary Chinese Journalism*, 83–84.

65. "To Our Readers," *People's Daily*, July 1, 1956, cited in Fang and Chen, *A History of Contemporary Chinese Journalism*, 82.

66. For a more detailed discussion of the 1956 media reform, see Jinglu Yu, "The Abortive 1956 Reform of Chinese Journalism," *Journalism Quarterly* 65.2 (Summer 1988): 328–34.

67. Kenneth Starck and Yu Xu, "Loud Thunder, Small Raindrops: The Reform Movement and the Press in China," *Gazette* 42.3 (1988): 146.

68. Fang and Chen, *A History of Contemporary Chinese Journalism*, 182.

69. Ibid., 223.

Chapter 2: The Trajectory of Media Reform

1. Gan Xifen, "Debates Contribute to the Development of the Journalistic Science," *Journal of Communication* 44.3 (Summer 1994): 45.

2. Bradley S. Greenberg and Tuen-Yu Lau, "The Revolution in Journalism and Communication Education in the People's Republic of China," *Gazette* 45.1 (1990): 23.

3. For overviews of news media reform in the 1980s, see Kenneth Starck and Yu Xu, "Loud Thunder, Small Raindrops: The Reform Movement and the Press in China," *Gazette* 42.3 (1988): 143–59; Junhao Hong and Marlene Cuthbert, "Media Reform in China since 1978: Background Factors, Problems, and Future Trends," *Gazette* 47.3 (1991): 141–58.

4. Judy Polumbaum, "The Chinese Press and Its Discontents," *China Exchange News* 16.4 (1988): 4.

5. Hu Yaobang, "On the Party's Journalism Work," *People's Daily*, Aug. 14, 1985, 1.

6. Judy Polumbaum, "The Tribulations of China's Journalists after a Decade of Reform," in *Voices of China: The Interplay of Politics and Journalism*, ed. Chin-Chuan Lee (New York: Guilford, 1990), 41.

7. Ibid., 42.

8. Liu Binyan, "Press Freedom: Particles in the Air," in *Voices of China*, 135. Gerald B. Sperling provides many interesting examples of openness in the Chinese press during this period. See "'Glasnost' in the Chinese Press," in *Encounter '87: Media, Democracy, and Development*, ed. Peter Desbarats and Robert Henderson (London, Ontario: Graduate School of Journalism, University of Western Ontario, 1988), 39–46.

9. Judy Polumbaum notes that whereas the phrase "freedom of the press" was used by only a few bold pathbreakers early in the 1980s, by the fall of 1987, journalists and scholars were talking casually about it. See Polumbaum, "Tribulations of China's Journalists," 43.

10. Hu Jiwei, "There Will Be No Genuine Stability without Press Freedom," *World Economic Herald*, May 8, 1989, 8.

11. "Mainland Scholars Talk Freely about Freedom of the Press," *Da Gong Bao*, July 29, 1988, 2.

12. Hu, "There Will Be No Genuine Stability without Press Freedom," 8.

13. *World Economic Herald*, May 8, 1989, 8.

14. "Hu Jiwei Says That Freedom of the Press Must Not Be Wrongly Regarded as an Unstable Factor," *China News Service*, Mar. 27, 1989, translated in Foreign Broadcasting Information Service, *Daily Report: China* (hereafter FBIS-*China*), Mar. 27, 1989, 47–48.

15. Gan, "Debates," 41–42.

16. Qian Xinbo, "Media Supervision Is the Duty, Not a Favor Granted to the Media," *World Economic Herald*, Apr. 24, 1989, 3, translated in FBIS-*China*, May 25, 1989, 44–46.

17. Quoted in Zhang Kewen, "Role of the News Media: A Debate," *China Daily,* Jan. 22, 1988, 4.

18. Wu Tingjun, "Rethinking the 'Mouthpiece' Theory," *Journalism Research Material* 46 (1989): 143–52.

19. Ibid., 152.

20. Mo Ru, "Acting according to Laws of Journalism," *Chinese Journalists* (Mar. 1989): 1.

21. Gan, "Debates," 44.

22. Liu Binyan, a well-known investigative journalist, was more straightforward in using the Western model as the standard of journalism. He pointed out that "China's newspapers are not newspapers at all" and argued that they must eventually follow the Western model by becoming the "Fourth Estate." Quoted in Lu Mu, "Adhere to Our newspapers' Party Principle—Comments on Liu Binyan's Views on the Nature of Newspapers," *Journalism Front* (Feb. 1987): 3–4.

23. Quoted in Marlowe Hood, "Effects of Press Law Reform on Media Viewed," *South China Sunday Morning Post,* Apr. 24, 1988, 4, reprinted in FBIS-*China,* Apr. 25, 1988, 25–26.

24. Gan, "Debates," 45.

25. While the term *minban* certainly includes private newspaper ownership by an individual, it can also mean other forms of nonstate ownership, such as nongovernmental organizations. Although some reformers used the narrow term "newspapers run by private individuals" (*siren banbao*), others used the broad term *minban* in the news media reform literature.

26. "The Government Must Be Constrained by the Public," *World Economic Herald,* May 8, 1989, 4, translated in FBIS-*China,* May 25, 1989, 50–51.

27. Journalism Research Institute of the Chinese Academy of Social Sciences and the Survey Group of the Capital Journalism Society, "People's Calls, People's Expectations," in *A Perspective Study of Media Communication Effects in China,* ed. Chen Chongshan and Er Xiuling (Shenyang: Shenyang Publishing House, 1989), 85. See also Chen Lidan, "Why Has the Issue of Private Newspaper Ownership Been Avoided," *World Economic Herald,* May 8, 1989, 4.

28. Chen, "Why Has the Issue of Private Newspaper Ownership Been Avoided," 4.

29. This theory was put forward by two scholars in the Chinese Academy of Social Sciences. It received the endorsement of the Party in its Thirteenth National Congress in October 1987.

30. Timothy Cheek, "Redefining Propaganda: Debates on the Role of Journalism in Post-Mao Mainland China," *Issues and Studies* 25.2 (1989): 47–74.

31. Chen, "Why Has the Issue of Private Newspaper Ownership Been Avoided," 4.

32. The argument for "objective reporting" in Chinese journalism is part of the struggle for the relative autonomy of the news media in China. Viewed from this perspective, the call for the practice of Western-style objective journalism in China has a progressive face. For an account of the pursuit of "objective reporting" in Chinese journalism, see Li Liangrong, "The Historical Fate of 'Objective Reporting' in China," in *China's Media, Media's China,* ed. Chin-Chuan Lee (Boulder: Westview Press, 1994), 225–37.

33. See Chen Yang, *People's Daily,* overseas ed., Apr. 5, 1990, 2.

34. Mark P. Petracca and Mong Xiong, "The Concept of Chinese Neo-Authoritarianism: An Exploration and Democratic Critique," *Asian Survey* 30.11 (Nov. 1990): 1112–13. This article provides a concise overview of the main thrusts of the neo-authoritarian and democratic perspectives on China. The following account of these two schools are drawn from this article.

35. Wu Jiaxiang, "Neo-Authoritarianism: A Special Express Train to Democratization," in *Neo-Authoritarianism: Debate on Theories of Reform,* ed. Liu Ling and Liu Jun (Beijing: Economic Institution Press, 1989), 45–46, cited in Petracca and Mong, "The Concept of Chinese Neo-Authoritarianism," 1109.

36. See Li Cheng and Lynn T. White III, "China's Technocratic Movement and the *World Economic Herald,*" *Modern China* 17.3 (July 1991): 344. This article provides an excellent analysis of China's technocratic movement in the mid-1980s and its relationship with the democracy movement in 1989 and the *World Economic Herald,* which was the main forum of this technocratic movement.

37. Petracca and Mong, "The Concept of Chinese Neo-Authoritarianism," 1111.

38. Ibid., 1112.

39. Ibid.

40. For an excellent analysis of the different political orientations of China's intellectuals and conflicts and divisions between government technocrats and dissident intellectuals, see Cheng and White, "China's Technocratic Movement."

41. Chen Yizi, Wang Xiaoqiang, and Li Jun, "Establishing the Developmental Model of a Hard Government and a Soft Economy," in *Neo-Authoritarianism,* ed. Liu Yuan and Li Qing (Beijing: Institute of Economics, 1989), 248.

42. Ruan Ming, "Press Freedom and Neoauthoritarianism: A Reflection on China's Democracy Movement," in *Voices of China,* 130.

43. Ibid., 127–29. Ruan attributes the passivity of Party reformers to their embrace of the neo-authoritarian theory.

44. Alison L. Jernow, *Don't Force Us to Lie: The Struggle of Chinese Journalists in the Reform Era* (New York: Committee to Protect Journalists, 1993), 158.

45. Quoted in ibid., 158–59.

46. Sun Xupei has written extensively on press legislation. See *New Theories of Journalism* (Beijing: Contemporary China Press, 1994), 131–71. Kenneth Starck and Yu Xu provide a brief summary of the democratic perspective on press legislation in "Loud Thunder, Small Raindrops," 153–55.

47. Jernow, *Don't Force Us to Lie,* 158.

48. Journalism Research Institute of the Chinese Academy of Social Sciences and the Survey Group of the Capital Journalism Society, "People's Calls, People's Expectations," 85. The difference between the NPC delegates and the CPPCC delegates on this issue can be explained by differences in the composition of the two groups. CPPCC delegates are mainly members of China's democratic parties or nonpartisan political, commercial, and cultural elites. NPC delegates, on the other hand, are elected on the basis of representation. In addition to Party and government officials, some of the NPC delegates are model workers, peasants, soldiers, and members of China's national minorities.

49. See Jernow, *Don't Force Us to Lie,* 58–63, for a more detailed discussion of the division between Hu Jiwei and Du Daozheng. Timothy Cheek also provides a good analysis of the different perspectives of Hu Jiwei and Du Daozheng. See "Redefining Propaganda," 58–63.

50. Cheek, "Redefining Propaganda," 59.

51. Joseph M. Chan, "Commercialization without Independence: Trends and Tensions of Media Development in China," in *China Review 1993,* ed. Joseph Cheng Yu-Skek and Maurice Brosseau (Hong Kong: Chinese University Press, 1993), 25.2.

52. Jiang Zemin, "Issues in the Party's Journalism Work," in *Selections from Documents on Journalism,* ed. Journalism Research Institute of Xinhua News Agency (Beijing: Xinhua Press, 1990), 189–200.

53. Li Ruihuan, "Stick to the Principle of Positive Propaganda," in *Selections,* 217–18.

54. See Chan, "Commercialization without Independence," 25.3, for a brief summary of the personnel changes in media and ideological fields after June 4.

55. See Jernow, *Don't Force Us to Lie,* 137, 140.

56. Chan, "Commercialization without Independence," 25.3.

57. According China's Statistics Bureau, the growth rate for 1990 was 3.9 percent. It reached 8.0 percent in 1991 and jumped to 13.6 percent in 1992. The rates for 1993 and 1994 were 13.4 percent and 10.1 percent, respectively. The average rate for the whole world for 1990–94 was 2.2 percent, 0.8 percent, 1.4 percent, 2.3 percent, and 3.1 percent, respectively, while that of the developed countries was 2.0 percent, 0.3 percent, 2.0 percent, 1.8 percent, and 2.7 percent, respectively. *People's Daily,* overseas ed., Aug. 31, 1995, 2.

58. Minxin Pei, *From Reform to Revolution: The Demise of Communism in China and the Soviet Union* (Cambridge, Mass.: Harvard University Press, 1994), 84.

59. Ibid.

60. Chan, "Commercialization without Independence," 25.3–25.4.

61. Anne Thurston, "Frenzy for Money Masks a Dynasty in Decline," in Jernow, *Don't Force Us to Lie,* 7–8.

62. Central Party Propaganda Department, "Suggestions for Improving News Reporting," in *Selections,* 305.

63. Confidential interview, Oct. 14, 1994, Beijing.

64. These newspapers were all available in Beijing on October 22, 1994. While some of these newspapers were published on the same day, many provincial newspapers arrived in Beijing one to a few days after the date of publication.

65. The only exception was the night of January 17, when the leading story concerned a commemoration of the sixtieth anniversary of the Party's Zunyi Meeting, when Mao assumed full leadership of the party. But the story was immediately followed by two reports of Jiang Zemin receiving foreign guests.

66. Liang Heng, "Newspaper Management under a Socialist Market Economy," *Chinese Journalists* (Dec. 1992): 5.

67. Ibid.

68. *Workers' Daily,* Nov. 17, 1992, 1.

69. Liang, "Newspaper Management under a Socialist Market Economy," 5.

70. For a range of articles on market economy and the news media, see Journalism Research Institute of the Chinese Academy of Social Sciences, *Wuxi Daily*, and the Propaganda Department of the Jiangyin City Party Committee, eds., *Market Economy and the News Media* (Beijing: Yanshan Press, 1993).

71. See, for example, Liu Xuede, "Market Economy and Journalism Reform," *Young Journalists* (Jan. 1993): 12–13; Li Chuangmin, "Market Economy and Journalism Reform," *Press and Publications Herald* (Feb. 1993): 20–22; Li Renchen, "Market Economy and Journalism Reform," *Journalism Front* (Feb. 1993): 7–9; and Shen Shiwei, "Socialist Market Economy and Journalism Reform," *Journalism Practice* (Jan. 1993): 4–6.

72. Yu Tonghao and Zhu Yan, "Market Economy and Broadcasting Reform," *Chinese Journal of Broadcasting* (Jan. 1993): 11.

Chapter 3: Media Commercialization with Chinese Characteristics

1. Fang Hanqi and Chen Yeshao, *A History of Contemporary Chinese Journalism* (Beijing: Xinhua Press, 1992), 65–66.

2. Robert Weil, "China at the Brink: Class Contradictions of 'Market Socialism'—Part 2," *Monthly Review* 46.8 (Jan. 1995): 11–43. According to Weil, nonevaluation or underevaluation of joint ventures alone is estimated to cost the government 30 billion yuan or U.S. $3.4 billion per year. Over the past decade, the total state assets lost by all means amounts to some 500 billion yuan, or U.S. $57.5 billion, despite overall growth of the public sector. In addition, the growing epidemic of outright tax evasion and nonreporting of income are estimated conservatively to be costing the state 100 billion yuan, or U.S. $17.2 billion a year.

3. Weil, "China at the Brink," 33.

4. By 1994, there were 86 color television sets per 100 urban households in China and 73.3 television sets (13.3 color sets) per 100 rural households. *People's Daily*, overseas ed., Oct. 2, 1995, 2.

5. Hao Jianzhong, "An Overview of Debates on Newspaper Management," in *China Journalism Yearbook 1987*, Journalism Research Institute of the Chinese Academy of Social Sciences (Beijing: China Social Sciences Press, 1988), 79.

6. The Jilin provincial Party organ, *Jilin Daily*, for example, stopped receiving government funds entirely in 1983. In 1985, it earned a net profit of more than 4 million yuan and paid the government more than 1 million yuan in taxes and profits. See Guang Dongzheng, "Reform of Newspaper Management," *China Journalism Yearbook 1987*, 95–96.

7. Shun Fudi, "A Preliminary Exploration into the Overall Benefits of Radio and Television Broadcasting," *Chinese Journal of Broadcasting* (June 1990): 45.

8. This issue is discussed in more detail in chap. 4.

9. Typical of the ideal being promulgated is the Wuma Township station in Sichuan Province. The financial subsidy from the township government was two thousand yuan per year, barely enough to pay the salaries of the two staff members. From 1985 onward, the station began to acquire capital for self-development. It started by opening up wasteland for grain and tobacco cultivation and then established a grain processing service, a grocery store, and finally a hotel, a restaurant, and a transportation service. With an annual net profit of more than 30,000 yuan from these business operations, the station was able to establish a stan-

dard broadcasting network, replace old broadcasting facilities, set up a satellite ground receiving station and relay stations, hire seventeen employees, and produce a variety of programs. By 1992, the station boasted 400,000 yuan worth of fixed capital. Its experience was widely promoted and the station became a model broadcasting station for the whole country. See He Douwen, "Once Again on Broadcasting from a Macro-Perspective," *Chinese Journal of Broadcasting* (June 1992): 89.

10. Xuejun Yu, "Government Policies toward Advertising in China (1979–1989)," *Gazette* 48.1 (1991): 20.

11. Central Administration for Industry and Commerce, "Provisional Regulations for Advertising Management" (Beijing: the State Council of China, 1982), cited in ibid., 21.

12. "Admen in China Get Red Carpet," *Advertising Age,* June 22, 1987, 89.

13. State Administration for Industry and Commerce and State Planning Commission, "An Outline of the Schedule for Speeding Up the Development of the Advertising Industry," *Chinese Advertising* (Apr. 1993): 6.

14. Television for the first time surpassed newspapers as the number one advertising medium in 1991, with a total advertising revenue of 1,000,520,000 yuan. Its 1992 figure of 2,054,708,000 yuan represented a 105.4 percent increase. See Guo Zhenzhi, "Broadcasting in a Market Economy," *Journalism and Communication Research* 1.3 (1994): 3; Wu Dongbin, "A Brief Introduction to China's Advertising Business in 1992," *Modern Advertising* (Jan. 1994): 18. Television advertising revenue continued to grow dramatically. Total Chinese television advertising revenue for 1994 was U.S. $0.65 billion and U.S. $1.31 billion for 1995. Forecasts for 1996 and 1997 are U.S. $2.43 billion and U.S. $4.11 billion, respectively. See Matthew Miller, "No Limit to China's Cable TV Market," *Asia Times,* Nov. 11, 1996, 16.

15. *People's Daily,* overseas ed., Oct. 21, 1993.

16. "The Country's Advertising Industry Grows Rapidly," *People's Daily,* overseas ed., Feb. 28, 1994, 2.

17. Pang Wangxiong, "An Analysis of Newspaper Marketization," *Journalism Knowledge* (Apr. 1994): 13.

18. *Press and Publications News,* Jan. 28, 1994, 7.

19. S. D. Seligman, "China's Fledgling Advertising Industry," *China Business Review* (Jan.–Feb. 1984), cited in Junhao Hong, "The Resurrection of Advertising in China: Developments, Problems, and Trends," *Asian Survey* 34.4 (1994): 329.

20. Hong, "The Resurrection of Advertising in China," 330.

21. Yu Huang, "Peaceful Evolution: The Case of Television Reform in Post-Mao China," *Media, Culture, and Society* 16.2 (1994): 229–30.

22. Miller, "No Limit to China's Cable TV Market," 16.

23. Ibid.

24. Zhan Jiang, "Riding the Tide," in *A Journalism Shock Wave,* ed. Zheng Xingdong, Chen Renfeng, and Zheng Chaoran (Beijing: Chinese People's University Press, 1994), 2.

25. There are no individual media tycoons yet since the government prohibits private newspaper ownership and allows only state and collective ownership. The country's government still monopolizes the broadcasting media by allowing only governments at each administrative level to operate broadcasting stations.

26. Mao Zedong, "Reasons for Publishing the *Political Journal,*" *Political Journal,* Dec. 5, 1925, reprinted in *Selections from Documents on Journalism,* ed. Journalism Research Institute of Xinhua News Agency (Beijing: Xinhua Press, 1990), 56.

27. This is the answer given by an applicant for a newspaper registration number. See Zhu Mingzou, "A Preliminary Analysis of the 'Newspaper Publishing Fever,'" *News Communication* (May 1994): 5.

28. The first one for newspapers occurred in the early 1980s. Between January 1980 and March 1985 1,008 newspapers were published, which is an average growth rate of one new newspaper every two days. See Journalism Research Institute of the Chinese Academy of Social Sciences and the Readership Survey Team of the Capital Journalism Society, "A General Survey of Newspapers in China," in *China Journalism Yearbook 1986,* Journalism Research Institute of the Chinese Academy of Social Sciences (Beijing: China Social Sciences Press, 1987), 121. In broadcasting, the first boom occurred in the second half of the 1980s as a result of commercialization and the government's policy of decentralization, which allowed municipal/prefecture and county governments to establish their own radio and television stations. The number of television stations, for example, grew from 93 in 1984 to 509 in 1990. Editorial Board of China Broadcasting Yearbook, *China Broadcasting Yearbook 1986* (Beijing: Beijing Broadcasting Institute Press, 1987) and *China Broadcasting Yearbook 1991* (Beijing: Beijing Broadcasting Institute Press, 1992).

29. China Statistics Bureau, *China Statistical Yearbook, 1993* (Beijing: China Statistics Press, 1993); Editorial Board of China Broadcasting Yearbook, *China Broadcasting Yearbook 1996* (Beijing: Beijing Broadcasting Institute Press, 1997), 623.

30. "Registered Newspapers Number 2,093 Nationwide," *China News Service,* Jan. 1, 1994, translated in FBIS-*China,* Jan. 14, 1994, 13.

31. "China in Transition," *Far Eastern Economic Review,* Oct. 3, 1996, 29.

32. Yang Wenzhen, "1992: A Wave of Newspaper Expansion," *Journalism Front* (Apr. 1992): 10.

33. "Newspapers Boost Issues, Pages Amid Competition," *Ming Bao,* Jan. 7, 1994, 7.

34. Sun Xianghui, "Rapid Growth in Television Advertising: Its Problems and Solutions," *Reference to Decision Making in Broadcasting* (Apr. 1992): 42.

35. Wu, "A Brief Introduction to China's Advertising Business," 18.

36. The cost of prime-time advertising in a thirty-second spot on CCTV grew from 11,000 yuan in 1992 to 25,000 yuan in 1993. By 1994, the highest prime-time advertising price had reached 42,000 yuan for a thirty-second spot. See CCTV Advertising Department, "CCTV Advertising Price List," Mar. 1, 1994.

37. Qian Jian, "Advertising on the Rise on China's Mainland," *Cultural Dialogue* 20 (Zhejiang Provincial People's Association for Friendship with Foreign Countries and Zhejiang International Cultural Exchange Association, Apr. 1996): 10.

38. Ibid.; See also Jing Hao, "The Readjustment of Advertising Prices on CCTV and Issues Related to Advertising on CCTV," *Chinese Advertising* 47 (Jan. 1993): 19.

39. The above information was based on my own monitoring of CCTV programming between January 16, 1995, and January 20, 1995.

40. In early January 1995, one such message promoted a particular brand of hard liquor, another promoted a brand of monosodium glutamate.

41. The most extreme example in January 1995 was a scene of Taiyuan City, the capital of Shanxi Province. There was no landmark of the city, just a common street scene with a huge red banner carrying the name of a local liquor manufacturer.

42. In 1988, a survey of three major Shanghai dailies found that their advertising space accounted for 23.4 percent of the total newspaper space. See Yu Zhengwei, "Newspaper Advertising: Trends, Patterns, and Characteristics," *Journal of Shanghai University,* social sciences ed. (June 1989): 104. There are no other statistics available for the 1990s. Since Shanghai newspapers are usually ahead of newspapers in the rest of the country in their extent of commercialization, this 1988 figure might be taken as the national average for the early 1990s. Examples of Party organs I read in late 1994 typically devoted approximately 30 percent of their space to advertising.

43. For example, *Beijing Daily* sold its entire front page to a foreign advertiser for U.S. $50,000; Shanghai's *Wenhui Bao* and *Liberation Daily* sold their entire front pages for $200,000 and $150,000, respectively. See Hong, "The Resurrection of Advertising," 334.

44. Ruo Chen, "A Report on the Auction of Advertising Space," *Journalist Monthly* (Aug. 1993): 39.

45. Ibid.

46. The program received several hundred letters and inquiries each day from its audience.

47. Yu Guanghua, Ma Chaozeng, and Mu Xiaofang, *A Brief History of CCTV* (Beijing: People's Publishing House, 1993), 140.

48. Lu Ye, "Chinese Television News amidst Reform" (Ph.D. diss., Fudan University, 1994), 11.

49. *People's Daily,* overseas ed., Dec. 18, 1992, 1.

50. Yu, *A Brief History of CCTV,* 144.

51. Perhaps because of this program's success and the need to avoid overlapping, CCTV reformatted "The Economy in Half an Hour" in February 1995 to focus more on macroeconomic news and broad market trends.

52. Yu, *A Brief History of CCTV,* 146.

53. Lu Hong, "A Television Program That Influences China's Economic Development," *Journalism Front* (Jan. 1993): 6.

54. Ibid., 5.

55. Quoted in ibid., 5.

56. Quoted in Yu, *A Brief History of CCTV,* 148.

57. Not surprisingly, the program attracted foreign media attention when it first appeared on the screen in November 1992. See Editorial Board of China Broadcasting Yearbook, *China Broadcasting Yearbook 1993* (Beijing: Beijing Broadcasting Institute Press, 1994), 174.

58. Zhuang Hongchang, "Using Market Mechanisms to Promote Reform in Broadcasting," *Chinese Journal of Broadcasting* (May 1993): 36.

59. For example, the Public Security Bureau would provide money to make a television

drama series that portrayed the "heroes on the public security front" or the State Family Planning Commission would provide funds for the production of an educational program on family planning.

60. Fang Zheng, "Questioning 'Co-sponsored Essay Competitions,'" *Journalism Front* (Mar. 1991): 23.

61. Chan Ming, "Sponsorship Makes One Rich," *Ming Bao,* Nov. 11, 1992, cited in Joseph M. Chan, "Commercialization without Independence: Trends and Tensions of Media Development in China," in *China Review 1993,* ed. Joseph Cheng Yu-Skek and Maurice Brosseau (Hong Kong: Chinese University Press, 1993), 25.6.

62. "Deputy Minister Xu Chonghua Demands Open-Mindedness and Income Growth by Taking Advantage of Broadcasting," *Reference to Decision Making in Broadcasting* (Sept. 1992): 1.

63. Shen Jiachun, "Developing Local Characteristics, Taking Full Advantage of Service Functions," *Chinese Journal of Broadcasting* (Jan. 1994): 17.

64. Indeed, so long as there is money, local stations can cooperate with virtually anyone. In the fall of 1994, the regular daily fare of joint programs on the county radio station in my hometown in Zhejiang Province, for example, included feature programs sponsored by the local beer brewer. These programs popularized knowledge about beer and beer drinking and celebrated the great nutritional and health values of the beverage.

65. Yang Wenzhen, *Press and Publications News,* Jan. 24, 1994.

66. "Our Country's First Shareholding Newspaper Was Born," *Wenhui Bao,* Feb. 5, 1993, 1.

67. These reports usually do not specify the exact names of the news organizations involved, although insiders can easily figure them out.

68. "New Times, New Tasks, and New Demands," *Chinese Journalists* (Apr. 1993): 10.

69. Confidential interviews, Oct. 1994, Beijing.

70. *Press and Publications News,* Sept. 5, 1994, 1.

71. Chen Rongshen, "A Reflection on the Suspension of the *Light Industry Herald*'s License," *Journalist Monthly* (Aug. 1993): 46–47.

72. Chan, "Commercialization without Independence," 25.7.

73. Yi Xudong and Xie Yuan, "The Printing Press in 1994: Makes Me Happy and Makes Me Worried," *Journalist Monthly* (Jan. 1994): 12.

74. Advertisement for *China Economic News Bulletin, People's Daily,* overseas ed., May 14, 1992, 8.

75. Many provincial Party organs also have a similar lineup of subsidiary newspapers and magazines, although not as many as *People's Daily.*

76. Li Xiangyang, "The Trend toward the Conglomeration of Broadcasting Organizations," *Chinese Journal of Broadcasting* (Jan. 1994): 5.

77. Ibid.

78. Speech by Vice Minister He Dongchi, *Reference to Decision Making in Broadcasting* (Sept. 1994): 8.

79. Li Xiangyang, "The Business Path to the Development of Radio and Television," *Reference to Decision Making in Broadcasting* (Dec. 1993): 2.

80. Li, "The Trend," 5.

81. Audience and readership surveys began in the mid-1980s, mostly initiated by journalism research institutes and news organizations to study media effects. Some of the influential surveys were reported in *A Perspective Study of Media Communication Effects in China*, ed. Chen Chongshan and Er Xiuling (Shenyang: Shenyang Publishing House, 1989).

82. Lu Yunpeng, "Audience Survey and Its Reality in Shanghai," *Radio and Television Research* 3 (Oct. 1995): 17–21.

83. Wang Fang, "Revelations from the Growth of Advertising in Guangdong Newspapers," *Fudan University Journalism Quarterly* (Fall 1994): 53.

84. Advertising income for peasant newspapers is generally very low. In 1992, for example, for *Changchun Rural News* (Changchun nongcun bao), it was only 40,000 yuan, for *Harbin Rural News* (Harbin nongcun bao), 80,000 yuan, for *Guizhou Peasant News* (Guizhou nongmin bao), 60,000 yuan, and for others even less. Most peasant newspapers were run at a deficit. *Chongqing Rural News* (Chongqing nongcun bao) had an advertising income of 150,000 yuan in 1992, but still had a deficit of 10,000 yuan, and the amount of deficit for 1993 was estimated at 200,000 yuan. See Xiong Qingyuan, "Peasant Newspapers under the Market Economy," *Chinese Journalists* (June 1993): 33.

85. Xiong, "Peasant Newspapers," 33.

86. Wang Minsheng, "Peasant Papers Should Not Be Chopped," *Chinese Journalists* (Jan. 1993): 52.

87. Paul Siu-nam Lee, "Mass Communication and National Development in China: Media Roles Reconsidered," *Journal of Communication* 44.3 (Summer 1994): 24.

88. Ibid., 25.

89. See, for example, Hunan Provincial Government Joint Survey Team, "The Role of Rural Wired-Radio Networks under the New Conditions and Their Current Problems," *Reference to Decision Making in Broadcasting* (Jan.–Feb. 1994): 71–74.

90. Jia Yifan, "Cool Thinking on Media Hot Lines," *Journalist Monthly* (July 1994): 29–32.

91. Zhang Heling, Wang Xiaotuan, and Wei Minghuang, "*Yichang News* Sets Up a Foundation to Solicit Business Participation in Newspaper Work," in *China Journalism Yearbook 1988*, Journalism Research Institute of the Chinese Academy of Social Sciences (Beijing: China Social Sciences Press, 1989), 144.

Chapter 4: Corruption

1. Robert Weil, "China at the Brink: Class Contradictions of 'Market Socialism'—Part 2," *Monthly Review* 46.8 (Jan. 1995): 30.

2. This was admitted by one media official in a confidential interview, Oct. 1994, Beijing.

3. The Hong Kong–based newspaper *Ming Bao* reported in July 1993 that approximately ten individuals from *People's Daily* were detained for investigation that revolved around five charges of corruption in the central Party organ. (1) Individual journalists from the newspaper's economic department and the economic department itself were involved in a gigantic illegal fund-raising scandal with Great Wall Machinery and Electronics Corporation in which they accepted bribes from the company and published promotional material for

it. (2) A subsidiary of the newspaper was under investigation for smuggling illegal immigrants into Japan. They charged 150,000 yuan for a single individual, of which one-third of the money went to the company itself, while the rest was used for bribes and traveling expenses. (3) A middle-level official, who had been transferred to the newspaper from the army during the reorganization after June 4, 1989, took advantage of his original relationship with the army to illegally sell cars with army licenses to various localities and take commissions from the deals. (4) The director of the newspaper's advertising department took advantage of his position to set up his own advertising firm and contracted the newspaper's advertising through his firm to channel funds into his own pocket. (5) *Tide of the Times,* a magazine run by the newspaper's political department, had repeatedly published articles about prostitutes and their clients to boost sales. It had also published an article calling for tolerance of prostitution under the market economy. See *Ming Bao,* July 22, 1993, 9, translated in FBIS-*China,* July 23, 1993, 13–14.

4. "Being a Journalist and Uncorrupted: The Story of Hebei People's Radio Reporter Li Wenhuai," *Press and Publications News,* Aug. 1, 1994, 2.

5. Lu Zheng, "'Noses' and 'Leashes': A Preliminary Discussion of 'Three-Warranty Reporting,'" *Journalism Front* (Apr. 1992): 20.

6. Ibid.

7. "On the Adherence to Journalism Ethics and Several Other Policy Issues," *Reference to Decision Making in Broadcasting* (Apr. 1992): 2.

8. "State to Increase Supervision over Advertising," *China Daily,* Aug. 4, 1993, 4.

9. Li Zhirong, "The Falling of the Crown from the 'Uncrowned King,'" *The Nineties* (Sept. 1993): 64.

10. Tian Fangmu, "On Journalists' Ethical Choices," *Chinese Journal of Broadcasting* (May 1989): 21.

11. Wang Fang, "Reflections on the Growth of Advertising in Guangdong Newspapers," *Fudan University Journalism Quarterly* (Fall 1994): 52.

12. Wang Xing, "The Advantages and Disadvantages of the Responsibility System in the News Media," *Chinese Journalists* (Oct. 1993): 19.

13. While there is no official document that permits individual journalists to undertake this kind of business, a 1987 government regulation permitted news organizations to undertake public relation functions. In fact, whatever the government regulations may be, individual journalists and news media organizations appear unconcerned.

14. Wang Qing, "Tainted Sanctity," *Journalism World* (Mar. 1994): 33.

15. Gu Tu, "Dealing with the Problem at the Root," *Journalism Front* (Oct. 1993): 26.

16. "Mini-treasury" (*xiao jinku*) to a department in a Chinese institution is similar to pocket money to an individual in a family. This money is not accounted by the unit and a unit usually collectively spends the money for extra benefits of staff members, such as dining and gifts on holidays. Sometimes, this money is simply allocated to staff members as extra cash income.

17. *People's Daily,* Aug. 5, 1993, 1.

18. While the stories recounted in this paragraph are hearsay, the fact that such stories are circulating in journalism circles is significant in itself regardless of whether the accounts can be verified.

19. Zhou Yunlong, "'Paid' without News," *Journalists* (Nov. 1993): 31.

20. *Ming Bao*, July 22, 1993, translated in FBIS-*China*, July 23, 1993, 14.

21. Wang Shuang, "Overcoming 'Paid Journalism' Involves System Engineering," *Journalism Knowledge* (Aug. 1994): 18.

22. A national media outlet is more likely to have a special page about a city or a county, whereas a local media outlet will more likely deal with the township level.

23. The most bizarre case is perhaps the publication of two different editions of *China Human Resources News* (Zhongguo rencai bao) on June 11, 1987; one was the regular version that was distributed nationally, the other contained "special pages" of promotional news about rural enterprises solicited by two reporters from two counties in Beijing. Of the 20,000 copies of this special version, most were distributed in the two counties. The counties paid a total of 21,500 yuan to the newspaper only to find that these "special pages" were produced only for their own consumption. See "The Selling of the Journalistic Conscience," *China Youth News*, Sept. 29, 1987, cited in Chang Xiuying, *A Hundred Cases of Poor News Writing* (Beijing: Agricultural Readings Press, 1989), 4–5.

24. Yi Ren, "Who Is a 'News Broker?'" *Journalism Front* (Jan. 1992): 17; see also Bai Shui, "Watching Out for 'News Brokers,'" *Press and Publications Herald* (Jan. 1994): 53. The following case, based on information obtained through a confidential interview, describes a "news broker" in action. This particular broker was working in the office of a Party committee. He knew many reporters and editors because of his training and job and also knew many potential "news clients" because of his background and socialization. Thus he could act as a link between the two. One day, he received copies of a ready-to-publish news story about the establishment of a new business and copies of a feature story on the subject. He also received a retainer from his client to cover the necessary spending, including cash for editors. His task was to personally deliver one or the other item to ten major national newspapers in Beijing. He put the news story and the feature into separate envelopes. The envelopes with the news story included 300 yuan cash, the feature story envelopes contained 500 yuan. He put the two types of envelopes in separate pockets. Depending on whether an editor had news or feature space available, he would hand in the appropriate piece with the appropriate amount of money. Of course, he does not have personal connections in all the ten newspapers. So he gave part of the retainer to someone with better connections to do the job. After all the items had been delivered, he waited for their publication. When he had collected all the newspapers with the requested coverage, he would receive a handsome sum from his client as compensation for his labor.

25. I collected many such examples from confidential interviews. However, due to the sensitivity of the issue, I decided to include only the examples reported in the news media and in authoritative journalism trade journals. In the age of paid journalism, one wonders about the credibility of news stories in the Chinese news media. But when a piece is critical, the level of credibility should be higher, because few people want to spend money to get negative publicity. The same rule also applies to news reports about the news media themselves. The many examples I gathered from interviews lend credibility to these reports.

26. Deng Lipin, "Why Do Journalists No Longer 'Get to the Grass Roots?'" *Journalism Front* (Feb. 1994): 23.

27. Wang, "Tainted Sanctity," 34.

28. In fact, journalists and officials are always collecting receipts. During my visit to Beijing in early 1995, I took an individual in the government bureaucracy to dinner. I paid the taxi and restaurant bills and when the receipts were issued, he accepted them and kept them without any hesitation. Like many journalists, my guest could get the receipts reimbursed somewhere. A public relations agent revealed in a confidential interview that journalists sometimes hand in up to 500 yuan worth of receipts for reimbursement in the name of "transportation fees" during an assignment, even when the assignment does not require leaving the city.

29. Wang, "Tainted Sanctity," 33.

30. Zhou, "'Paid' without News," 31.

31. "Under the Lure of Money," *People's Daily,* overseas ed., Apr. 14, 1994, 3; see also "Reporters Arrested in Financial Scandal," *Ming Bao,* May 28, 1993, reprinted in FBIS-*China,* June 11, 1993, 25–26.

32. State Council General Office, "Circular on Strengthening Advertising Management," Oct. 13, 1982, in *A Concise and Practical Guide to Laws and Regulations on Press and Publications in China, 1949–1994,* ed. Policy and Regulations Bureau, State Press and Publications Administration (Beijing: Chinese Books Press, 1994), 262.

33. See, for example, "Regulations for Advertising Management," issued by the State Council in Oct. 1987; the "Circular on Further Strengthening Advertising Management on Television," jointly issued by the Ministry of Radio, Film, and Television and the State Administration for Industry and Commerce in Jan. 1988; "Regulations for the Undertaking of Advertising Business by Newspapers, Periodicals, and Publishing Houses," jointly issued by the State Administration of Industry and Commerce and the State Press and Publications Administration in Mar. 1990; and "Provisional Regulations for Newspaper Management" issued by the State Press and Publications Administration in Dec. 1990. See Policy and Regulations Bureau, *Guide,* 264, 271, 278–79.

34. Ibid., 271.

35. Ibid., 279.

36. "State Issues Supplement on News Briefings," *Xinhua Domestic Service,* Aug. 13, 1993, translated in FBIS-*China,* Aug. 13, 1993, 12.

37. Chinese Journalists Association, "Professional Ethical Principles of Chinese Journalists," Jan. 1991, cited in Yi Xinwen, "Market Economy and 'Paid Journalism,'" *News Correspondence* (May 1993): 9; the Apr. 1994 amended version is in *Journalism Front* (July 1994): 18–19.

38. Chinese Journalists Association, "Professional Ethical Principles of Chinese Journalists," *Journalism Front* (July 1994): 19.

39. "False Advertising Angers Consumers," *Beijing Review,* July 29, 1985, 8.

40. Han Wenhui, "'Paid Journalism' Must Be Eliminated Both from the Inside and from the Outside," *Xinjiang Press Circles* (May 1993): 6.

41. Propaganda Department of the Central Committee of the Chinese Communist Party, State Press and Publications Administration, "Circular on Enhancing Professional Ethics in Journalism and Prohibiting 'Paid Journalism,'" *People's Daily,* overseas ed., Aug. 5, 1993, 3, translated in FBIS-*China,* Aug. 5, 1993, 19.

42. Lu Rongxiang, "Reflections upon 'Notices,'" *Journalism Front* (Mar. 1994): 23.

43. Confidential interview, Oct. 28, 1994, Beijing.

44. "Paper Pays Journalists to Attend News Conference," *AFP in English*, Oct. 20, 1993, reprinted in FBIS-*China*, Oct. 20, 1993, 16.

45. *People's Daily*, overseas ed., Apr. 26, 1994.

46. Xia Shangzhou, "From 'Paid Journalism' to Unfair Competition," *News Communication* (Feb. 1994): 7.

47. Confidential interview, Hangzhou, Nov. 13, 1994.

48. Li Jie, "The Confusion in Journalism Circles," *Chinese Journalists* (July 1993): 8.

49. Of course, partisan journalism in the United States was rather different from Party journalism in China. For one, the American partisan press was made up of competing political parties rather than a single ruling party; for another, American political parties did not necessarily directly own and control the press, as is the case in China. For a description of the American partisan press, see Frank L. Mott, *American Journalism: A History of Newspapers in the United States through 260 Years, 1690–1950* (New York: Macmillan, 1959); for analyses of the rising of the American penny press, see Michael Schudson, *Discovering the News: A Social History of American Newspapers* (New York: Basic Books, 1978), and Dan Schiller, *Objectivity and the News: The Public and the Rise of Commercial Journalism* (Philadelphia: University of Pennsylvania Press, 1981).

50. Confidential interview, Beijing, Oct. 20, 1994.

51. A news producer in a provincial capital city made the following calculation for me. There are approximately thirty national and local media outlets in the city. Assuming that a business gives each journalist from each media outlet two hundred yuan in a publicity event, the company only spends six thousand yuan. Such an amount can hardly buy much advertising space in a single medium. But such an amount in the form of a bribe may get the company's news across a wide range of outlets in the whole city.

52. A company manager reportedly spent 170,000 yuan on twenty newspapers and magazines, which published tens of thousands of words to publicize him. See Wang Huiquan, "Developing a Commodity Economy and Building a Team of Journalism Professionals," *Journalism Front* (Mar. 1992): 19.

53. Contract responsibility systems whereby individual workshops in manufacturing plants and shops assume responsibility for their own profits and losses have been introduced throughout China as part of the enterprise management reforms since the early 1980s.

54. Wang, "The Advantages and Disadvantages of the Responsibility System," 19.

55. Li, "The Confusion in Journalism Circles," 7.

56. Ibid.

57. Ibid.

58. Zhang Jianxing, "Which Class of Journalists to Be?" *Journalism Front* (Apr. 1993): 14.

59. A reporter I interviewed on October 31, 1994, in Beijing described the mentality of news division chiefs in this way: "What will make them happy is to see that all the reporters under their supervision are sitting in the news room and not going out to stir up political troubles. They will be most happy if they frequently have bonuses to hand out to the reporters."

60. This trend is true of workers in other cultural industries as well, for example, writers and filmmakers.

61. Zhang, "Which Class of Journalists to Be?" 14.

62. Wang, "Reflections on the Growth of Advertising," 52.

63. This point was suggested to me by a number of journalism scholars and journalists I interviewed in Beijing. They said that since journalists were not allowed to exercise their sense of social responsibility in news reporting, they turned to gaining practical material benefits for themselves. Political repression is an important reason for corruption in journalism.

64. Joseph M. Chan, "Commercialization without Independence: Trends and Tensions of Media Development in China," in *China Review 1993*, ed. Joseph Cheng Yu-Skek and Maurice Brosseau (Hong Kong: Chinese University Press, 1993), 25.1.

65. The following excerpt from a news story in *Heilongjiang Daily* (Oct. 14, 1994, 1) provides a detailed view of how local Party authorities carry out their subscription drive. "Jixi city held the 1995 newspaper subscription meeting. On behalf of the city Party committee, Jixi city Party propaganda department chief signed Party newspapers and journals subscription responsibility contracts with Party committees from 124 units. The city's Party committee issued compulsory subscription orders to these party committees. . . . The city's Party propaganda department and the city's finance bureau jointly issued a circular on the use of funds for newspaper subscriptions in 1995. The circular stipulated that units can use Party membership dues, youth league membership dues, meeting funds, operational funds, research funds, education funds, and other public funds to subscribe to Party newspapers and Party journals. . . . Jixi city also suggested that Party committees at various levels should withdraw the honorary status a unit has previously acquired if it fails to fulfil subscription quotas for its Party newspapers and journals."

66. "Sichuan Declares War against Corrupt Practices in Newspaper Subscriptions," *Guangming Daily*, Dec. 23, 1991, 3.

67. Wang Xiaomei and Li Feizhi, "The Disfigured Child of Newspaper Self-Distribution," *Guangming Daily*, Dec. 10, 1991, 3.

68. "Sichuan Declares War."

69. Confidential interview with a teacher from the school, Jinyun County, Zhejian Province, Jan. 5, 1995.

70. Wang, "Overcoming 'Paid Journalism' Involves System Engineering," 20.

71. "Promoting Quality Consciousness among the Population," *Journalism Front* (Apr. 1992): 6–7.

72. Lu Ye, "Chinese Television News amidst Reform" (Ph.D. diss., Fudan University, 1994), 56.

73. Twenty national media outlets issued the same report on the same day plus a Xinhua release and local media transmission.

74. Even Ai Feng, *People's Daily*'s high profile journalist and chairperson of the "ten thousand li journey" organizing committee, met one such fake reporting team on his tour. Wang, "Tainted Sanctity," 34.

75. Ibid.

76. Confidential interview, Beijing, Oct. 14, 1994.

77. Ruan Guanrong, *A Macro-Perspective on Broadcasting Policy* (Beijing: China Broadcasting Press, 1991), 183–84.

78. Such complaints are well expressed in popular sayings such as "watch out for fires, burglars, and journalists." See Lu Xiaohuang, "Two Kinds of 'Watching Out for Journalists,'" *Chinese Journalists* (Dec. 1993): 29. See also Li, "The Confusion in Journalism Circles," 7.

79. A manager from a Beijing business company provided astonishing statistics. On April 28, 1993, the company received a total of thirty-three visitors and visiting teams. Altogether they demanded a total of 500,000 yuan in various forms. The company could not afford to offend any of these uninvited guests. Among these, at least one-third were news media or media-related organizations. See *Reference to Decision Making in Broadcasting* (July 1993): 9.

80. *People's Daily*, overseas ed., Aug. 5, 1993, 1.

Chapter 5: Broadcasting Reform amidst Commercialization

1. Luo Hongdao, "From 'Official Model' to 'Popular Model': Reform at Pearl River Economic Radio," *Chinese Journal of Broadcasting* (Mar. 1983): 11–12.

2. Chen Dahai, "Competition: The Motivating Force for Radio Reform," *Chinese Journal of Broadcasting* (Jan. 1988): 71.

3. Guangdong People's Radio, "Strive to Establish Broadcasting with Southern Chinese Characteristics," *South China Radio and Television Research* 3 (1988): 10–16, cited in Joseph M. Chan, "Media Internationalization in China: Processes and Tensions," *Journal of Communication* 44.3 (Summer 1994): 76.

4. Yu Tonghao, "The Birth of Pearl River Economic Radio and Its Practices in the Past Year," *Chinese Journal of Broadcasting* (Jan. 1988): 10.

5. In 1990, the two Hong Kong commercial radio stations that were very influential in the Guangzhou area changed their language of broadcasting from Cantonese to English and thus basically withdrew from Guangdong territories. Guangdong People's Radio claimed that its withdrawal was the result of the loss of audiences to PRER. See Guangdong People's Radio and Pearl River Economic Radio, "Sticking to the Perspective of Both Being Correct and Lively, Strive to Do a Good Job in Running Economic Radio Stations," *Reference to Decision Making in Broadcasting* (June 1991): 43.

6. Yu, "The Birth of Pearl River Economic Radio," 10; see also Qian Xinbo, "Revelations from Pearl River Economic Radio's Reform," *Chinese Journal of Broadcasting* (Mar. 1988): 8–9.

7. Yu, "The Birth of Pearl River Economic Radio," 11.

8. Ibid.

9. In May 1995, the work week for a large part of wage workers in China was reduced to five days, Monday to Friday.

10. Zheng Guangxing, "The Overall Function and Effectiveness of Broadcasting," *Chinese Journal of Broadcasting* (Jan. 1988): 35.

11. Luo, "From 'Official Model' to 'Popular Model,'" 14–15.

12. Liu Wei, "On the 'Dilution' of Radio Information Programming," *Chinese Journal of Broadcasting* (Jan. 1988): 68–70.

13. Zhu Yan, "The Current Conditions and Prospects for China's Economic Radio Stations," *Reference to Decision Making in Broadcasting* (Feb. 1992): 5.

14. The term "economic" (*jingji*) primarily refers to the station's content orientation. However, it can also carry a connotation related to the operational orientation of the station, i.e., for profit.

15. Zeng Guangsheng, "The Programming Principles of Pearl River Economic Radio," *Chinese Journal of Broadcasting* (Jan. 1988): 65.

16. Zhu Yan, "Guangdong Radio's Policies and Practices in Establishing Specialized Radio Stations," *Reference to Decision Making in Broadcasting* (Feb. 1990): 23.

17. Yu, "The Birth of Pearl River Economic Radio," 11; Luo, "From 'Official Model' to 'Popular Model,'" 10.

18. Zeng, "The Programming Principles of Pearl River Economic Radio," 65.

19. Zhu, "Guangdong Radio's Policies and Practices," 23.

20. Ibid., 26.

21. Ibid.

22. Li Xiangyang, "The Path to the Industrialization of Broadcasting," *Reference to Decision Making in Broadcasting* (Dec. 1993): 2.

23. Guangdong People's Radio and Pearl River Economic Radio, "Sticking to the Perspective of Both Being Correct and Lively," 43.

24. Chen Shenglai, "Riding the Wind of Reform and Setting Out to Sail," *Journalists* (Jan. 1993): 24.

25. Yun Minghuang, "This Group of 'East People,'" *Journalists* (Jan. 1993): 29.

26. According to an insider I interviewed in Beijing, on October 20, 1994, East Radio and East Television were specially approved by the central Party authorities (*zhongyang tepi*).

27. "Shanghai East Radio Begins Broadcasting," *Chinese Journal of Broadcasting* (June 1992): 102.

28. Selection and competition were limited to Shanghai Radio, Film, and Television Bureau staff members.

29. The above information is based on a confidential interview with an official with the All China Journalists Association in Beijing, October 26, 1994. See also Yun, "This Group of 'East People,'" 29; and Hu Jia, "Objective: Connecting to the World Track," *Journalism Front* (Aug. 1993): 45. This sort of consultative selection process is quite uncommon in Chinese enterprises, not to mention in political institutions such as the news media.

30. "Connecting to the world track" (*yu shijie jiegui*) is political jargon that has been circulating in official political and economic discourse in China since 1992. Using the metaphor of the train track, the phrase is a euphemism for changing China's economic system and bringing it into the world order.

31. Wang Wei, "A Brief One-Month Note on 'The Night Eagle Hot Line,'" *Journalists* (Jan. 1993): 34.

32. Chen Shenglai, "The Calling of a New Radio Age," *Chinese Journal of Broadcasting* (Mar. 1994): 49.

33. Ibid.

34. Yu Chuanshi, "The Shock Wave of East Radio," *Chinese Journalists* (Mar. 1993): 17.

35. Li Xiang, Yang Yang, and Yang Daquan, "We Listen to East Radio," *Journalists* (Jan. 1993): 37.

36. Yun, "This Group of 'East People,'" 31.

37. Chen, "Riding the Wind of Reform," 27.

38. Ibid.

39. This information is based on the *Journal of Beijing Broadcasting Institute*'s interview with Wang Zhiping, which ran without a byline. See "The Deputy Director of Shanghai East Radio's News Department Talks about Explorations and Improvements in Using Telephone Participation in News Programming," *Journal of Beijing Broadcasting Institute* (Feb. 1993): 9–11.

40. Yu, "The Shock Wave of East Radio," 16. These two categories accounted for 80 percent of the 400 calls actually broadcast by the station in the first month.

41. Chen, "Riding the Wind of Reform," 26.

42. Ibid.

43. "Deputy Director," 10.

44. Ibid.

45. Xu Wei, "'Today's News' Answers Four Questions for You," *Journalists* (Jan. 1993): 34.

46. Yun, "This Group of 'East People,'" 29.

47. Ibid., 28–29.

48. "Theoretical Responses to the 'East Radio Shock,'" *Journal of Beijing Broadcasting Institute* (Feb. 1993): 16–19; see also Jia Yifan, "East Radio in the Eyes of News Executives," *Journalists* (Jan. 1993): 39.

49. "Theoretical Responses," 39.

50. A program consultant at East Television told me in an interview that audience rating is very important to the stations. A producer reported to her the actual rating figure just before she prepared a television talk show, which made her nervous.

51. Chen Jiezhang, "Building a Bridge between Citizens and Mayors," *Journalists* (Apr. 1993): 26.

52. Ibid., 27.

53. Ibid., 29.

54. In other provincial capitals, the only all-interest newspaper is typically the provincial Party organ. The evening paper for the capital city is usually published by the same Party organ. In Shanghai, due to its pre-1949 history as the center of commercial newspapers in China, in addition to the Party organ, *Liberation Daily,* there are two other major newspapers, *Wenhui Bao,* and *Xinmin Evening News.*

55. Lu Xiaohuang and Wen Lu, "Competition and Cooperation," *Chinese Journalists* (Aug. 1994): 5.

56. Ibid., 7.

57. Actually, the program does include women. Gender-biased language is still common in the news media in China.

58. These four phrases are the slogans of the program.

59. CCTV audience rating figures during the week of October 9–15, 1994, were published in the department's newsletter, *Empty Talk* 18 (Oct. 31, 1994).

60. Confidential interview with a media official, Beijing, Oct. 20, 1994.

61. News Department, CCTV General Editorial Office, "Television Audience Survey Report," in *A Perspective Study of Media Communication Effects in China*, ed. Chen Chong-shan and Er Xiuling (Shenyang: Shenyang Publishing House, 1989), 402–4.

62. The CCTV News Center is responsible for news and current affairs programming.

63. Luo Hongdao and Lu Min, "'East Time and Space': What Are You After?" *Chinese Journal of Broadcasting* (Mar. 1994): 89.

64. Wen Lu and Liu Yanguang, "Interview with 'Focus,'" *Chinese Journalists* (July 1994): 14.

65. Xiao Rong, "Why Not the Best?" *Chinese Journalists* (June 1994): 20–21.

66. The logo features an eye similar to that of CBS's, with blue on the top and green on the bottom. According to one journalist, it symbolizes integrity, standing firmly on the green ground and up straight against the blue sky. The logo has become a trademark of the program.

67. The huge screen allegedly even made Ted Turner feel humble, who reportedly said during his tour of CCTV that he did not have such a big one for CNN. See Guo Xiuyuan, "'Focus': A New Scene in CCTV's Reform," *Journalism Front* (June 1994): 44.

68. These "laws of communication," as discussed in chap. 2, are actually mainstream journalism practices and production values in the West.

69. Luo and Lu, "'East Time and Space,'" 92.

70. Ibid.

71. Ibid.

72. See, for example, John Hartley, *Understanding News* (New York: Routledge, 1982).

73. Luo and Lu, "'East Time and Space,'" 89. The elitist "high culture" and "low culture" or "high taste" and "low taste" distinction is common in Chinese discussions of popular culture.

74. Yang Weiguang, "Sticking to the Principle of Correct Opinion Guidance Is the Key to Good 'Focus' Programs," *Reference to Decision Making in Broadcasting* (Sept. 1994): 3.

75. These topics were recorded by Chen Fuqing in *Television News* (Beijing: China Broadcasting Press, 1994), 214.

76. These topics were surveyed during the course of fieldwork. The topic sentence is mainly CCTV's, with minor modifications for clarity.

77. Quoted in Xiao, "Why Not the Best?" 21.

78. Li Zhengyan, "Random Notes on 'Focus,'" *Press and Publications News*, Sept. 3, 1994, 1.

79. For example, while rich parents in urban areas pay tens of thousands of yuan to send their children to private boarding "aristocratic" schools, poor peasants in many parts of the countryside are still unable to send their children to school at all.

80. Li, "Random Notes on 'Focus,'" 1.

81. Zhou Hongjun, "Tell the Ordinary Folks' Own Stories," *Press and Publications News,* July 2, 1994, 1.

82. See, for example, Luo and Lu, "'East Time and Space,'" 90–91.

83. I am only speaking of a question of degree, of course.

84. Paraphrased by Luo and Lu in "'East Time and Space,'" 93.

85. Confidential interview, Beijing, Nov. 3, 1994.

86. "Focus" follows CCTV's 7:00 P.M. news, separated by eight minutes of commercials. Thus the contrast is quite evident.

87. Xiao, "Why Not the Best?" 21.

88. Confidential interview with a media official, Beijing, Oct. 20, 1994.

89. This comment was clearly made in response to a perceived problem. Elsewhere, Yang Weiguang instructed the whole CCTV staff: "Don't ask experts and scholars to discuss the gains and losses of the reforms on television, even less should we let experts predict the problems that may arise out of the reforms." See Yang Weiguang, "Carrying Out the Spirit of the National Meeting on Propaganda Work Completely, Make Our Station into an Important Front for the Construction of Socialist Spirit Civilization," *Television Research* (Apr. 1994): 17.

90. Of course, as Yang Weiguang and his audience were clearly aware, many people were forced by the Party to speak against their will in the past, particularly during the anti-rightist campaign in 1957 and the Cultural Revolution between 1966 and 1976.

91. Yang, "Sticking to the Principle," 2.

92. See, for example, Todd Gitlin, *The Whole World Is Watching: Mass Media in the Making and Unmaking of the New Left* (Berkeley: University of California Press, 1980); and Stuart Hall, Chas Critcher, Tony Jefferson, John Clarke, and Brian Robert, *Policing the Crisis: Mugging, the State, and Law and Order* (New York: Macmillan, 1978). Robert A. Hackett provided a summary of the literature on state institutions as "primary definers" of public issues in the Western news media. See *News and Dissent: The Press and the Politics of Peace in Canada* (Norwood, N.J.: Ablex, 1991), 71–73.

93. Yang, "Sticking to the Principle," 1.

94. Lei Weizheng, "Enlightenment from *Living Space*'s Process of Re-positioning Itself," *Television Research* (Apr. 1994): 30–31.

95. Du Xueliang, "An Overview of the Development of Local Broadcasting in China in 1992," *China Journalism Yearbook 1993,* Journalism Research Institute of the Chinese Academy of Social Sciences (Beijing: Chinese Social Sciences Press, 1994), 8.

96. Zhang Zhongyi and Wang Yong, "A Successful Experiment with Radio Reform at the Provincial Level," *Reference to Decision Making in Broadcasting* (Jan.–Feb. 1993): 85.

97. For a more complete overview of specialization in radio broadcasting, see Liu Yujun, "The Distribution of Specialized Radio Stations and Their Prospects," in *Reform and Developments in Chinese Broadcasting across the Century,* ed. Luo Hongdao and Liu Yujun (Beijing: China Broadcasting Press, 1994), 122.

98. Ibid., 120–22.

99. Xiu Mu, "Speaking about Important News," *Journalism Front* (Nov. 1994): 14.

100. For example, Luo and Lu reported that leaders of a major Beijing news organization suggested to their journalists that their news should be written like the news on "Living Space." A Xinhua News Agency official said that the agency has felt the challenges posed by the journalism orientation of "Living Space." See Luo and Lu, "'East Time and Space,'" 89; Lei, "Enlightenment from *Living Space*'s Process of Re-positioning Itself," 30.

Chapter 6: Newspapers for the Market

1. State Press and Publications Administration, "Provisional Regulations on Newspaper Management," issued on Dec. 25, 1990, in *A Concise and Practical Guide to Laws and Regulations on Press and Publications in China, 1949–1994*, ed. Policy and Regulations Bureau, State Press and Publications Administration (Beijing: China Books Press, 1994), 135–45.

2. The print shops of large newspapers undertake contract jobs from smaller newspapers in an effort to increase revenue.

3. Joseph M. Chan, "Commercialization without Independence: Trends and Tensions of Media Development in China," in *China Review 1993*, ed. Joseph Cheng Yu-Skek and Maurice Brosseau (Hong Kong: Chinese University Press, 1993), 25.9.

4. Ibid.

5. Wen Lu, "Capital City: 1,200 News-Stands," *Chinese Journalists* (Aug. 1992): 18–20.

6. The sample was collected on different dates by purchasing all issues available at one retail outlet. The Shanghai sample was collected on September 7, 1994, from a post office–owned newspaper booth contracted out to a male retiree near one of Shanghai's major long-distance bus depots. The Beijing sample was purchased from a female retiree on a busy intersection in central Beijing on October 7, 1994. The Hangzhou sample was obtained from a young man selling papers in a market area in the city center on February 9, 1995.

7. Journalism Research Institute of the Chinese Academy of Social Sciences, *China Journalism Yearbook 1993* (Beijing: Chinese Social Sciences Press, 1993), 413.

8. Qian Xinbao, ed., *A Handbook for News Correspondents* (Dalian: Dalian Press, 1992), 92.

9. Lynn T. White III provides a very insightful analysis of the similarities and differences between the main Party organ, *Liberation Daily*, and the evening paper, *Xinmin Evening News*, in Shanghai. See his "All the News: Structure and Politics in Shanghai's Reform Media," in *Voices of China: The Interplay of Politics and Journalism*, ed. Chin-Chuan Lee (New York: Guilford Press, 1990), 88–110.

10. *China Journalism Yearbook 1993*, 413.

11. Wang Zhereng, "Carry Forward the Party Press's Fine Tradition of Closely Connecting to the People," *Journalism Front* (Dec. 1994): 3.

12. In 1992, circulation of *Beijing Daily* was 650,000, whereas that of *Beijing Evening News* was 800,000. In Tianjin, circulation of *Tianjin Daily* was 412,000, whereas the city's evening paper, *Tonight's News*, had a circulation of 450,000. In Shanghai, *Liberation Daily*'s circulation figure was 655,000, whereas that of *Xinmin Evening News* was 1,590,000. Similarly, whereas *Guangzhou Daily* had a circulation of 430,000, that of *Yangcheng Evening News* was 1,130,000. *China Journalism Yearbook 1993*, 374–75, 413.

13. Editorial Committee of *Yangtze Evening News*, "Think Highly of Readers, Understand Readers, and Be Close to Readers," *Chinese Journalists* (Jan. 1993): 17.

14. Ibid.

15. Wang, "Carry Forward the Party Press's Fine Tradition," 3.

16. Ibid.

17. Editorial Committee of *Yangtze Evening News,* "Think Highly of Readers," 17.

18. Papers published in folio size whose content fits this category are also treated as tabloids. On the other hand, although evening papers are tabloids in size, they are not generally regarded as tabloids in the second sense.

19. For a brief description and analysis of street tabloids in 1984–85, see Robert Bishop, *Qi Lai: Mobilizing a Billion* (Ames: Iowa State University Press, 1989).

20. See, for example, "Guangxi Urges Supervision of Small Newspapers," *Nanning Guangxi Regional Service,* Dec. 18, 1984, translated in FBIS-*China,* Dec. 21, 1984, P1; "Sichuan Urges Tighter Control of Newspapers," *Chengdu Sichuan Provincial Service,* Dec. 16, 1984, translated in FBIS-*China,* Dec. 18, 1984; "Guangdong Regulates Tabloids' Market Management," *Yangcheng Evening News,* Apr. 10, 1985, 1, translated in FBIS-*China,* Apr. 18, 1985, P1.

21. For example, some were from Shenyang, Fushun, and Jilin in the northeast, Xi'an in the northwest, Baotou in Inner Mongolia, Chengdu and Nanning in the southwest, and Zhuhai, Haikou, and Guangzhou in the south.

22. Unlike all other pieces in the paper, this one does not name an original source and is therefore not a "news digest."

23. While dailies typically publish "weekend editions," weeklies publish "end-of-month editions" (*yuemo ban*) or "midmonth editions" (*yuezhong ban*). For the sake of simplicity, all these papers will be referred to as "weekend editions" hereafter, unless specified otherwise.

24. "Over Four Hundred Weekend Editions in the Country," *Press and Publications News,* Jan. 21, 1994, 1.

25. Bi Yang, "An Analysis of Weekend Editions," *Journalism Front* (Dec. 1994): 44.

26. Ibid.

27. Si Tong, "Weekend Editions: Exploring the Path for a Long Journey," *Journalism Front* (Feb. 1994): 21.

28. Deng Xinxin, "An Analysis of the Weekend Edition Phenomenon," *Journalism Front* (May 1992): 31.

29. Bi, "An Analysis of Weekend Editions," 44.

30. Si, "Weekend Edition," 22.

31. Zuo Fang, "The Nature and Orientations of Weekend Papers," *Journalism Front* (July 1994): 15.

32. One story, about fires in 1993, for example, revealed the startling statistics that in 1993 alone, there were 38,094 fires in the country in which 2,467 people were killed and direct economic losses amounted to more than 1.12 billion yuan. The analysis points out that bureaucraticism is the primary cause of loss of human lives and property, and yet implicated bureaucrats remain protected from prosecution.

33. This particular end-of-the-month issue is the best, most critical, and most informative Chinese newspaper I have ever read.

34. Shi Tongyu, "The Perplexed and Flustered Social News in China," *Journal of Beijing Broadcasting Institute* (Jan. 1994): 15.

35. This paper, however, is not unique, either in form or content. The weekend edition of *Light Industry Shopping Guide* (Qinggong gouwu daobao), a paper whose official publisher is the government authority responsible for light industries, is another case in point. Again, the sensational titles of articles are in bigger type and more a attention-grabbing color than the masthead; articles on the inside pages are put at the masthead's position. The contents have nothing to do with either light industries, shopping, or the weekend. The headlines of the front page articles are "The Lives of the Republic's Generals with Maimed Arms and Legs," "Living Buddha Found in Taiwan," "Kidnapping Case Shakes Zhongnan-hai," and "Deng Xiaoping and His Relatives." The inside pages are filled with other sensational stories such as "A Female Prosecutor and Her Criminal Husband," "The Bizarre Marriage of a Female Ph.D.," and other human interest stories about well-known personalities, both past and present, domestic and international, including Michael Jackson's hobbies, and the lives of American presidents' daughters in the White House. Pictures of sexy women (often blonde) appear, often without any relevance to the stories themselves.

36. Yang Zicai, "Newspaper Peddlers Previewing Newspapers? Wait a Moment!" *Press and Publications News,* Jan. 15, 1994, 1.

37. "Control Over Publications Reportedly Tightened," *China News Service,* May 14, 1993, translated in FBIS-*China,* May 17, 1993, 19.

38. Zha Xiduo, "From 'Orioles Sing and Swallows Dart' to 'Flower-Decorated Streets and Willow-Lined Alleys': The Flooding of Popular Tabloids," *The Nineties* (Aug. 1993): 12–13.

39. The details of the contracted amount is based on Chan, "Commercialization without Independence," 25.9. Chan used an article on page 27 of the January 13, 1993, issue of *Ming Bao* as his source. My own source, Zhaxiduo's "From 'Orioles Sing and Swallows Dart,'" however, reported that the contracted amount was 470,000 a year.

40. See "Ministry Closes Newspaper over Nudity Article," *Tokyo KYODO* in English, Jan. 13, 1993, reprinted in FBIS-*China,* Jan. 13, 1993, 13.

41. Confidential interview, Beijing, Oct. 27, 1994.

42. "*Renmin Ribao* Official Removed for 'Improper Remarks,'" *Ming Bao,* Aug. 23, 1993, 2, translated in FBIS-*China,* Aug. 23, 1993, 24.

43. Shi, "The Perplexed and Flustered Social News in China," 15.

44. Ibid.

45. Ibid.

46. Propaganda Department of the Chinese Communist Party Central Committee and the State Press and Publications Administration, "Circular on Strengthening the Management of the Weekend Editions," Mar. 15, 1994, in *Guide,* 152–54.

47. Zuo Fang, a writer from *Nanfang Weekend,* refused to put his paper and other weekend editions of major Party organs in the same category as tabloids on the streets. Although they are sold on the streets, Zuo emphasizes that they are not the same as tabloids but rather are a small army sent by the Party organs to conquer the newspaper market on the streets. See "The Nature and Orientations of Weekend Editions," 14. While it is certainly true that the weekend editions of major Party organs have less pornographic, violent, and fabricated material, they are not devoid of such content.

48. Confidential interview, Beijing, Oct. 14, 1994.

49. Liu Hongsheng, "Fascinating or Hopeless? Some Cool-Headed Thinking on the Weekend Edition Phenomenon," *Journalism Front* (Sept. 1992): 62.

50. In China, the conventional hierarchy of power units at the same jurisdictional level is the Party, the government, the trade union, the Youth League, and the Women's Federation.

51. The paper is unable to get permissions to report important political events, for example.

52. Political and cultural elites often get their children and relatives appointed jobs in journalism even though they do not have the necessary qualifications.

53. For a more detailed description of these management reforms at *Beijing Youth News*, see Yang Lixin, "Developing Potentials: The 'Dao' of Human Resource Management in *Beijing Youth News*," in *A Journalism Shock Wave: Scanning the Beijing Youth News Phenomenon*, ed. Zheng Xingdong, Chen Renfeng, and Zheng Chaoran (Beijing: Chinese People's University Press, 1994), 298–312.

54. Zhao Xiaofeng, "The Macro-Management Perspective of the *Beijing Youth News*," in *A Journalism Shock Wave*, 314.

55. Ibid., 319.

56. Zhan Jiang, "Riding the Tide," in *A Journalism Shock Wave*, 5.

57. In addition to the main newspaper, the news organization also publishes three specialized papers, targeting school students at different levels. Its businesses include a book store, an arts center, a high-tech firm, a public relations firm, a grocery store, a medical clinic, and a resort.

58. Yu Guoming, "*Beijing Youth News* in the Eyes of the 'Gods': A Readership Survey Report of the *Beijing Youth News*," in *A Journalism Shock Wave*, 37. For example, 93 percent of the readers of *Beijing Daily* spend thirty minutes or less on that paper. See the Public Opinion Research Institute of Chinese People's University, "A Survey Report of the *Beijing Daily* Readership," in *A Perspective Study of Media Communication Effects in China*, ed. Chen Chongshan and Er Xiuling (Shenyang: Shenyang Publishing House, 1989), 431.

59. For example, 81.8 percent of *Beijing Daily*'s circulation is official subscriptions. Private subscriptions account for 7.9 percent of its total subscriptions, while only 2.8 percent of its readership obtain the paper through street sales. See Yu, "*Beijing Youth News* in the Eyes of the 'Gods,'" 36; and Public Opinion Research Institute of the Chinese People's University, "Survey Report," 429.

60. Yu, "*Beijing Youth News* in the Eyes of the 'Gods,'" 20.

61. Pu Wei, "Understanding the Characteristics of the Readership and Improving the Newspaper: An Analysis of *People's Daily*'s Readership," *Journalism Front* (Mar. 1994): 42.

62. The *People's Daily* Readership Survey Team, "*People's Daily* Readership Survey," in *China Journalism Yearbook 1993*, Journalism Research Institute of the Chinese Academy of Social Sciences (Beijing: Chinese Social Sciences Press, 1994), 185.

63. Zhan, "Riding the Tide," 6–7.

64. A dispatch by Agence France Presse, for example, mentioned that although the paper was not as influential as *People's Daily*, its articles deserve attention. Zhan, "Riding the Tide," 6.

65. See John Hartley, *Understanding News* (New York: Routledge, 1982), for a list and an analysis of news values in Western journalism.

66. Cited in Wang Junchao, "The Difficult Transformation to a Daily," in *A Journalism Shock Wave*, 159–60.

67. Ownership of a private car is the biggest dream of the rising urban consumer class, and the paper has frequently pursued this dream. A story in 1993 had carried the headline "With 10,000 Yuan, Drive the Car Home," and the 1994 feature cited above is apparently a reinforcement of the dream. The leather jacket is part of the dress code of fashion conscious Beijing yuppies. Prices are ridiculously high.

68. Ye Guobiao, "Glories and Dreams," in *A Journalism Shock Wave*, 98.

69. These four examples were purchased from the streets of Beijing. They are not randomly selected samples, but there is some sense of randomness to it: they were purchased by convenience whenever I was close to a newsstand that carried the paper.

70. This story illustrates the reporting approach of the paper's new editor-in-chief, Xiao Pei: "There is no such thing as pure objectivity in in-depth reporting. Since such a thing does not exist, it is meaningless to pursue it. Rather, it is better to perfect the propaganda art of conveying a point of view without it being perceived as such." See Xiao Pei, "Working Hard to Build a Highly Qualified Journalist Team," *Beijing Youth News*, special promotional ed., 1994–95.

71. Feng Yaoxiang, "Writing about the Heroes of the New Times," in *A Journalism Shock Wave*, 225.

72. Feng Yaoxiang, "You Have Educated a Whole Generation!" in *A Journalism Shock Wave*, 201.

73. Ibid., 201–2.

74. Ibid., 200.

75. Quoted in Wen, "Capital City: 1,200 News-Stands," 20.

76. Chen Renfeng, "Behind All the Talk," in *A Journalism Shock Wave*, 77.

77. Ibid., 76.

78. For example, the paper almost drew a formal protest from a national research institute when it published an unfounded story about budget cuts to the social sciences.

79. Ye, "Glories and Dreams," 100–101.

80. Quoted in Zhan, "Riding the Tide," 12.

81. Yu, "*Beijing Youth News* in the Eyes of the 'Gods,'" 41.

Chapter 7: Toward a Propagandist/Commercial Model of Journalism?

1. "New Art in China, 1989–1994," Apr. 12–May 28, 1995, Vancouver Art Gallery. The exhibition was organized by the Hanart TZ Gallery in Hong Kong and the American Federation of the Arts in New York.

2. "Mickey Mao," *The Economist*, Aug. 3, 1996, 32, reprinted in *Globe and Mail*, Aug. 6, 1996, A6.

3. Xu Yu, "Professionalization without Guarantees: Changes of the Chinese Press in Post-1989 Years," *Gazette* 53.1–2 (1994): 36.

4. Confidential interview, Vancouver, Aug. 5, 1995.

5. Confidential interview, Beijing, Oct. 16, 1994.

6. Confidential interview, Beijing, Nov. 3, 1994.

7. Yang Ji, "Newspapers Need More Environmental Awareness," *Beijing Review* 39.29 (July 15–21, 1996): 22.

8. Ibid.

9. *People's Daily,* overseas ed., May 1, 1995, 1.

10. "Guangdong Suspended Golf Course Developments," *People's Daily,* overseas ed., June 21, 1995, 6. This brief news story was based on a Guangdong provincial government announcement. There is no follow-up as to how these projects were started in the first place or why the Guangdong provincial government suspended only seven of them.

11. Alison L. Jernow, *Don't Force Us to Lie: The Struggle of Chinese Journalists in the Reform Era* (New York: Committee to Protect Journalists, 1993), 85.

12. The popular saying "Eating meat when holding the bowl, shouting abuses when putting down the bowl" (duanzhe wan chirou, fangxia wan maniang) captures this situation of a rising living standard and rising frustration very well.

13. "Urban Residents Wish to Triple Their Income," *Ming Bao,* Nov. 10, 1996, B4.

14. "Levels of Satisfaction," *Beijing Review* 39.31 (July 29–Aug. 4, 1996): 22.

15. For the purpose of this discussion, "audience" should be read as including readers, listeners, and viewers of different news media.

16. PRER has to compete with Hong Kong stations. The two East stations have to compete with Shanghai's two old stations. The newly established specialized stations have to compete with stations within the framework of the people's radio station. In the newspaper market, the evening papers have to compete with the dailies, and *Beijing Youth News* is in a competitive market by the very fact that there are so many media outlets available in the capital.

17. Chen Shenglai, "Riding the Wind of Reform and Setting Out to Sail," *Journalists* (Jan. 1993): 26.

18. See "The Discovery of the Secret Weapon and the Rise of the Second Wave of Broadcasting Reform," *Journal of Beijing Broadcasting Institute* (Feb. 1993): 1–5.

19. There were only 3 telephones per 1,000 people in China in 1995. The comparable figure for Hong Kong is 123.3 per 1,000. Simon Fluendy, "Markets Call for Freedom," *Far Eastern Economic Review,* Oct. 17, 1996, 40–41.

20. Chen, "Riding the Wind of Reform," 26.

21. Leonard L. Chu, "Continuity and Change in China's Media Reform," *Journal of Communication* 44.3 (Summer 1994): 9.

22. Minxin Pei, *From Reform to Revolution* (Cambridge, Mass.: Harvard University Press, 1994), 165.

23. Ibid., 174.

24. Ibid., 165.

25. Zhao Xiaofeng, "The Macro-Management Perspective of the *Beijing Youth News,*" in *A Journalism Shock Wave: Scanning the Beijing Youth News Phenomenon,* ed. Zheng Xing dong, Chen Renfeng, and Zheng Chaoran (Beijing: Chinese People's University Press, 1994), 330.

26. Li Cheng and Lynn T. White III, "China's Technocratic Movement and the *World Economic Herald*," *Modern China* 17.3 (July 1991): 365, 364.

27. It is worthwhile to note that Sun Yusheng, director of CCTV's News Commentary Department, was declared one of "China's Ten Most Distinguished Youth" in 1995. See *People's Daily*, overseas ed., Sept. 19, 1995, 1. This prestigious annual competition is sponsored by China Youth Federation, China Youth and Juvenile Development Fund, and ten major national news media organizations. It honors young role models who have made an outstanding contribution to the country and whose achievements are widely recognized by society. Sun is the first journalist to win such a title. It indicates that Sun has indeed successfully put up a good television show while "dancing with chains."

28. Qin Nin, "Gong Xueping on Broadcasting Reform: Both Mouthpieces and Business Operations," *Journalists* (Jan. 1993): 5.

29. Confidential interview.

30. Confidential interview.

31. Michael Schudson provides an excellent analysis of the differences between "news as information" and "news as entertainment" in American journalism. See *Discovering the News: A Social History of American Newspapers* (New York: Basic Books, 1978).

32. Zhao, "The Macro-Management Perspective of the *Beijing Youth News*," 317.

Chapter 8: Challenges and Responses

1. For a more detailed description of the case, see Alison L. Jernow, *Don't Force Us to Lie: The Struggle of Chinese Journalists in the Reform Era* (New York: Committee to Protect Journalists, 1993), 90–91.

2. Qian Bocheng, "All Should Concern Themselves with This Lawsuit," *Liberation Daily*, Sept. 9, 1992, 2, quoted in Jernow, *Don't Force Us to Lie*, 91.

3. Gan Xifen, "New Situations Call for Reform in the News Media System," *Journalism Circles* (Feb. 1993): 4–6.

4. Ibid., 5.

5. Ibid., 6.

6. The article was first published in *Viewpoint* (Shidian) (Feb. 10, 1993): 25–27, a current affairs magazine published by China News Service. At the request of Gan himself, it was reprinted in *Journalism Circles* (Xinwen jie), a journalism trade journal in Sichuan Province, Gan's place of origin. Both journals have small circulations.

7. Sun Xupei was allowed, however, to travel to the United States as a visiting scholar.

8. "Beijing Magazine Calls Official Press 'Dull,'" *AFP in English*, Jan. 29, 1993, reprinted in FBIS-*China*, Jan. 28, 1993, 8.

9. Ibid.

10. "Authorities Cancel Radio 'Phone-in Show,'" *South China Sunday Morning Post*, Aug. 8, 1993, 1, reprinted in FBIS-*China*, Aug. 10, 1993, 21.

11. Liu Youli, "A Study of Cable Regulations in the Mainland," *Journalism and Communication* (Jan. 1994): 70.

12. Matthew Miller, "No Limit to China's Cable TV Market," *Asia Times*, Nov. 11, 1996, 16. *China and North Asia Monitor* provided a different set of data. It reported that by July

1996, an estimated 45 million Chinese households have connected to cable television, and the figure is expected to reach 80 million by the year 2000. See "StarTV Bypassed by Cable Boom," *China and North Asia Monitor* (Oct. 1996): 7.

13. "CCTV Vice President Yang Weiguang on Television Propaganda," *Reference to Decision Making in Broadcasting* (Feb. 1991): 17.

14. Zhang Chi, "County-Level Television Station Must Transmit the Complete Set of CCTV-1 Programming," *Reference to Decision Making in Broadcasting* (Feb. 1992): 46.

15. Sheng Wen, "Give Me Back the Right to Watch CCTV Programming," *Reference to Decision Making in Broadcasting* (Feb. 1992): 46.

16. "CCTV Vice President Yang Weiguang on Television Propaganda," 17–18.

17. Huang Handong, "A Preliminary Analysis of the Development of Cable Television Programming in Coastal Cities," *Chinese Journal of Broadcasting* (Feb. 1994): 57.

18. Cited in Guo Runtian, "The Cable Television Fever and the Search for Programming," *Chinese Journal of Broadcasting* (Feb. 1993): 67.

19. See Jin Wenxiong, "A Comparison of the Influences of Foreign Radio and Foreign Television on China," *Reference to Decision Making in Broadcasting* (Oct. 1993): 17.

20. Zhao Shuifu, "Several Issues on Foreign Broadcasting," *Reference to Decision Making in Broadcasting* (Mar. 1994): 20.

21. The national average audience rate for foreign stations is 0.5 to 3.0 percent lower than in Beijing. Ibid.

22. Zhao, "Challenges from Foreign Radio and Television," *Reference to Decision Making in Broadcasting* (Oct. 1993): 20.

23. Hu Yaoting, "From Radio Free Europe to Radio Free Asia," *Chinese Journal of Broadcasting* (May 1994): 24.

24. See Jin Gaochu, "Situations, Analysis, and Strategies," *Reference to Decision Making in Broadcasting* (Sept. 1993): 6.

25. Nigel Holloway, "Troubled Persuader," *Far Eastern Economic Review,* Aug. 1, 1996, 23; Reuters, Oct. 31, 1996. Other information about Radio Free Asia was gathered from various sources on the Internet, including its home page.

26. See, for example, Guang Fu, "Why Does the United States Want to Set up Radio Free Asia," *Chinese Journalists* (Mar. 1994); Hu, "From Radio Free Europe to Radio Free Asia."

27. Hu, "From Radio Free Europe to Radio Free Asia," 24.

28. Li Ze, "Reforms and Developments at the CCTV in 1994," *Chinese Journal of Broadcasting* (Mar. 1994): 24.

29. "Don't Publicize Private Satellite Receiving Facilities," *Reference to Decision Making in Broadcasting* (Feb. 1992): 45.

30. Zhao, "Several Issues on Foreign Broadcasting," 10.

31. Liu Xiliang, "New Demands on Program Hosts Posed by Developments in Broadcasting in the 1990s," *Chinese Journal of Broadcasting* (May 1994): 9.

32. For more detailed information on StarTV and its influence on Asia, see Joseph M. Chan, "National Responses and Accessibility of STAR TV in Asia," *Journal of Communication* 44.3 (Summer 1994): 112–31.

33. Liu, "New Demands on Program Hosts," 10.

34. Chan, "National Responses and Accessibility," 117–18.

35. The State Council of China, "Regulations on the Management of Satellite Television Ground Reception Facilities," Oct. 5, 1993, reprinted in *Reference to Decision Making in Broadcasting* (Nov. 1993): 1–2.

36. "Shandong Provincial Party Committee and Provincial Government Issued a Joint Order to Stop Transmission of All Foreign Satellite Broadcasting," *Reference to Decision Making in Broadcasting* (July 1994): 44.

37. "State Suspends Beijing Cable TV Sports Channel," *United News* (Lianhe bao), Feb. 8, 1994, 10, translated in FBIS-*China*, Feb. 10, 1994, 23.

38. Chan, "National Responses and Accessibility," 118.

39. Ibid.

40. "Beijing Blacks Out Internet Sites," *Asia Times*, Sept. 10, 1996, 2.

41. News Media and Chinese Modernization Research Team, *News Media and Chinese Modernization* (Beijing: Xinhua Press, 1992).

42. Xu Zhankun, "An Overall Perspective on News Media Reform," *Journalism Circles* (Jan. 1993): 4.

43. Joseph Fewsmith, "Institutions, Informal Politics, and Political Transition in China," *Asian Survey* 36.3 (Mar. 1996): 245, emphasis in the original.

44. Some academic writers still have to use pen names to publish their articles on news media reform. For example, a scholar gave me an article he had published under a pen name and asked me not to disclose his actual name in China.

45. Although a written document about the six no's was not available, the order was widely circulated in journalism circles in Beijing. This information was obtained through confidential interviews with several authoritative sources in Beijing during October and November 1994.

46. See Joseph M. Chan, "Media Commercialization without Independence," in *China Review 1993*, ed. Joseph Cheng Yu-Skek and Maurice Brosseau (Hong Kong: Chinese University Press, 1993), 25.10.

47. Joe Kahn, "China Chokes News Flows," *Globe and Mail*, Jan. 17, 1996, B9.

48. Ibid.

49. "China Finds New Way to Thwart StarTV," *Asia Times*, Sept. 10, 1996, 1.

50. "StarTV Bypassed by Cable Boom," 7.

51. This statement was made by Li Kehan, a deputy director at the Ministry of Radio, Film, and Television and first quoted in Britain's *Financial Times*. See "China Finds New Way to Thwart StarTV," 3.

52. "Publish and Be Ideologically Damned," *The Economist*, Oct. 26–Nov. 1, 1996, 41.

53. Ibid.; see also "More Magazines Face Censors' Scrutiny," *Asia Times*, Nov. 11, 1996, 2.

54. *People's Daily*, overseas ed., Nov. 27, 1996, 1; the full text of Jiang's speech was printed in *People's Daily*, overseas ed., Oct. 21, 1996, 1.

55. "Resolution of the Chinese Communist Party Central Committee on Several Important Issues Regarding Strengthening the Construction of Socialist Spiritual Civilization," *People's Daily*, overseas ed., Oct. 14, 1996, 1, 4.

56. The English text of Jiang's report is in *China Daily,* Sept. 23, 1997.

57. An internal Party circular acknowledges that many members are helping to disseminate "rumors" about differences of opinion among central leaders in China. "China in Transition," *Far Eastern Economic Review,* Oct. 17, 1996, 31.

Chapter 9: Media Reform beyond Commercialization

1. John Keane, *The Media and Democracy* (Cambridge, Mass.: Blackwell, 1991), 153.

2. Ibid., 152–53.

3. See, for example, Robert G. Picard, *The Press and the Decline of Democracy: The Democratic Socialist Response in Public Policy* (Westport, Conn.: Greenwood Press, 1985); Douglas Kellner, *Television and the Crisis of Democracy* (Boulder: Westview Press, 1990); and Ross M. Entman, *Democracy without Citizens: Media and the Decay of American Politics* (New York: Oxford University Press, 1989). James Curran provides a critical assessment of the traditional liberal arguments about the democratic role of the news media in "Mass Media and Democracy: A Reappraisal," in *Mass Media and Society,* ed. James Curran and Michael Gurevitch (London: Edward Arnold, 1991), 82–117. John Keane's critique of the blind spots in liberal conceptions of press freedom and limitations of the commercial logic is particularly relevant in this context. See *The Media and Democracy.*

4. James Curran, "The Impact of Advertising on the British Mass Media," *Media, Culture, and Society* 3.1 (1981): 43–69; James Curran, "The Press as an Agency of Social Control: An Historical Perspective," in *Newspaper History: From the Seventeenth Century to the Present Day,* ed. George Boyce, James Curran, and Pauline Wingate (London: Constable, 1978), 51–75.

5. Robert Hackett, Richard Pinet, and Myles Ruggles, "From Audience-Community to Audience Community: Mass Media in B.C.," in *Seeing Ourselves: Media Power and Policy,* ed. Helen Holmes and David Taras (Toronto: HBJ Canada, 1986), 13.

6. Keane, *The Media and Democracy,* 90.

7. Ibid., 91.

8. John H. McManus, *Market-Driven Journalism: Let the Citizen Beware?* (Thousand Oaks, Calif.: Sage, 1994), 90.

9. Ibid., 200.

10. Hackett, Pinet, and Ruggles, "From Audience-Community to Audience Community," 13. For an extended critique of the limitations of commercial logic, see Robert A. Hackett and Yuezhi Zhao, *Sustaining Democracy? Journalism and the Politics of Objectivity* (Toronto: Garamond Press, 1997).

11. Quoted in Keane, *The Media and Democracy,* 150.

12. Fred S. Siebert, Theodore Peterson, and Wilbur Schramm, *Four Theories of the Press* (Urbana: University of Illinois Press, 1956).

13. Raymond Williams's four communications systems were first discussed in 1962. See *Communications,* rev. ed. (London: Chatto and Windus, 1966).

14. Denis McQuail, *Mass Communication Theory: An Introduction* (London: Sage, 1987).

15. Picard, *The Press and the Decline of Democracy.*

16. James Curran, "Rethinking the Media as a Public Sphere," in *Communication and Citizenship: Journalism and the Public Sphere,* ed. Peter Dahlgren and Colin Sparks (London: Routledge, 1991), 27–57.

17. John C. Nerone, ed., *Last Rights: Revisiting Four Theories of the Press* (Urbana: University of Illinois Press, 1995).

18. Ibid., 146.

19. Huang Mingxing, "Reform Brings Change," *Journalists* (Apr. 1993): 5.

20. Maxwell E. McCombs, "Concentration, Monopoly, and Content," in *Press Concentration and Monopoly: New Perspectives on Newspaper Ownership and Operation,* ed. Robert Picard, James Winter, and Maxwell McCombs (Norwood, N.J.: Ablex, 1988), 133.

21. Slavko Splichal, *Media beyond Socialism: Theory and Practice in East-Central Europe* (Boulder: Westview Press, 1994), 135–36.

22. Journalism Research Institute of the Chinese Academy of Social Sciences and the Survey Group of the Capital Journalism Society, "People's Calls, People's Expectations," in *A Perspective Study of Media Communication Effects in China,* ed. Chen Chongshan and Er Xiuling (Shenyang: Shenyang Publishing House, 1989), 85.

23. Denis McQuail, *Media Performance* (London: Sage, 1992), 103.

24. Ibid.

25. See Splichal, *Media beyond Socialism,* for an excellent analysis of media theory and practice in post-socialist societies in east-central Europe. See also articles on media in eastern Europe in the winter 1995 issue of the *Canadian Journal of Communication.* Minxin Pei provides an excellent analysis of the transformation of the Soviet mass media in *From Reform to Revolution: The Demise of Communism in China and the Soviet Union* (Cambridge, Mass.: Harvard University Press, 1994), 179–204.

26. Andrei G. Richter, "The Russian Press after *Perestroika,*" *Canadian Journal of Communication* 20.1 (Winter 1995): 21.

27. I am indebted to one of the University of Illinois Press's anonymous reviewers for the formulation of this sentence.

28. Pat Howard, *Breaking the Iron Rice Bowl: Prospects for Socialism in China's Countryside* (Armonk, N.Y.: M. E. Sharpe, 1988), 191.

29. Marie Cambon relates such a case in her fieldwork in China in the early 1990s on Chinese responses to foreign media imports. See "The Dream Palace of Shanghai: American Films in China's Largest Metropolis, 1920–1950" (M.A. thesis, Simon Fraser University, 1993), 261–62.

30. This comment was made to me by a Chinese visiting scholar on his tour to Canada in 1992.

31. Liu Binyan, for example, noted in June 1995 that the hundreds of Chinese dissidents overseas have not seriously reflected upon the 1989 democracy movement and drawn lessons from it. See "Controversies Over Chai Ling Are Not Over," *Ming Bao,* June 18, 1995, C16.

32. Ibid.

33. Robert A. Hackett, *News and Dissent: The Press and the Politics of Peace in Canada* (Norwood, N.J.: Ablex, 1991), 286.

34. Ruan Ming, "Press Freedom and Neoauthoritarianism," in *Voices of China: The Interplay of Politics of Journalism,* ed. Chin-Chuan Lee (New York: Guilford Press, 1990), 131.

35. Political theorist C. B. Macpherson, for example, has made a strong point that a range of political movements, ideologies, and systems could lay claim to the mantle of democracy. See *The Real World of Democracy* (Canada: Canadian Broadcasting Corporation, 1966).

36. For more discussion of these ideas, see Hackett and Zhao, *Sustaining Democracy.*

37. Macpherson, *The Real World of Democracy,* 20, 22.

38. Splichal, *Media beyond Socialism,* 1.

39. See, for example, Su Shaozhi, "Problems of Democratic Reform in China," Stephen Manning, "Social and Cultural Prerequisites of Democratization: Generalizing from China," and Edward Friedman, "Conclusion," all in *The Politics of Democratization: Generalizing East Asian Experiences,* ed. Edward Friedman (Boulder: Westview Press, 1994), 221–58. See also Edward Friedman, *National Identity and Democratic Prospects in Socialist China* (Armonk, N.Y.: M. E. Sharpe, 1995).

40. Chandra Muzaffar, "Human Rights: The Case for an Integrated Approach," *Commonwealth Currents* (Mar. 1996): 6.

41. Ibid.

42. Splichal, *Media beyond Socialism,* 3, emphasis in the original.

43. Ibid., emphasis in the original.

44. Williams, *Communications,* 124.

45. McQuail, *Media Performance,* 65–80. See also Denis McQuail, "Mass Media in the Public Interest: Toward a Framework of Norms for Media Performance," in *Mass Media and Society,* 68–81.

46. In 1992, population coverage was 75.6 percent for radio and 81.3 percent for television. China Statistics Bureau, *China Statistical Yearbook, 1993* (Beijing: China Statistics Press, 1993), 785. The rate of growth has been very slow since then, however. In 1993, for example, the rates grew 0.8 percent for television and 0.7 percent for radio. See Ai Zhisheng, "Speech at National Broadcasting Working Conference," Jan. 27, 1994, reprinted in *Reference to Decision Making in Broadcasting* (Jan.–Feb. 1994): 13.

47. Journalism Research Institute of the Chinese Academy of Social Sciences and the Survey Group of the Capital Journalism Society, "People's Calls, People's Expectations," 99.

48. Curran, "Mass Media and Democracy," 105.

49. Sun Xupei, *New Theories of Journalism* (Beijing: Contemporary China Press, 1994), 109.

50. This point was made by the Journalism Research Institute of the Chinese Academy of Social Sciences and the Survey Group of the Capital Journalism Society in "People's Calls, People's Expectations," 113.

51. This point was made by a National People's Congress delegate, quoted in ibid., 113.

Selected Bibliography

Bell, Daniel. *The End of Ideology.* New York: Free Press, 1960.

Bishop, Robert. *Qi Lai: Mobilizing a Billion.* Ames: Iowa State University Press, 1989.

Cambon, Marie. "The Dream Palace of Shanghai: American Films in China's Largest Metropolis, 1920–1950." M.A. thesis, Simon Fraser University, 1993.

Chan, Joseph M. "Commercialization without Independence: Trends and Tensions of Media Development in China." In *China Review 1993,* ed. Joseph Cheng Yu-Skek and Maurice Brosseau. Hong Kong: Chinese University Press, 1993. 25.1–25.21.

———. "Media Internationalization in China: Processes and Tensions." *Journal of Communication* 44.3 (Summer 1994): 70–88.

———. "National Responses and Accessibility of STAR TV in Asia." *Journal of Communication* 44.3 (Summer 1994): 112–31.

Chang, Tsan-Kuo, Chin-Hsien Chen, and Guo-Qiang Zhang. "Rethinking the Mass Propaganda Model: Evidence from the Chinese Regional Press." *Gazette* 51.3 (1993): 173–95.

Chang Xiuying. *A Hundred Cases of Poor News Writing.* Beijing: Agricultural Readings Press, 1989.

Cheek, Timothy. "Redefining Propaganda: Debates on the Role of Journalism in Post-Mao Mainland China." *Issues and Studies* 25.2 (1989): 47–74.

Chen Chongshan and Er Xiuling, eds. *A Perspective Study of Media Communication Effects in China* (Zhongguo chuanbo xiaoguo toushi). Shenyang: Shenyang Publishing House, 1989.

Chen Fuqing. *Television News* (Dianshi xinwen). Beijing: China Broadcasting Press, 1994.

Cheng, Li, and Lynn T. White III. "China's Technocratic Movement and the *World Economic Herald.*" *Modern China* 17.3 (July 1991): 342–88.

Chen Lidan. "Why Has the Issue of Private Newspaper Ownership Been Avoided." *World Economic Herald* (Shijie jingji daobao), May 8, 1989, 4.

Chen Renfeng. "Behind All the Talk." In *A Journalism Shock Wave: Scanning the Beijing Youth News Phenomenon* (Xinwen chongji bo: Beijing qingnian bo xianxiang saomiao), ed. Zheng Xingdong, Chen Renfeng, and Zheng Chaoran. Beijing: Chinese People's University Press, 1994. 66–79.

China Statistics Bureau. *China Statistical Yearbook, 1993.* Beijing: China Statistics Press, 1993.

Chu, Leonard L. "Continuity and Change in China's Media Reform." *Journal of Communication* 44.3 (Summer 1994): 4–21.

Curran, James. "The Impact of Advertising on the British Mass Media." *Media, Culture, and Society* 3.1 (1981): 43–69.

———. "Mass Media and Democracy: A Reappraisal." In *Mass Media and Society,* ed. James Curran and Michael Gurevitch. London: Edward Arnold, 1991. 82–117.

———. "The Press as an Agency of Social Control: An Historical Perspective." In *Newspaper History: From the Seventeenth Century to the Present Day,* ed. George Boyce, James Curran, and Pauline Wingate. London: Constable, 1978. 51–75.

———. "Rethinking the Media as a Public Sphere." In *Communication and Citizenship: Journalism and the Public Sphere,* ed. Peter Dahlgren and Colin Sparks. London: Routledge, 1991. 27–57.

Dittmer, Lowell. *China under Reform.* Boulder: Westview Press, 1994.

———. "The Politics of Publicity in Reform China." In *China's Media, Media's China,* ed. Chin-Chuan Lee. Boulder: Westview Press, 1994. 89–112.

Entman, Ross M. *Democracy without Citizens: Media and the Decay of American Politics.* New York: Oxford University Press, 1989.

Fang Hanqi and Chen Yeshao. *A History of Contemporary Chinese Journalism, 1949–1988* (Zhongguo dangdai xinwen shiye shi 1949–1988). Beijing: Xinhua Press, 1992.

Fang Hanqi, Chen Yeshao, and Zhang Zhihua. *A Brief History of Chinese Journalism* (Zhongguo xinwen shiye jianshi). Beijing: Chinese People's University Press, 1982.

Feng Yaoxiang. "Writing about the Heroes of the New Times." In *A Journalism Shock Wave: Scanning the Beijing Youth News Phenomenon* (Xinwen chongji bo: Beijing qingnian bo xianxiang saomiao), ed. Zheng Xingdong, Chen Renfeng, and Zheng Chaoran. Beijing: Chinese People's University Press, 1994. 177–216.

———. "You Have Educated a Whole Generation!" In *A Journalism Shock Wave: Scanning the Beijing Youth News Phenomenon* (Xinwen chongji bo: Beijing qingnian bo xianxiang saomiao), ed. Zheng Xingdong, Chen Renfeng, and Zheng Chaoran. Beijing: Chinese People's University Press, 1994. 217–33.

Fewsmith, Joseph. "Institutions, Informal Politics, and Political Transition in China." *Asian Survey* 36.3 (Mar. 1996): 230–45.

Fluendy, Simon. "Markets Call for Freedom." *Far Eastern Economic Review,* Oct. 17, 1996, 40–41.

Friedman, Edward. "Conclusion." In *The Politics of Democratization: Generalizing East Asian Experiences,* ed. Edward Friedman. Boulder: Westview Press, 1994. 249–58.

———. *National Identity and Democratic Prospects in Socialist China.* Armonk, N.Y.: M. E. Sharpe, 1995.

———. "The Oppositional Decoding of China's Leninist Media." In *China's Media, Media's China,* ed. Chin-Chuan Lee. Boulder: Westview Press, 1994. 129–46.

Fukuyama, Francis. *The End of History and the Last Man.* New York: Free Press, 1992.

Gan Xifen. "Debates Contribute to the Development of the Journalistic Science." *Journal of Communication* 44:3 (Summer 1994): 38–51.

———. "New Situations Call for Reform in the News Media System." *Viewpoint* (Shidian) (Feb. 10, 1993): 4–6.

Gitlin, Todd. *The Whole World Is Watching: Mass Media in the Making and Unmaking of the New Left.* Berkeley: University of California Press, 1980.

Goldman, Merle. "The Role of the Press in Post-Mao Political Struggles." In *China's Media, Media's China,* ed. Chin-Chuan Lee. Boulder: Westview Press, 1994. 23–35.

Greenberg, Bradley S., and Tuen-Yu Lau. "The Revolution in Journalism and Communication Education in the People's Republic of China." *Gazette* 45.1 (1990): 19–31.

Guo Zhenzhi. "Broadcasting in a Market Economy." *Journalism and Communication Research* (Xinwen yu chuanbao yanjiu) 1.3 (1994): 2–8.

Hackett, Robert A. *News and Dissent: The Press and the Politics of Peace in Canada.* Norwood, N.J.: Ablex, 1991.

Hackett, Robert, Richard Pinet, and Myles Ruggles. "From Audience-Community to Audience Community: Mass Media in B.C." In *Seeing Ourselves: Media Power and Policy,* ed. Helen Holmes and David Taras. Toronto: HBJ Canada, 1986. 10–20.

Hackett, Robert A., and Yuezhi Zhao. "Are Ethics Enough? Objectivity versus Substainable Democracy." In *Deadlines and Diversity: Journalism Ethics in a Changing World,* ed. Valerie Alia, Brian Brennan, and Barry Hoffmaster. Halifax: Fernwood, 1995. 44–58.

———. *Sustaining Democracy? Journalism and the Politics of Objectivity.* Toronto: Garamond Press, 1997.

Hall, Stuart. "Culture, the Media, and the 'Ideological Effect.'" In *Mass Communication and Society,* ed. James Curran, Michael Gurevitch, and Janet Woollacott. London: Arnold, 1977. 315–48.

———. "The Rediscovery of 'Ideology': Return of the Repressed in Media Studies." In *Culture, Society, and the Media,* ed. Michael Gurevitch, Tony Bennett, James Curran, and Janet Woollacott. New York: Routledge, 1982. 56–90.

Hall, Stuart, Chas Critcher, Tony Jefferson, John Clarke, and Brian Robert. *Policing the Crisis: Mugging, the State, and Law and Order.* New York: Macmillan, 1978.

Hartley, John. "Ideology." In *Key Concepts in Communication and Cultural Studies,* ed. Tim O'Sullivan, John Hartley, Danny Saunders, Martin Montgomery, and John Fiske. 2d ed. New York: Routledge, 1994. 139–43.

———. *Understanding News.* New York: Routledge, 1982.

Holloway, Nigel. "Troubled Persuader." *Far Eastern Economic Review,* Aug. 1, 1996, 22–23.

Hong, Junhao. "The Resurrection of Advertising in China: Developments, Problems, and Trends." *Asian Survey* 34.4 (1994): 326–42.

Hong, Junhao, and Marlene Cuthbert. "Media Reform in China since 1978: Background Factors, Problems, and Future Trends." *Gazette* 47.3 (1991): 141–58.

Hood, Marlowe. "The Use and Abuse of Mass Media by Chinese Leaders during the 1980s." In *China's Media, Media's China,* ed. Chin-Chuan Lee. Boulder: Westview Press, 1994. 37–57.

Houn, Franklin. *To Change a Nation.* New York: Free Press, 1961.

Howard, Pat. *Breaking the Iron Rice Bowl: Prospects for Socialism in China's Countryside.* Armonk, N.Y.: M. E. Sharpe, 1988.

Hsiao Ching-Chang and Yang Mei-Rong. "Don't Force Us to Lie: The Case of the *World*

Economic Herald." In *Voices of China: The Interplay of Politics and Journalism,* ed. Chin-Chuan Lee. New York: Guilford Press, 1990. 111–21.

Huang, Yu. "Peaceful Evolution: The Case of Television Reform in Post-Mao China." *Media, Culture, and Society* 16.2 (1994): 217–41.

Hu Jiwei. "There Will Be No Genuine Stability without Press Freedom." *World Economic Herald* (Shijie jingji daobao), May 8, 1989, 8.

Jernow, Alison L. *Don't Force Us to Lie: The Struggle of Chinese Journalists in the Reform Era.* New York: Committee to Protect Journalists, 1993.

Journalism Research Institute of the Chinese Academy of Social Sciences and the Survey Group of the Capital Journalism Society. "People's Calls, People's Expectations." In *A Perspective Study of Media Communication Effects in China* (Zhongguo chuanbo xiaoguo toushi), ed. Chen Chongshan and Er Xiuling. Shenyang: Shenyang Publishing House, 1989. 29–102.

Journalism Research Institute of the Chinese Academy of Social Sciences, *Wuxi Daily,* and the Propaganda Department of the Jiangyin City Party Committee, eds. *Market Economy and the News Media* (Shichang jingji yu xinwen shiye). Beijing: Yanshan Press, 1993.

Journalism Research Institute of Xinhua News Agency, ed. *Selections from Documents on Journalism* (Xinwen gongzuo wenxian xuanbian). Beijing: Xinhua Press, 1990.

Keane, John. *The Media and Democracy.* Cambridge, Mass.: Blackwell, 1991.

Kellner, Douglas. *Television and the Crisis of Democracy.* Boulder: Westview Press, 1990.

Kim, Seung-Soo. "The Communication Industries in Modern China: between Maoism and the Market." Ph.D. diss., University of Leicester, 1987.

Lee, Chin-Chuan. "Ambiguities and Contradictions: Issues in China's Changing Political Communication." In *China's Media, Media's China,* ed. Chin-Chuan Lee. Boulder: Westview Press, 1994. 3–20.

———, ed. *China's Media, Media's China.* Boulder: Westview Press, 1994.

———. "Mass Media: Of China, about China." In *Voices of China: The Interplay of Politics and Journalism,* ed. Chin-Chuan Lee. New York: Guilford Press, 1990. 3–32.

Lee, Paul Siu-nam. "Mass Communication and National Development in China: Media Roles Reconsidered." *Journal of Communication* 44.3 (Summer 1994): 22–37.

Levy, Mark R. "Editor's Note." *Journal of Communication* 44.3 (Summer 1994): 3.

Lewis, Glen, and Sun Wanning. "Discourses about 'Learning from Japan' in Post-1979 Mainland Chinese Management Journals." *Issues and Studies* 30.5 (May 1994): 63–76.

Li Liangrong. "The Historical Fate of 'Objective Reporting' in China." In *China's Media, Media's China,* ed. Chin-Chuan Lee. Boulder: Westview Press, 1994. 225–37.

———. *Theory and Practice of the Chinese Press* (Zhongguo baozhi de lilun yu shijian). Shanghai: Fudan University Press, 1992.

Liu, Alan P. L. *Communication and National Integration in Communist China.* Berkeley: University of California Press, 1971.

Liu, Binyan. "Press Freedom: Particles in the Air." In *Voices of China: The Interplay of Politics and Journalism,* ed. Chin-Chuan Lee. New York: Guilford Press, 1990. 132–39.

Li Zhirong. "The Falling of the Crown from the 'Uncrowned King,'" *The Nineties* (Jiushi niandai) (Sept. 1993): 62–64.

Lull, James. *China Turned On: Television, Reform, and Resistance.* London: Routledge, 1991.

Luo Hongdao and Liu Yujun. *Reform and Developments in Chinese Broadcasting across the Century* (Kua shiji Zhongguo guangbo dianshi gaige yu fazhan). Beijing: China Broadcasting Press, 1994.

Lu Ye. "Chinese Television News amidst Reform" (Gaige zhong de Zhongguo dianshi xinwen). Ph.D. diss., Fudan University, 1994.

Macpherson, C. B. *The Real World of Democracy.* Toronto: Canadian Broadcasting Corporation, 1965.

Manning, Stephen. "Social and Cultural Prerequisites of Democratization: Generalizing from China." In *The Politics of Democratization: Generalizing East Asian Experiences,* ed. Edward Friedman. Boulder: Westview Press, 1994. 232–48.

Mao Zedong. *Selected Works.* 5 vols. Beijing: Foreign Languages Press, 1961–77.

McCombs, Maxwell E. "Concentration, Monopoly, and Content." In *Press Concentration and Monopoly: New Perspectives on Newspaper Ownership and Operation,* ed. Robert Picard, James Winter, and Maxell McCombs. Norwood, N.J.: Ablex, 1988. 129–37.

McManus, John H. *Market-Driven Journalism: Let the Citizen Beware?* Thousand Oaks, Calif.: Sage Publications, 1994.

McQuail, Denis. *Mass Communication Theory: An Introduction.* London: Sage, 1987.

———. "Mass Media in the Public Interest: Toward a Framework of Norms for Media Performance." In *Mass Media and Society,* ed. James Curran and Michael Gurevitch. London: Edward Arnold, 1991. 68–81.

———. *Media Performance.* London: Sage, 1992.

Mott, Frank L. *American Journalism: A History of Newspapers in the United States through 260 Years, 1690–1950.* New York: Macmillan, 1959.

Muzaffar, Chandra. "Human Rights: The Case for an Integrated Approach." *Commonwealth Currents* (Mar. 1996): 6–7.

Nathan, Andrew J. *Chinese Democracy.* Berkeley: University of California Press, 1985.

Nerone, John C., ed. *Last Rights: Revisiting Four Theories of the Press.* Urbana: University of Illinois Press, 1995.

News Media and Chinese Modernization Research Team. *News Media and Chinese Modernization* (Xinwen shiye yu Zhongguo xiedai hua). Beijing: Xinhua Press, 1992.

Pei, Minxin. *From Reform to Revolution: The Demise of Communism in China and the Soviet Union.* Cambridge, Mass.: Harvard University Press, 1994.

Petracca, Mark P., and Mong Xiong. "The Concept of Chinese Neo-Authoritarianism: An Exploration and Democratic Critique." *Asian Survey* 30.11 (Nov. 1990): 1099–1117.

Picard, Robert G. *The Press and the Decline of Democracy: The Democratic Socialist Response in Public Policy.* Westport, Conn.: Greenwood Press, 1985.

———. *The Ravens of Odin: The Press in the Nordic Nations.* Ames: Iowa State University Press, 1988.

Policy and Regulations Bureau, State Press and Publications Administration, ed. *A Concise and Practical Guide to Laws and Regulations on Press and Publications in China, 1949–1994* (Zhongguo xinwen chuban fagui jianming shiyong shouce 1949–1994). Beijing: Chinese Books Press, 1994.

Polumbaum, Judy. "The Chinese Press and Its Discontents." *China Exchange News* 16.4 (1988): 2–5.

——. "Outpaced by Events: Learning, Unlearning, and Relearning to Be a Journalist in Post–Cultural Revolution China." *Gazette* 48.2 (1991): 129–46.

——. "Striving for Predictability: The Bureaucratization of Media Management in China." In *China's Media, Media's China,* ed. Chin-Chuan Lee. Boulder: Westview Press, 1994. 113–28.

——. "The Tribulations of China's Journalists after a Decade of Reform." In *Voices of China: The Interplay of Politics and Journalism,* ed. Chin-Chuan Lee. New York: Guilford Press, 1990. 33–68.

Portis, Larry. "On the Rise and Decline of Totalitarian Liberalism: Schlesinger, Bell, Larouche." *Canadian Journal of Political and Social Theory* 12:3 (1988): 20–36.

Public Opinion Research Institute of Chinese People's University. "A Survey Report of the *Beijing Daily* Readership." In *A Perspective Study of Media Communication Effects in China* (Zhongguo chuanbo xiaoguo toushi), ed. Chen Chongshan and Er Xiuling. Shenyang: Shenyang Publishing House, 1989. 428–41.

Qian Xinbao, ed. *A Handbook for News Correspondents* (Xinwen tongxunyuan shouce). Dalian: Dalian Press, 1992.

——. "Media Supervision Is a Duty, Not a Favor Granted to the Media." *World Economic Herald* (Shijie jingji daobao), Apr. 24, 1989, 3. Translated in Foreign Broadcasting Information Service, *Daily Report: China,* May 25, 1989, 44–46.

Richter, Andrei G. "The Russian Press after *Perestroika.*" *Canadian Journal of Communication* 20.1 (Winter 1995): 7–24.

Ruan Guanrong. *A Macro-Perspective on Broadcasting Policy* (Guangbo dianshi hongguan juece sikao). Beijing: China Broadcasting Press, 1991.

Ruan Ming. "Press Freedom and Neoauthoritarianism." In *Voices of China: The Interplay of Politics of Journalism,* ed. Chin-Chuan Lee. New York: Guilford Press, 1990. 122–31.

Ruo Chen. "A Report on the Auction of Advertising Space." *Journalist Monthly* (Aug. 1993): 38–39.

Ryan, Alan. "Professor Hegel Goes to Washington." *New York Review of Books,* Mar. 26, 1992, 7–13.

Schiller, Dan. *Objectivity and the News: The Public and the Rise of Commercial Journalism.* Philadelphia: University of Pennsylvania Press, 1981.

Schudson, Michael. *Discovering the News: A Social History of American Newspapers.* New York: Basic Books, 1978.

Shen Lianggui. *Exploring Laws of Journalism* (Xinwen kaitou guilu tan). Beijing: Xinhua Press, 1991.

Siebert, Fred, Theodore Peterson, and Wilbur Schramm. *Four Theories of the Press.* Urbana: University of Illinois Press, 1956.

Song Qiangqiang, Zhang Zangzang, and Qiao Bian. *China Can Say No: Political and Emotional Choices in the Post–Cold War Era* (Zhongguo keyi shuobu: Lengzhan huoshidai de zhengzhi yu qinggan xuanze). Beijing: China Industrial and Commercial Association Press, 1996.

Sperling, Gerald B. "'Glasnost' in the Chinese Press." In *Encounter '87: Media, Democracy, and Development,* ed. Peter Desbarats and Robert Henderson. London, Ontario: Graduate School of Journalism, University of Western Ontario, 1988. 39–46.

Splichal, Slavko. *Media beyond Socialism: Theory and Practice in East-Central Europe.* Boulder: Westview Press, 1994.

Starck, Kenneth, and Yu Xu. "Loud Thunder, Small Raindrops: The Reform Movement and the Press in China." *Gazette* 42.3 (1988): 143–59.

Stranahan, Patricia. *Modeling the Medium: The Chinese Communist Party and the Liberation Daily.* Armonk, N.Y.: M.E. Sharpe, 1990.

Sun Xupei. *New Theories of Journalism* (Xinwenxue xinlun). Bejing: Contemporary China Press, 1994.

———. "The Take-over and Transformation of the Old Press in the Years after Liberation." *Journalism Research Material* (Xinwen yanjiu ziliao) 43 (Sept. 1988): 48–61.

Su Shaozhi. "Chinese Communist Ideology and Media Control." In *China's Media, Media's China,* ed. Chin-Chuan Lee. Boulder: Westview Press, 1994. 75–88.

———. "Problems of Democratic Reform in China." In *The Politics of Democratization: Generalizing East Asian Experiences,* ed. Edward Friedman. Boulder: Westview Press, 1994. 221–31.

Thompson, John B. *Ideology and Modern Culture: Critical Social Theory in the Era of Mass Communication.* Stanford: Stanford University Press, 1990.

Tong Bing and Cheng Mei. *A Teaching Program for Journalism Theory* (Xinwen lilun jiaocheng). Bejing: Chinese People's Univerity Press, 1993.

Wang Junchao. "The Difficult Transformation to a Daily." In *A Journalism Shock Wave: Scanning the Beijing Youth News Phenomenon* (Xinwen chongji bo: Beijing qingnian bo xianxiang saomiao), ed. Zheng Xingdong, Chen Renfeng, and Zheng Chaoran. Beijing: Chinese People's University Press, 1994. 155–76.

Wang Qing. "Tainted Sanctity." *Journalism World* (Xinwen shijie) (Mar. 1994): 33–36, 43.

Weil, Robert. "China at the Brink: Class Contradictions of 'Market Socialism'—Part 2." *Monthly Review* 46.8 (Jan. 1995): 11–43.

White, Lynn T., III. "All the News: Structure and Politics in Shanghai's Reform Media." In *Voices of China: The Interplay of Politics and Journalism,* ed. Chin-Chuan Lee. New York: Guilford Press, 1990. 88–110.

Williams, Raymond. *Communications.* Rev. ed. London: Chatto and Windus, 1966.

Wright, Kate. "The Political Fortunes of Shanghai's *World Economic Herald.*" *Australian Journal of Chinese Affairs* 23 (Jan. 1990): 121–32.

Wu Dongbin. "A Brief Introduction to China's Advertising Business in 1992." *Modern Advertising* (Jan. 1994): 18–19.

Wu Jianguo, Chen Xiankui, Liu Xiao, and Yang Fengcheng. *Ideological Winds in Contemporary China* (Dangdai Zhongguo yishixingtai fengyunlu). Beijing: Police Education Press, 1993.

Wu Tingjun. "Rethinking the 'Mouthpiece Theory.'" *Journalism Research Material* (Xinwen yanjiu ziliao) 46 (1989): 143–52.

Yang Lixin. "Developing Potentials: The 'Dao' of Human Resource Management in *Beijing*

Youth News." In *A Journalism Shock Wave: Scanning the Beijing Youth News Phenomenon* (Xinwen chongji bo: Beijing qingnian bo xianxiang saomiao), ed. Zheng Xingdong, Chen Renfeng, and Zheng Chaoran. Beijing: Chinese People's University Press, 1994. 298–312.

Ye Guobiao. "Glories and Dreams." In *A Journalism Shock Wave: Scanning the Beijing Youth News Phenomenon* (Xinwen chongji bo: Beijing qingnian bo xianxiang saomiao), ed. Zheng Xingdong, Chen Renfeng, and Zheng Chaoran. Beijing: Chinese People's University Press, 1994. 94–107.

Yu, Frederick T. C. *Mass Persuasion in Communist China.* New York: Frederick A. Praeger, 1964.

Yu, Jinglu. "The Abortive 1956 Reform of Chinese Journalism." *Journalism Quarterly* 65.2 (Summer 1988): 328–34.

———. "The Structure and Function of Chinese Television, 1979–1989." In *Voices of China: The Interplay of Politics and Journalism,* ed. Chin-Chuan Lee. New York: Guilford Press, 1990. 69–87.

Yu, Xu. "Professionalization without Guarantees: Changes of the Chinese Press in Post-1989 Years." *Gazette* 53.1–2 (1994): 23–41.

Yu, Xuejun. "Government Policies toward Advertising in China (1979–1989)." *Gazette* 48.1 (1991): 17–39.

Yu Guanghua, Ma Chaozeng, and Mu Xiaofang. *A Brief History of CCTV* (Zhongyang Dianshitai jianshi). Beijing: People's Publishing House, 1993.

Yu Guoming. "*Beijing Youth News* in the Eyes of the 'Gods': A Readership Survey Report of the *Beijing Youth News.*" In *A Journalism Shock Wave: Scanning the Beijing Youth News Phenomenon* (Xinwen chongji bo: Beijing qingnian bo xianxiang saomiao), ed. Zheng Xingdong, Chen Renfeng, and Zheng Chaoran. Beijing: Chinese People's University Press, 1994. 17–63.

Zhang Tao. *A History of Journalism in the People's Republic of China* (Zhonghua Renming Gongheguo xinwen shi). Beijing: Economic Daily Press, 1992.

Zhan Jiang. "Riding the Tide." In *A Journalism Shock Wave: Scanning the Beijing Youth News Phenomenon* (Xinwen chongji bo: Beijing qingnian bo xianxiang saomiao), ed. Zheng Xingdong, Chen Renfeng, and Zheng Chaoran. Beijing: Chinese People's University Press, 1994. 2–16.

Zhao, Yuezhi. "The 'End of Ideology' Again? The Concept of Ideology in the Era of Post-Modern Theory." *Canadian Journal of Sociology* 18.1 (Winter 1993): 70–85.

Zhao Xiaofeng. "The Macro-Management Perspective of the *Beijing Youth News.*" In *A Journalism Shock Wave: Scanning the Beijing Youth News Phenomenon* (Xinwen chongji bo: Beijing qingnian bo xianxiang saomiao), ed. Zheng Xingdong, Chen Renfeng, and Zheng Chaoran. Beijing: Chinese People's University Press, 1994. 313–38.

Zha Xiduo. "From 'Orioles Sing and Swallows Dart' to 'Flower-Decorated Streets and Willow-Lined Alleys': The Flooding of Popular Tabloids." *The Nineties* (Jiushi niandai) (Aug. 1993): 12–13.

Chinese Academic and Trade Journals

Beijing Broadcasting Institute. *Journal of Beijing Broadcasting Institute* (Beijing guangbo xueyuan xuebao).

Beijing Daily. *Journalism and Writing* (Xinwen yu xiezuo).

Beijing Journalism Society. *News Correspondence* (Xinwen tongxun).

China Central Television. *Television Research* (Dianshi yanjiu).

Chinese Advertising Association. *Chinese Advertising* (Zhongguo guanggao).

Chinese People's University. *Photocopied Material from Newspapers and Periodicals: Journalism* (Baokan fuyin zhilao: xinwen xue).

Chinese Radio and Television Society. *Chinese Journal of Broadcasting* (Zhongguo guangbo dianshi xuekan).

Guangdong Broadcasting Society. *South China Broadcasting Research* (Lingnan guangbo dianshi yanjiu).

Heilongjiang Journalism Society. *News Communication* (Xinwen tongxun).

Journalism Research Institute of the Chinese Academy of Social Sciences. *Journalism* (Xinwen xuekan).

———. *Journalism and Communication Research* (Xinwen yu chuanbo yanjiu).

———. *Journalism Research Material* (Xinwen yanjiu ziliao).

People's Daily. Journalism Front (Xinwen zhanxian).

Policy and Regulations Bureau, Ministry of Radio, Film, and Television. *Reference to Decision Making in Broadcasting* (Guangbo dianshi juece cankao).

School of Journalism, Fudan University. *Fudan University Journalism Quarterly* (Xinwen daxue).

Shaanxi Association of Journalists. *Journalism Knowledge* (Xinwen zhishi).

Shandong Press and Publications Bureau. *Press and Publications Herald* (Xinwen chuban daokan).

Shanghai Association of Journalists. *Journalists* (Xinwen jizhe).

Shanghai Radio, Film, and Television Bureau, *Radio and Television Research* (Guangbo dianshi yanjiu).

Xinhua News Agency. *Chinese Journalists* (Zhongguo jizhe).

Xinjiang Association of Journalists. *Xinjiang Journalism Circles* (Xinjiang xinwenjie).

Index

YUEZHI ZHAO has published articles on media and ideology as well as *Sustaining Democracy? Journalism and the Politics of Objectivity* with Robert A. Hackett. She is currently an assistant professor in the Department of Communication at the University of California at San Diego.

Books in The History of Communication Series

Selling Free Enterprise: The Business Assault on Labor and Liberalism, 1945–60
  Elizabeth A. Fones-Wolf

Last Rights: Revisiting *Four Theories of the Press*
  Edited by John C. Nerone

"We Called Each Other Comrade": Charles H. Kerr & Company, Radical Publishers
  Allen Ruff

WCFL, Chicago's Voice of Labor, 1926–78
  Nathan Godfried

Taking the Risk Out of Democracy: Corporate Propaganda versus Freedom and Liberty
  Alex Carey; edited by Andrew Lohrey

Media, Market, and Democracy in China: Between the Party Line and the Bottom Line
  Yuezhi Zhao